Modern Language Associatio

Approaches to Teaching World Literature

Joseph Gibaldi, Series Editor

---

1. Joseph Gibaldi, ed. *Approaches to Teaching Chaucer's* Canterbury Tales. 1980.
2. Carole Slade, ed. *Approaches to Teaching Dante's* Divine Comedy. 1982.
3. Richard Bjornson, ed. *Approaches to Teaching Cervantes'* Don Quixote. 1984.
4. Jess B. Bessinger, Jr., and Robert F. Yeager, eds. *Approaches to Teaching* Beowulf. 1984.
5. Richard J. Dunn, ed. *Approaches to Teaching Dickens'* David Copperfield. 1984.
6. Steven G. Kellman, ed. *Approaches to Teaching Camus's* The Plague. 1985.
7. Yvonne Shafer, ed. *Approaches to Teaching Ibsen's* A Doll House. 1985.
8. Martin Bickman, ed. *Approaches to Teaching Melville's* Moby-Dick. 1985.
9. Miriam Youngerman Miller and Jane Chance, eds. *Approaches to Teaching* Sir Gawain and the Green Knight. 1986.
10. Galbraith M. Crump, ed. *Approaches to Teaching Milton's* Paradise Lost. 1986.
11. Spencer Hall, with Jonathan Ramsey, eds. *Approaches to Teaching Wordsworth's Poetry.* 1986.
12. Robert H. Ray, ed. *Approaches to Teaching Shakespeare's* King Lear. 1986.
13. Kostas Myrsiades, ed. *Approaches to Teaching Homer's* Iliad *and* Odyssey. 1987.
14. Douglas J. McMillan, ed. *Approaches to Teaching Goethe's* Faust. 1987.
15. Renée Waldinger, ed. *Approaches to Teaching Voltaire's* Candide. 1987.
16. Bernard Koloski, ed. *Approaches to Teaching Chopin's* The Awakening. 1988.
17. Kenneth M. Roemer, ed. *Approaches to Teaching Momaday's* The Way to Rainy Mountain. 1988.
18. Edward J. Rielly, ed. *Approaches to Teaching Swift's* Gulliver's Travels. 1988.

19. Jewel Spears Brooker, ed. *Approaches to Teaching Eliot's Poetry and Plays*. 1988.
20. Melvyn New, ed. *Approaches to Teaching Sterne's* Tristram Shandy. 1989.
21. Robert F. Gleckner and Mark L. Greenberg, eds. *Approaches to Teaching Blake's* Songs of Innocence and of Experience. 1989.
22. Susan J. Rosowski, ed. *Approaches to Teaching Cather's* My Ántonia. 1989.
23. Carey Kaplan and Ellen Cronan Rose, eds. *Approaches to Teaching Lessing's* The Golden Notebook. 1989.
24. Susan Resneck Parr and Pancho Savery, eds. *Approaches to Teaching Ellison's* Invisible Man. 1989.
25. Barry N. Olshen and Yael S. Feldman, eds. *Approaches to Teaching the Hebrew Bible as Literature in Translation*. 1989.
26. Robin Riley Fast and Christine Mack Gordon, eds. *Approaches to Teaching Dickinson's Poetry*. 1989.
27. Spencer Hall, ed. *Approaches to Teaching Shelley's Poetry*. 1990.

Approaches to Teaching Shelley's Poetry

Edited by

Spencer Hall

The Modern Language Association of America
New York   1990

Library of Congress Cataloging-in-Publication Data

Approaches to teaching Shelley's poetry / edited by Spencer Hall.
      p.   cm. — (Approaches to teaching world literature : 27)
    Includes bibliographical references.
    ISBN 0-87352-527-2   ISBN 0-87352-528-0 (pbk.)
    1. Shelley, Percy Bysshe, 1792–1822—Study and teaching.
  2. Shelley, Percy Bysshe, 1792–1822—Criticism and interpretation.
I. Hall, Spencer, 1942– . II. Series.
PR5438.A66   1990
821'.7—dc20   89-13425

Cover illustration of the paperback edition: J. M. W. Turner, *The Angel Standing in the Sun*, Tate Gallery, London, 1846. Photograph: Tate Gallery/Art Resource.

Published by The Modern Language Association of America
10 Astor Place, New York, NY 10003-6981

CONTENTS

Preface to the Series   viii

Preface to the Volume   ix

PART ONE: MATERIALS *Spencer Hall*

Editions   3

   Teaching Editions: Selections and Collections   3
   Teaching Editions: Anthologies   5
   Reference and Critical Editions   7

Readings for Students and Teachers   9

   Reference Works   9
   Recommended Readings   11
   Romantic Contexts   12
   Studies of Shelley   17

Aids to Teaching   22

PART TWO: APPROACHES

Introduction   27

Selected Pedagogical Approaches

Shelley's Grasp upon the Actual
   Stuart Curran   28

"The Mind in Creation": Life as Metaphor
   Ross Woodman   32

Shelley's Workmanship of Style
   William Keach   36

Shelley for Sophomores
   Nancy Moore Goslee   41

Knowing a Romantic Poem: A Sequenced Research Project
   Mary A. Quinn   44

Writing-across-the-Curriculum Techniques for Teaching Shelley
   Art Young   49

Teaching Individual Texts

Two Voices: Narrator and Poet in *Alastor*
   Stephen C. Behrendt   54

vi   CONTENTS

Contrasting Styles: Teaching "Mont Blanc" with Coleridge's
   "Hymn before Sun-Rise"
   Adam J. Frisch   59

Myths of Power and the Poet: Teaching "Hymn to Intellectual
   Beauty"
   Spencer Hall   62

Look on My Words, Ye Mighty, but Don't Despair: Teaching
   "Ozymandias"
   Gyde Christine Martin   65

Julian and Maddalo: An Introduction to Shelley
   Charles Rzepka   67

Aggression and Regression in Prometheus Unbound
   Thomas R. Frosch   70

Love and Egocentricity: Teaching Alastor and Prometheus
   Unbound with Mary Shelley's Frankenstein
   Betty T. Bennett   76

Windows of Meaning in "Ode to the West Wind"
   Seraphia D. Leyda   79

Teaching "To a Sky-Lark" in Relation to Shelley's Defence
   John L. Mahoney   83

Shelley as Poet and Dramatist in The Cenci
   Vincent F. Petronella   86

Teaching Shelley's Anatomy of Anarchy
   Stuart Peterfreund   90

Shelley and Androgyny: Teaching "The Witch of Atlas"
   Diane Long Hoeveler   93

Epipsychidion and Romantic Passion Love
   Jeffrey C. Robinson   96

Teaching Adonais as Pastoral Elegy
   Judith W. Page   100

Shelley's Portrayals of Emotion in the Lyrics to Jane Williams
   Constance Walker   103

Transformability in "The Triumph of Life"
   Jean Hall   107

Teaching "On Life": An Introduction to Shelley's Skeptical
   Poetics
   Brooke Hopkins   111

The Poetics of Re-vision: Teaching A Defence of Poetry
   Jerrold E. Hogle   114

Literary and Historical Contexts

Shelley in His Times
  Donald H. Reiman   120

Wordsworth and the Shelleyan Self
  Leon Waldoff   127

The Younger Romantics: Teaching Shelley with Byron and Keats
  John A. Hodgson   132

Shelley and Modern Poetry
  George Bornstein   137

Critical Perspectives

Shelley and Current Critical Debates
  Paul Magnuson   142

Shelley's Endings: Formalist and Postformalist Perspectives
  Susan J. Wolfson   146

Teaching and Un-teaching Shelley's Texts: Textual Criticism in
    the Classroom
  Neil Fraistat   152

A Feminist Approach to Teaching Shelley
  Barbara Charlesworth Gelpi   157

Contributors and Survey Participants   163

Works Cited   165

Index of Works by Shelley   183

Index of Names   185

PREFACE TO THE SERIES

In *The Art of Teaching* Gilbert Highet wrote, "Bad teaching wastes a great deal of effort, and spoils many lives which might have been full of energy and happiness." All too many teachers have failed in their work, Highet argued, simply "because they have not thought about it." We hope that the Approaches to Teaching World Literature series, sponsored by the Modern Language Association's Committee on Teaching and Related Professional Activities, will not only improve the craft—as well as the art—of teaching but also encourage serious and continuing discussion of the aims and methods of teaching literature.

The principal objective of the series is to collect within each volume different points of view on teaching a specific literary work, a literary tradition, or a writer widely taught at the undergraduate level. The preparation of each volume begins with a wide-ranging survey of instructors, thus enabling us to include in the volume the philosophies and approaches, thoughts and methods of scores of experienced teachers. The result is a sourcebook of material, information, and ideas on teaching the subject of the volume to undergraduates.

The series is intended to serve nonspecialists as well as specialists, inexperienced as well as experienced teachers, graduate students who wish to learn effective ways of teaching as well as senior professors who wish to compare their own approaches with the approaches of colleagues in other schools. Of course, no volume in the series can ever substitute for erudition, intelligence, creativity, and sensitivity in teaching. We hope merely that each book will point readers in useful directions; at most each will offer only a first step in the long journey to successful teaching.

Joseph Gibaldi
Series Editor

PREFACE TO THE VOLUME

Shelley is arguably the most difficult of the major English Romantic poets to teach. The unique, often problematical combinations of emotion and philosophy, effusive metaphor and subtle intellectuality, personal expression and extensive literary and cultural allusiveness, subjectivity and historical awareness, idealism and skepticism that mark his genius offer a special challenge to student and teacher alike. As a result, Shelley has all too often been presented as the poet of a few intense lyrics, to the exclusion of his longer works, or his extraordinary stylistic and conceptual variety has been reduced to one or another critical generalization.

As the hold of the New Criticism has waned, however, Shelley has re-emerged in contemporary theoretical, critical, and scholarly debate as a major figure in American undergraduate literary education. Whether taught in introductory poetry courses, literature surveys, classes on critical theory, or special-topics classes or, increasingly, presented as the paradigmatic second-generation poet in Romantic-period courses, his work has assumed an importance that will grow, one suspects, in the 1990s.

I hope that this volume will assist beginning and nonspecialist instructors, to whom it is primarily addressed, as well as older hands, to meet the considerable challenge of teaching Shelley's poetry well. The first part of the volume ("Materials") provides information on teaching and reference editions and on secondary readings for both students and instructors. It reflects the preferences of respondents to the questionnaire that preceded the preparation of this volume, but it is by no means a thorough bibliography. The second part of the volume ("Approaches") contains thirty-two essays describing various approaches to teaching Shelley's poetry, including essays on most of the longer poems and lyrics usually taught in undergraduate classes. A list of participants in the survey, a bibliography of works cited, and an index complete the volume. Wherever possible, quotations from Shelley's poetry and prose have been taken from *Shelley's Poetry and Prose*, edited by Donald H. Reiman and Sharon B. Powers.

I wish to thank the many participants in the Modern Language Association survey, whose commitment both to Shelley and to undergraduate teaching made this volume possible. Particular thanks are due to Joseph Gibaldi, general editor of the series, to Elizabeth Holland and her colleagues on the MLA editorial staff, and to Frank Jordan and Muriel Mellown for their careful and encouraging reading of the manuscript. I also wish to express my gratitude to the Faculty Research Committee at Rhode Island College for its support of work on this project.

SH

Part One

MATERIALS

Spencer Hall

Editions

The editing of Shelley's works is a fascinating story. Beginning with Mary Shelley and continuing to the present day, it has been marked by strong personalities, violent disputes, unexpected discoveries, pirated texts, suppressed or altered evidence, and even the odd forgery. Because so much of Shelley's poetry was either published without his supervision, during his exile in Italy, or published posthumously, culled from scattered manuscripts and notebooks that are sometimes almost indecipherable, he has proved the most difficult of the English Romantics to edit. At present, as one authority wrote, "neither Shelley's poetry nor his prose is completely available in a reliable version" (Curran, "Shelley" 598), and many of the versions commonly used in the classroom are clearly out-of-date. Teachers should be aware that new Shelley texts—poetry, prose, and letters—and significant corrections to existing texts are continually appearing in scholarly journals and book-length studies.

Presented below is a guide to the editions now used for teaching Shelley, as reported by survey respondents. No attempt has been made to provide a complete list; the editions listed here are those works that respondents most frequently consult, require for class use, place on library reserve, and recommend to students. These editions are divided into three categories: teaching editions of Shelley's poetry and prose, anthologies, and reference and critical editions.

Teaching Editions: Selections and Collections

By far the most frequently used teaching edition of Shelley's poetry, recommended by respondents by a margin of more than ten to one, is Donald H. Reiman and Sharon B. Powers's Norton Critical Editions paperback *Shelley's Poetry and Prose*. Universally praised for its authoritative texts, it has become a standard edition for critics and scholars, as well as teachers. Reiman and Powers present an extensive and more than representative selection of works, including juvenilia from the Esdaile Notebook; *Queen Mab* (excepting Shelley's notes), *Prometheus Unbound*, *The Cenci*, and *Hellas* in their entireties; virtually all the shorter narrative and lyric poems usually taught in the undergraduate classroom; and three prose essays, "On Love," "On Life," and *A Defence of Poetry*. (A number of respondents would in fact like to see more of Shelley's prose in the volume.) Also included, in accordance with the Norton Critical Editions format, are fifteen essays or parts of books on Shelley's thought and art and on individual poems. The volume concludes with a selected bibliography.

Reiman and Powers provide copious headnotes and annotations, both factual and interpretive, the latter placed conveniently on the bottom of the page. Most respondents found the notes informative and helpful for both student and teacher, although some expressed a concern that the notes are occasionally misleading or too sharply opinionated and that they may pre-determine a student's reading of the text. "Helpful" was also repeatedly used to describe the critical essays. Several respondents did suggest, however, that, while excellent in themselves, the essays have begun to "show their age." (This situation should soon be addressed in a forthcoming edition.) All in all, the Reiman-Powers selection stands alone in the field as a model teaching text; its only major drawback is that it is not a complete collected edition. (One aesthetically minded respondent did complain that it "has an awful cover.")

Several once-popular paperback teaching editions of Shelley's poetry have gone out of print, including those edited by Carlos Baker and Neville Rogers. The editions that remain, with the exception of the Reiman-Powers book, are more or less outdated in texts and, when offered, in notes and bibli-ographies as well. Harold Bloom's Meridian paperback *The Selected Poetry and Prose of Shelley* includes a representative sampling of Shelley's poetry, sufficient to most undergraduate needs, although it omits several longer poems and excerpts some others. Its annotation is minimal, but the volume does boast an influential, widely reprinted introductory essay.

Kenneth Neill Cameron's paperback *Percy Bysshe Shelley: Selected Poetry and Prose*, although almost forty years old, is still interesting for its topical organization, which groups selected poems, prose, and letters under six headings. The selection includes an especially generous amount of Shelley's prose, although often in abridged form, and valuable notes on the poet's social and political commitments. The Penguin paperback *Shelley: Poems*, selected by Isabel Quigly, is an inexpensive teaching text whose value is greatly diminished by the total absence of annotations and its excerpting of major poems. Stephen Spender's slight and idiosyncratic paperback *A Choice of Shelley's Verse* may be chosen for the bedside table but not for the classroom. Unfortunately, Timothy Webb's authoritatively edited Everyman paperback *Shelley: Selected Poems* is not in print in the United States.

The standard single-volume edition of the collected poetry for teachers and critics alike is *The Complete Poetical Works of Percy Bysshe Shelley* edited for the Oxford Standard Authors series by Thomas Hutchinson and corrected by G. M. Matthews. Several respondents reported using the vol-ume in specialized undergraduate and graduate classes, even though it is no longer available in paperback. The edition has not been revised to in-corporate newly discovered poems and textual recensions made since 1905, and the notes to individual poems are almost exclusively editorial. Hutchinson does include Mary Shelley's "Notes to the Poems" from the first collected edition of 1839.

Another one-volume collection recommended by several respondents is Newell Ford's Cambridge edition *The Poetical Works of Shelley.* The text and the notes are those of G. E. Woodberry's original Cambridge edition of 1901, although Ford added a new introduction and five selections from Shelley's prose. The Cambridge edition is textually less reliable and less complete than the Oxford Standard Authors' edition, but its commentary on individual poems is more helpful for students. One respondent called the Modern Library edition of *The Complete Poems of Keats and Shelley* "a great buy," but it lacks any apparatus, except for Mary Shelley's "Notes."

The standard teaching and critical edition of Shelley's prose for many years, David Lee Clark's book *Shelley's Prose: Or, The Trumpet of a Prophecy,* has gone out of print. That status is not an unmixed evil, since the book was notorious for inaccuracies in texts, dating, and commentary. There is currently no teaching edition of the complete prose. Three selected editions were mentioned by respondents; each emphasizes a different group of Shelley's prose writings, although all three include *A Defence of Poetry.*

Roland A. Duerksen's paperback *Shelley: Political Writings* focuses, as the title says, on the poet's political and social thought; it contains a helpful introduction detailing Shelley's lifelong commitment to social reform. Bruce R. McElderry's book *Shelley's Critical Prose,* no longer available in paperback, emphasizes Shelley's literary and critical ideas and includes Thomas Love Peacock's "Four Ages of Poetry" to complement *A Defence.* John Shawcross's 1909 book *Shelley's Literary and Philosophical Criticism* has also been reprinted.

Unlike Wordsworth's *Lyrical Ballads* and *Prelude,* Shelley's major poems and poetic volumes have not been widely taught in editions of their own. One can hope in the light of current editing projects that the situation will change and that an inexpensive and up-to-date teaching text of, say, *Prometheus Unbound* will appear. Finally, a new paperback edition of Shelley's two juvenile Gothic novels, *Zastrozzi* and *St. Irvyne,* has been prepared by Stephen Behrendt.

Teaching Editions: Anthologies

It is impossible to list here all the anthologies in which Shelley's lyrics and other poetry find a place. According to the survey, however, two anthologies are clearly preferred above all others; each is connected with a particular course appearing in most English curricula across the country. For the lower-division introductory survey of English literature, taken by both majors and nonmajors, volume 2 of *The Norton Anthology of English Literature,* under the general editorship of M. H. Abrams, is the text of choice. For the upper-division Romantic survey and other more specialized courses dealing with English Romanticism, the most often used anthology is David Perkins's *English Romantic Writers*.

The respondents uniformly praised the introductions and the notes to Shelley's poetry by Abrams and Jack Stillinger in the fifth edition of the *Norton Anthology*, as well as the up-to-date texts. Opinions were less uniform concerning the selections. While some respondents thought that the *Norton Anthology* has steadily improved its Shelley selections, others complained that it has too many lyrics and not enough long poems. Perkins's *English Romantic Writers*, by contrast, was generally thought to offer adequate coverage but to need updating. The respondents found the general introduction to Shelley and the headnotes to the individual poems helpful but wished for more extensive annotations. The notes, the bibliography, and the texts all need to be brought up to date, and several respondents strongly recommended a new edition.

Teachers reported using two other anthologies besides *The Norton Anthology of English Literature* in the English literature survey course and in comparable lower-division introductory courses: volume 2 of *The Norton Anthology of World Masterpieces*, the Romanticism section edited by Howard E. Hugo, with Maynard Mack as general editor, and the *Romantic Poetry and Prose* volume of *The Oxford Anthology of English Literature*, edited by Harold Bloom and Lionel Trilling. Those using the *Norton World Masterpieces* found the Shelley selections deficient. The selections in the *Oxford Anthology* are better, although many of the longer poems are cut and the annotations are uneven.

Three other anthologies, in addition to Perkins's, were recommended for use in Romantic survey and period courses: Russell Noyes's *English Romantic Poetry and Prose*, William Heath's *Major British Poets of the Romantic Period*, and John L. Mahoney's *English Romantics: Major Poetry and Critical Theory*. Whereas Perkins and especially Noyes seek to cover the Romantic period in some depth, Heath and Mahoney include only the six major Romantic poets (plus, in the case of Mahoney, a selection of Hazlitt's criticism). Heath's anthology is particularly noteworthy for the range and the number of his Shelley selections. Two features of Mahoney's book are the inclusion of selected critical essays and its availability in paperback.

Several respondents who teach *A Defence of Poetry* in literary criticism courses recommended Hazard Adams's anthology of criticism, *Critical Theory since Plato*. Adams includes Peacock's "Four Ages of Poetry" as well as Shelley's *Defence of Poetry*, thus allowing students to compare the two. John E. Jordan's useful paperback editon of the two essays is unfortunately out of print, but Carl Woodring's inclusive Riverside paperback *Prose of the*

Romantic Period, which contains both essays and a selection from Shelley's *Philosophical View of Reform*, happily is not out of print.

Reference and Critical Editions

The Reiman-Powers, Hutchinson, and Ford editions of Shelley's poetry have already been mentioned under "Teaching Editions." While Reiman-Powers is textually definitive for those works it prints and while Hutchinson is still the most often used complete edition of the poetry, the standard reference edition remains, despite its outdated texts and canon, Roger Ingpen and Walter E. Peck's ten-volume *Complete Works of Percy Bysshe Shelley*. Known as the Julian Edition, it conveniently brings together in one set Shelley's poetry (vols. 1–4), prose (vols. 5–7), and letters (vols. 8–10), together with Mary Shelley's prefaces and notes. Of the three groups of texts, the prose is the least unreliable, and the letters are the most unreliable. Neville Rogers's Oxford English Texts edition *The Complete Poetical Works of Percy Bysshe Shelley*, which returned to the manuscript sources and was meant to fill the glaring need for a standard, up-to-date collected edition of the poetry, has not been a success. Only two of its four projected volumes have appeared; volume 1 covers the period 1802–13, volume 2 covers 1814–17. It should be noted, however, that a complete edition of the poems, edited in three volumes by G. M. Matthews and Kelvin Everest for Longman, is now under way. Volume 1, covering the years 1804–17, was published in late 1989.

Among the specialized critical editions mentioned in the survey, Judith Chernaik's *Lyrics of Shelley* was highly recommended both for its scrupulously edited texts and for its instructive critical commentary. Chernaik includes and discusses twenty-four of Shelley's best-known lyrics. The Esdaile Notebook, the collection of fifty-seven early poems that Shelley considered releasing as a volume and that became available for publication only in the 1960s, has been produced twice in book-length editions: by Kenneth Neill Cameron in *The Esdaile Notebook* and by Neville Rogers in *The Esdaile Poems*. A definitive edition, edited by Cameron, also appears in volume 4 of *Shelley and His Circle* (see below).

Shelley's great lyrical drama *Prometheus Unbound* has been edited twice by the same person, Lawrence J. Zillman, first in 1959 in *Shelley's Prometheus Unbound: A Variorum Edition* and then in 1968 in *Shelley's Prometheus Unbound: The Texts and Drafts*. The two texts are based on different editorial practices, and neither is entirely satisfactory, but the *Variorum Edition* is useful to students and teachers wishing to survey the divergent interpretations of the poem over the years. Donald H. Reiman's book *Shelley's "The Triumph of Life": A Critical Study* presents a newly edited text of Shelley's last poem (later somewhat revised in Reiman's Norton Critical Edition), plus extensive textual notes, a reading of the poem, and an informative commentary on Shelley's thought and art. Anthony Knerr's 1984 book *Shelley's* Adonais: *A Critical Edition* provides a sound text, line-by-line annotations, helpful literary and biographical information on the Keats-Shelley relationship, and a survey of critical opinion on the poem.

Once known only to scholars and advanced students of Shelley, the poet's wide-ranging translations from Greek, German, Spanish, and Italian have begun to find a limited place in the undergraduate classroom. That increased interest is due, in part, to Timothy Webb's study of Shelley's theory and practice of translation, *The Violet in the Crucible*, which, although it does not give complete versions of Shelley's translations, does offer many crucial passages in full. James Notopoulos includes reliable texts of Shelley's renderings of Plato in *The Platonism of Shelley*, and in *The German Literary Influence on Shelley* Roxana Klapper quotes Shelley's long literal prose translations from Goethe's *Faust*.

Undergraduate teachers are teaching more of Shelley's extensive and subtle prose writings, other than *A Defence of Poetry*, than they were in the not-too-distant past. Several editions of the prose were mentioned in "Teaching Editions." Unfortunately, the state of Shelley's prose is even less reliable than the state of his poetry, and the standard reference edition remains, by default, volumes 5–7 of Ingpen and Peck's outdated Julian Edition. A new complete edition, edited by E. B. Murray and Timothy Webb for the Clarendon Press, Oxford, is under way, however, and should begin to appear shortly. With reference to *A Defence*, Fanny Delisle's textual and critical evaluation is helpful for both the teacher and the advanced student. The standard edition of Shelley's letters, although incomplete and sometimes inaccurate, is Frederick L. Jones's two-volume *The Letters of Percy Bysshe Shelley*.

Finally, the major American collection of Shelley manuscripts is in the Carl H. Pforzheimer Library, now housed in the New York Public Library. The collection—which includes manuscripts by Shelley and his circle of friends, family, and literary acquaintances—is being systematically published in *Shelley and His Circle, 1773–1822*. Of the twelve volumes projected for this monumental edition, eight have appeared, the first four under the general editorship of Kenneth Neill Cameron and subsequent volumes under the general editorship of Donald H. Reiman. The volumes contain not only definitively edited texts of Shelley's letters, prose, and poetry in the collection but also wide-ranging critical, biographical, and historical commentaries, as well as maps, illustrations, and facsimiles of manuscripts.

Readings for Students and Teachers

The following list of readings is by no means a thorough review of the scholarship in the field. Specialists in Shelley and the Romantics will note many omissions. Most obviously and with only a few exceptions, journal articles have been excluded for lack of space; that is a particularly important exclusion because much of the best that has been written on Shelley has been published in journals. My aim in compiling this list has been neither completeness nor a scrupulous selectivity; rather, I have tried to present a representative reading list reflecting the results of the survey that preceded the writing of this volume. I have weighted that list toward comparatively recent scholarship and criticism and have tried, in particular, to include some recent works that have already begun or will soon begin to influence the teaching of Shelley's poetry.

Readers are encouraged to consult more detailed bibliographies and reviews of criticism and to explore the wealth of current Shelley studies in the scholarly journals. The *Keats-Shelley Journal*, published annually by the Keats-Shelley Association of America and edited by Stuart Curran, deserves particular mention.

This section is divided into four categories: reference works, recommended readings, Romantic contexts, and studies of Shelley. The distinction between the last two categories is largely one of convenience. I have placed in "Romantic Contexts" book-length studies that examine several different writers, including Shelley, or explore topics pertinent to him. I have placed in "Studies of Shelley" book-length works devoted entirely or largely to him. Readers interested in particular topics or approaches should consult both categories, as well as the titles listed under "Recommended Readings."

Reference Works

Modern bibliographical records for Shelley began to be systematically compiled in 1951 in the *Keats-Shelley Journal*. Teachers can rely on that journal for thorough, updated, partially annotated annual bibliographies. The first twelve annual bibliographies, covering the period from 1 July 1950 to 30 June 1962, were collected and edited by David Bonnell Green and Edwin Graves Wilson; the next thirteen bibliographies, from 1 July 1962 to 31 December 1974, were collected and edited by Robert A. Hartley.

More than three thousand references before 1950 to Shelley and his works are listed, indexed, and cross-referenced in Clement Dunbar's compendious *Bibliography of Shelley Studies: 1823–1950*. Dunbar updated his work in *Shelley Studies, 1950–1984: An Annotated Bibliography*. The respondents especially recommended three general bibliographies of the Romantic period for their comprehensiveness and annotations. They are Stuart Curran's chapter on Shelley in the fourth edition of *The English Romantic Poets: A Review of Research and Criticism,* edited by Frank Jordan; Donald H. Reiman's *English Romantic Poetry, 1800–1835: A Guide to Information Sources;* and *The Romantic Movement: A Selective and Critical Bibliography,* a continuing series edited by David Erdman and others and published, since 1979, as separate volumes in the Garland Reference Library for the Humanities.

Annotated bibliographies of Shelley and the Romantic period appeared annually in *ELH* from 1937 to 1949, in *Philological Quarterly* from 1950 to 1964, and in *English Language Notes* from 1965 to 1978. The annual *MLA International Bibliography* is relatively complete but attempts no annotations; *The Year's Work in English Studies* does provide commentary. Reviews of major Shelley and Romantic studies also appear regularly in the Autumn issues of *Studies in English Literature* and the *Wordsworth Circle,* in *Studies in Romanticism,* and in the *Keats-Shelley Journal.*

Increasing numbers of teachers are including contemporary reviews in their presentations of Shelley's poetry. Widely available collections of contemporary Romantic criticism include Newman Ivey White's *Unextinguished Hearth,* long a standard reference for notices of the poet during his lifetime; James E. Barcus's *Shelley: The Critical Heritage;* John O. Hayden's *Romantic Bards and British Reviewers;* and Theodore Redpath's *Young Romantics and Critical Opinion 1807–1824.* The most comprehensive of the collections is Donald H. Reiman's nine-volume series, *The Romantics Reviewed: Contemporary Reviews of British Romantic Writers, 1793–1830.* Volumes 8 and 9 reprint facsimile reviews of Shelley, Keats, and their circles to 1830.

Among comparatively recent literary histories that the respondents mentioned for their coverage of Shelley are Ian Jack's *English Literature, 1815–1832,* volume 10 of the Oxford History of English Literature; James Robert de J. Jackson's *Poetry of the Romantic Period,* volume 4 of the Routledge History of English Poetry; Boris Ford's *From Blake to Byron,* reissued as volume 5 of the New Pelican Guide to English Literature; and, the most recent entry on the list, J. R. Watson's *English Poetry of the Romantic Period, 1789–1830,* in the Longman Literature in English Series. To those general literary-historical introductions for the student should be added A. D. Harvey's *English Poetry in a Changing Society, 1780–1825* and Marilyn Gaull's *English Romanticism: The Human Context.* Finally, the standard concordance to Shelley's poetry by F. S. Ellis, first published in 1892, is dependable for what it does, but it is outdated and incomplete.

Recommended Readings

The respondents were asked to recommend the background and critical studies on Shelley that they thought would be most useful to beginning teachers and to students. Biographies dominated the list of recommended background works, thus suggesting the perennial attraction of Shelley's eventful and unorthodox life and the importance given by many teachers to placing Shelley in the context of his contemporaries and his cultural milieu. The four biographical studies mentioned most frequently were Newman Ivey White's two-volume *Shelley*, Richard Holmes's *Shelley: The Pursuit*, and two works by Kenneth Neill Cameron, *The Young Shelley: Genesis of a Radical* and *Shelley: The Golden Years*.

White's scholarly and judicious life of Shelley (also available in a one-volume edition, *Portrait of Shelley*, without the extensive footnotes and appendixes) has been the standard biography for almost half a century. Holmes's life, which sets out to give a more human view of the poet, is an informative and readable, if sometimes sensationalized, account. (Holmes records his adventures as a Romantic biographer of Shelley in an autobiographical travel book, *Footsteps*.) Cameron's two learned volumes—*The Young Shelley* traces the poet's life and the development of his ideas from 1809 to the publication of *Queen Mab* in 1813, and *The Golden Years* continues his life from the breakup of Shelley's first marriage in 1814 to his death in 1822—systematically develop an image of the poet as a proto-Marxist political and social thinker vitally in tune with the events of his times and devoted to the cause of radical reform. Only the first part of *Shelley: The Golden Years* is biography; the second and third parts are biographically and historically oriented criticism of Shelley's later prose and poetry.

By far the most frequently cited critical study of Shelley's poetry is Earl Wasserman's *Shelley: A Critical Reading*. The book—which incorporates in more or less revised form virtually everything Wasserman had published previously on the subject, including his book-length study of *Prometheus Unbound* and his influential and extended analyses of "Mont Blanc," "The Sensitive-Plant," and *Adonais* from *The Subtler Language*—is arguably the most important critical study of Shelley published in the last half century. Wasserman's close, philosophically oriented expositions, like virtually all modern criticism of Shelley, owe a substantial debt to C. E. Pulos's study *The Deep Truth*, which was also frequently mentioned by the respondents. That slender monograph argues that Shelley's skepticism is "the logical center of his thought, the point where his empiricism terminates and his idealism begins" (i).

Another highly recommended work, Harold Bloom's book *Shelley's Myth-making*, holds that the poet's Humean skepticism about metaphysical absolutes coincides with and in part sponsors his characteristic mythopoeic tendencies. Like Bloom's *Visionary Company*, a reading of Shelley and the other English Romantics that was also highly recommended by the respondents, the enduring value of *Shelley's Mythmaking* is in its close and provocative interpretations of particular texts. Shelley's skepticism is also vital to another highly recommended study, Stuart Curran's book *Shelley's Annus Mirabilis*. Curran argues that the great poetry from late 1818 to early 1820 is the "maturing of an epic vision" in which Shelley, adapting his extensive knowledge of syncretic mythology and esoteric thought, pictures the purgatorial struggle of the poet who sees both the fallen nature of European culture and the possibilities of its redemption.

The most recent of the critical studies most often recommended by the respondents is William Keach's work *Shelley's Style*, a sensitive and informed analysis not only of the poet's characteristic artistic and linguistic techniques but also of his highly ambivalent view of language itself. Carlos Baker's book *Shelley's Major Poetry*, although forty years old, is still frequently cited. Its Platonic bias is critically out-of-date, but the book remains valuable for demonstrating Shelley's creative assimilation of Renaissance literary traditions. Another frequently cited work, *The Lyrics of Shelley* by Judith Chernaik, has already been mentioned in "Reference and Critical Editions."

Several teachers reported using the books by Chernaik and Baker as students' general critical introductions to Shelley. Two highly recommended works specifically designed for that purpose are Donald H. Reiman's *Percy Bysshe Shelley* in the Twayne English Authors Series and Timothy Webb's *Shelley: A Voice Not Understood*. The Reiman book interweaves a chronological account of Shelley's life with helpful thematic analyses of his major writings that emphasize their philosophical skepticism and their social and political content. The Webb book also focuses on Shelley as a progressive thinker who built on an extensive knowledge of Western culture and literature, both classical and Christian.

Romantic Contexts

According to the survey, no general studies of Romantic theory and practice have been more influential in the classroom over the last quarter century than M. H. Abrams's two classic works, *Natural Supernaturalism* and *The Mirror and the Lamp*. Although the second-generation English poets are somewhat marginal to Abrams's formulation of European Romanticism in *Natural Supernaturalism*, Shelley's poetry, principally *Prometheus Unbound*, is noted for its apocalyptic imaginings and for its affirmation of a philosophical and spiritual Romantic love. *The Mirror and the Lamp* identifies Shelley, primarily because of *A Defence of Poetry*, as an exponent of Romantic Platonism. A 1981 overview by Marilyn Butler, *Romantics, Rebels and Reactionaries*—which emphasizes Shelley's classicism, humanism, and paganism, including his frank avowal of erotic love—was also highly recommended. (Butler's somewhat revisionist estimates of Shelley are also elaborated in a study of Thomas Love Peacock and his circle.) Lillian R. Furst's comparative study of English, French, and German Romanticism, *Romanticism in Perspective*, should also be mentioned here.

In *English Romanticism: The Grounds of Belief*, John Clubbe and Ernest J. Lovell, Jr., recognize the religious skepticism in the second-generation poets but reaffirm the ethical and humanistic grounds of Romantic poetry against poststructuralist readings. Likewise, Michael Cooke's *Acts of Inclusion* is sensitive to the ironies inherent in Shelley and Romantic literature but defines Romantic irony as a program of "radical reconciliation." Other recent studies of irony in Shelley and the Romantics take a more deconstructionist view. David Simpson, for example, in *Irony and Authority in Romantic Poetry*, discovers a problematic indeterminacy, an ongoing tension between the assertion and the subversion of authorial meanings. Closer still to the main current of American deconstructionism is Tilottama Rajan's *Dark Interpreter: The Discourse of Romanticism*, which argues that Shelley's subtextual skepticism continually undercuts his textual idealism.

Among Shelley's poems, "The Triumph of Life" has become a target text for deconstructionist critics, as three books from the "Yale school" indicate. The contributions to *Deconstruction and Criticism*, edited by Harold Bloom and others, center on "The Triumph." From that collection, Paul de Man reprinted his essay "Shelley Disfigured" in his own book of essays *The Rhetoric of Romanticism*. J. Hillis Miller's chapter on Shelley in *The Linguistic Moment* is also devoted to Shelley's unfinished final work. Cynthia Chase's 1986 book *Decomposing Figures* is among the most recent deconstructionist readings of Romantic tradition mentioned by the respondents. Two recent collections of essays that bear on Shelley from that perspective are *Romanticism and Language*, edited by Arden Reed, and *Romanticism and Contemporary Criticism*, edited by Morris Eaves and Michael Fischer.

An important Romantic context for the teacher of undergraduates is the social and political history of the age, an age still defined for many respondents almost exclusively by those two definitive revolutions, the French and the industrial. Several classic studies of the industrial revolution from socialist perspectives were especially praised in the survey. The studies include E. P. Thompson's *Making of the English Working Class* and two books by Raymond Williams, *Culture and Society: 1780–1950* and *The Country and the City*. The social and political backgrounds are studied from other points of view by Asa Briggs in *The Age of Improvement, 1783–1867*; by R. J.

White in *Life in Regency England* and *From Waterloo to Peterloo*; by A. D. Harvey in *Britain in the Early Nineteenth Century*; and by John Roach in *Social Reform in England 1780–1880*. G. M. Trevelyan's hoary but still useful *British History of the Nineteenth Century*, E. J. Hobsbawm's *Age of Revolution 1789–1848*, and C. W. Crawley's *War and Peace in an Age of Upheaval, 1793–1830* are informative general histories of the period with particular relevance to the French Revolution and its aftermath.

Not all the books just mentioned bear directly on Romanticism as a cultural movement, but others do, such as Howard Mumford Jones's *Revolution and Romanticism*, R. W. Harris's *Romanticism and the Social Order, 1780–1830*, and Allan Rodway's *Romantic Conflict*. By far the most often recommended and most comprehensive study of the interconnections between politics and poetry in the period is Carl Woodring's *Politics in English Romantic Poetry*.

Thomas R. Edwards takes Shelley and the Romantics to task in *Imagination and Power* for deflecting actual political issues into poetic myth. Indeed, a new kind of historical criticism is emerging in which the Romantic's own claims to revolutionary principles are being questioned. A 1981 work that finds Shelley and other Romantics to be both self-deceived and deceiving in that way is *Romanticism and Ideology* by David Aers, Jonathan Cook, and David Punter. Along the same lines, although more comprehensive in scope, is Jerome J. McGann's influential new historicist critical investigation of Romantic ideology.

Literary history, whether old or new, is a Romantic context of particular importance to Shelley, whose relation to predecessors, contemporaries, and heirs is frequently a topic in undergraduate classes. Several respondents recommended Walter Jackson Bate's authoritative study of poetic influence, *The Burden of the Past and the English Poet*; even more mentioned Harold Bloom's numerous meditations on the anxiety of influence. The works by Bloom cited as most helpful for Shelley were *The Anxiety of Influence, A Map of Misreading*, and *Poetry and Repression*.

The great predecessor poet for the Romantics in general was Milton, although Bloom and others identify Wordsworth as the source of Shelley's most fertile anxieties. Fairly recent studies of Milton's varied influence include Leslie Brisman's book *Milton's Poetry of Choice and Its Romantic Heirs*; a collection edited by Joseph Wittreich, Jr., *Milton and the Line of Vision*; and Nancy Moore Goslee's *"Uriel's Eye."* Roger Sales devotes a chapter to the effects of Wordsworth on Shelley and Keats in *Literary Inheritance*, and Jonathan Bate argues, in quite un-Bloomian fashion, the positive influence of Shakespeare on the English Romantics. Among studies of continuities between the Romantics and modern poetry, two can be mentioned here as particularly relevant to Shelley: George Bornstein's *Transformations of Romanticism in Yeats, Eliot, and Stevens* and Carlos Baker's *Echoing Green*.

For several reasons, the importance of genre in Romantic poetry has not been duly appreciated, a matter of particular interest for Shelley, whose creative use of varied poetic forms is unmatched in the period. Clearly, however, the situation has begun to change. Stuart Curran's 1986 book *Poetic Form and British Romanticism* is the most comprehensive and potentially influential study of the subject. In addition, numerous studies of particular literary forms consider relevant poems by Shelley in some detail. Among them are Paul Fry's book *The Poet's Calling in the English Ode*, Brian Wilkie's *Romantic Poets and Epic Tradition*, Roger Sales's *English Literature in History, 1780–1830: Pastoral and Politics*, Lore Metzger's *One Foot in Eden: Modes of Pastoral in Romantic Poetry*, Peter Sacks's *English Elegy*, Eric Smith's *By Mourning Tongues: Studies in English Elegy*, and Daniel Albright's *Lyricality in English Literature*.

Most comprehensive accounts of Romantic drama—such as those by Bertrand Evans, Richard M. Fletcher, Joseph Donohue, Terry Otten, and Erika Gottlieb—attend to *The Cenci*, whether from a literary or a theatrical perspective. In *English Comedy* Allan Rodway considers Shelley as a satirist, and both Shelley's Gothic fiction and *The Cenci* are discussed in James Twitchell's *Dreadful Pleasures*.

Shelley has figured significantly in the recent growth of critical interest in poetic fragments. "The Triumph of Life" immediately comes to mind, although Marjorie Levinson examines the juvenile "Posthumous Fragments of Margaret Nicholson" and *Julian and Maddalo* in *The Romantic Fragment Poem*. Balachandra Rajan takes up "The Triumph of Life" in *The Form of the Unfinished*. On the other hand, Neill Fraistat's study of Shelley's *Prometheus Unbound* volume in *The Poem and the Book* suggests an increased attention by critics and teachers to the relation of individual poems to the poetic volumes of which they are parts.

A new or renewed commitment to myth and symbol is a leading characteristic of Romantic poetry and is particularly important to the teaching of Shelley. While asserting the centrality of different mythic structures, M. H. Abrams's *Natural Supernaturalism*, Harold Bloom's *Visionary Company*, Northrop Frye's *Study of English Romanticism*, Leslie Brisman's *Romantic Origins*, and Paul Cantor's *Creature and Creator* all see the mythmaking impulse itself as essential to Romanticism. In *Mythology and the Romantic Tradition in English Poetry* Douglas Bush focuses on the uses made of Greek mythology, and Paul Korshin in *Typologies in England, 1650–1820* relates Shelley and others to mythological syncretism and categorizes types of Romantic imagery.

Among the studies of Romantic imagery and symbolism, many of which ground Shelley's symbolism in particular metaphysical systems, David Perkins's Platonic *The Quest for Permanence* was the one most frequently mentioned by the respondents. Other studies mentioned include G. Wilson

Knight's *Starlit Dome*, Albert Gerard's *English Romantic Poetry*, R. A. Foakes's *Romantic Assertion*, C. M. Bowra's *Romantic Imagination*, James Benziger's *Images of Eternity*, and Kathleen Raine's *Defending Ancient Springs*. Among studies of the origin and the nature of the creative Romantic imagination, that by James Engell was particularly recommended to teachers of Shelley.

The nature of the self was a topic singled out by the respondents as particularly relevant to Shelley. In *The Romantic Mother* Barbara Schapiro takes a psychoanalytic view of narcissistic patterns and images of women in Romantic literature, and James Applewhite's *Seas and Inland Journeys* examines images of the individuated self and the collective unconscious from a Jungian perspective. Harold Bloom's influential collection of essays *The Ringers in the Tower* views the Romantic tradition as the poet's internal quest for his true self, the creative imagination. Michael Cooke in *The Romantic Will* argues the centrality of the engaged, assertive will in Romantic—and Shelleyan—conceptions of the self.

Two studies of Romantic love that are of interest to teachers and students of Shelley are Gerald Enscoe's *Eros and the Romantics*, which proclaims the sexual nature of Romantic love, and Frederick Beaty's *Light from Heaven*, which emphasizes its social and spiritual aspects. In his comprehensive study of the philosophy of love in Western culture, Irving Singer places Shelley under the heading "Benign Romanticism."

Two other important philosophical topics in teaching Shelley's poetry are his concept of necessity and his skepticism, both of which have been much discussed in critical works on the poet. Two general studies bearing on those issues can be mentioned here: *Romantic Contraries: Freedom versus Destiny* by Peter Thorslev, Jr., and Donald H. Reiman's 1988 book *Intervals of Inspiration: The Skeptical Tradition and the Psychology of Romanticism*.

Several teachers mentioned the advantages of comparing Shelley's poetry with other forms of Romantic art. One informative study along those lines is James Twitchell's *Romantic Horizons*, in which Shelley is compared with Constable, the more usually noted resemblance being to Turner. The collection of essays *Images of Romanticism: Verbal and Visual Affinities*, edited by Karl Kroeber and William Walling, should also be mentioned, as should Stephen Larrabee's study of the relation between sculpture and poetry in the Romantic period. Music is both an important source of imagery and metaphor in Shelley's poetry and a genetic influence on it. Both aspects are taken up in Erland Anderson's *Harmonious Madness*, and Lawrence Kramer compares Shelley and Chopin formalistically and psychologically in *Music and Poetry*.

Among the recommended studies of the influence on English Romanticism of Greek and Italian culture are John Buxton's *Grecian Taste*, Kenneth Churchill's *Italy and English Literature, 1764–1930*, C. P. Brand's *Italy and the English Romantics*, and Steve Ellis's *Dante and English Poetry*. An influence of a different kind, that of audiences both real and imagined, is explored by Ian Jack in *The Poet and His Audience*.

Students and teachers of Shelley are fortunate to have at their disposal many excellent collections of critical and scholarly essays on English Romanticism. Although most of them date from the 1950s and 1960s, the number of recent entries is growing. The volumes edited by Reed, by Eaves and Fischer, and by Kroeber and Walling were mentioned earlier. The collection that teachers most often recommend to students and the one that they most often place on reserve lists is M. H. Abrams's *English Romantic Poets: Modern Essays in Criticism*, originally published in 1960 but extensively updated in 1975. Another collection revised in the 1970s is *Romanticism: Points of View*, edited by Robert Gleckner and Gerald Enscoe.

Among the earlier compilations of essays on Romantic literature are those edited by Shiv K. Kumar; Clarence D. Thorpe, Carlos Baker, and Bennett Weaver; Frederick Hilles and Harold Bloom; Northrop Frye; and John B. Halsted. More recent collections relevant to Shelley, including several from the 1980s, include those edited by George Bornstein; Stephen Prickett; R. T. Davies and B. G. Beatty; J. R. Watson; and Donald H. Reiman, Michael C. Jaye, and Betty T. Bennett. In addition to compiling the highly praised 1970 collection *Romanticism and Consciousness*, Harold Bloom has edited a 1986 anthology of criticism, *English Romantic Poets*, in the Chelsea House Critical Cosmos Series. The three essays on Shelley in that book also appear in the Chelsea House Modern Critical Views volume on Shelley, also edited by Bloom, cited in the "Studies of Shelley" section.

In addition to recommending collections of works by various hands, the respondents recommended several collections of essays by a single critic. Bloom's *Ringers in the Tower*, Abrams's *Correspondent Breeze*, and R. H. Fogle's *Permanent Pleasure* were mentioned most often for their various commentaries on Shelley, other Romantic writers, and Romantic literature in general. Shelley is featured prominently in an important 1987 collection by Donald H. Reiman, *Romantic Texts and Contexts*, which combines essays on the editing of Romantic texts with literary and historical criticism.

Studies of Shelley

Few teachers any longer take seriously the attacks leveled against Shelley earlier in this century by F. R. Leavis, T. S. Eliot, and other New Critics, new humanists, and Christian apologists. Partly in response to those ideologically motivated assessments of Shelley's moral irresponsibility and intellectual vacuity, critics and scholars around the mid-century began to argue that Shelley's poetry was at the very least a poetry of ideas whose difficult symbolism and imagery can be explained by a coherent body of thought. The privileged system of thought, until the mid-1960s, was Platonism, sometimes more, more often less, strictly defined.

Many teachers still recommend critical works of that kind—if not for their now out-of-fashion Platonic and Neoplatonic theses, then for their often penetrating local interpretations. Carl Grabo's ground-breaking critical biography, *The Magic Plant*, was mentioned by several respondents, as was James Notopoulos's *Platonism of Shelley*, which remains the definitive study of the poet's knowledge of Plato. Neville Rogers's *Shelley at Work*, based on an analysis of the poet's notebooks, seeks to determine "what Shelley took from Plato and how he absorbed and transmuted it" (23). In *Shelley's Later Poetry*, a study of the Italian years that focuses on *Prometheus Unbound*, Milton Wilson sees the poet's Platonism as unsystematic and not an "unmixed blessing" (298).

A tendency of all Platonic approaches to Shelley is to emphasize his commitment to the eternal and the transcendent, often at the expense of the temporal and the real. The mystical and religious impulses in Shelley's thought and their relation to his mythmaking and symbolism have been studied from widely differing points of view ever since Browning claimed that the poet would have become a Christian, had he lived, and Yeats called *Promethus Unbound* a "sacred book" (*Essays* 65). In *Shelley's Religion* Ellsworth Barnard affirms the compatibility of Shelley's poetry with modern, nontraditional versions of Christian teaching, and James Allsup argues in *The Magic Circle* that "Shelley is in essence a Christian poet" (ix) whose concept of love unites Platonic eros and Christian agape. Another kind of unity, the reconciliation of Christian prophecy and eighteenth-century epistemology, is posited of both Blake and Shelley by Terence Hoagwood in *Prophecy and the Philosophy of Mind*.

Ross Woodman invokes both Orphic mysticism and Platonism as determinant metaphysical contexts in *The Apocalyptic Vision in the Poetry of Shelley*. The esoteric nature of Shelley's thought is given perhaps its most extreme formulation in James Rieger's *Mutiny Within*. For Rieger, Shelley is a purposefully obscurantist writer who "derived many of his major symbols from . . . Gnostic and dualist Christian heresies" (14). The most recent study to emphasize Zoroastrian and Gnostic influences on Shelley is Andrew Welburn's *Power and Self-Consciousness in the Poetry of Shelley*.

A less esoteric but complex background for the poet's work is eighteenth-century French philosophy. One strand of that influence is explored by Edward Duffy in *Rousseau in England: The Context for Shelley's Critique of the Enlightenment*. Joseph Barrell demonstrates in *Shelley and the Thought of His Time* that the poet, like other contemporaries, was engaged by competing intellectual influences—Godwin and French rationalism on the one hand, Plato and the Greek revival on the other.

Shelley's interest in French rationalism is a major concern in many studies of the poet's political and social philosophy that place him as a liberal Whig or a philosophical anarchist or a Jacobinic revolutionary. Among such studies those most often recommended by the respondents are Gerald McNiece's *Shelley and the Revolutionary Idea*, P. M. S. Dawson's *Unacknowledged Legislator*, and Michael Henry Scrivener's *Radical Shelley*. Those works illuminate different political contexts, both English and Continental, in Shelley's writing, and they pay particular attention to his often topical, propagandistic prose. Art Young in *Shelley and Nonviolence* and Frank A. Lea in *Shelley and the Romantic Revolution* assess the poet's political anarchism, and Paul Foot's *Red Shelley* enlists the poet under the banner militant of proto-Marxism.

As evidenced by the works of Pulos, Wasserman, Bloom, Reiman, Curran, and Keach cited in "Recommended Readings," the most influential critical studies of Shelley's thought over the past quarter century or so have emphasized his philosophical skepticism, rather than his Platonism. In particular, recent critics have sought to relate his skepticism to his poetics, grounding in the skepticism the various kinds of openness, indeterminacy, relativism, and transformation they find in the poetics.

Several respondents mentioned the ground-breaking articles by Daniel J. Hughes on the fluidity of structure and symbol in Shelley's poetry. Shelley's poetics is also the subject of John Wright's book *Shelley's Myth of Metaphor*, and Earl J. Schulze stresses the idealist basis of Shelley's aesthetics in *Shelley's Theory of Poetry*. Two other often recommended studies of the major poems link poetic strategies to Shelley's underlying epistemological skepticism with very different conclusions: Lloyd Abbey's *Destroyer and Preserver* and Jean Hall's *Transforming Image*. Another recent interpretation of the major poems, Angela Leighton's *Shelley and the Sublime*, argues a relativism in the poetry that is at once aesthetic, political, and philosophical. In *Skepticism and Ideology*, Terence Hoagwood examines the philosophical context of Shelley's prose.

As mentioned previously in "Romantic Contexts," the skepticism and relativism of Shelley's poetry have begun to attract deconstructive analysis. Jerrold E. Hogle's 1988 book *Shelley's Process: Radical Transference and the Development of His Major Works* includes a number of Hogle's deconstructive essays on Shelley and may prove to be a major influence on undergraduate teaching in the future.

Many critical studies that concentrate on some aspect of Shelley's thought also have much to say about the formal and stylistic complexities of his art, the distinction between philosophy and poetics in Shelley's work being shadowy at best. Among the studies that focus on the poet's use of myth, symbol, imagery, and language, the respondents mentioned in particular Peter Butter's book *Shelley's Idols of the Cave*, R. H. Fogle's *Imagery of Keats and*

Shelley, and Glenn O'Malley's *Shelley and Synaesthesia*. Richard Cronin's book *Shelley's Poetic Thoughts* elucidates "Shelley's handling of language and poetic forms" (x) in relation to the poetry's intellectual content. The most recent study devoted to Shelley's manipulation of literary form is Ronald Tetreault's 1987 book *The Poetry of Life*, which sees the poetry moving chronologically toward ever-greater openness and indeterminacy.

Among the special topics in Shelley's poetry singled out for attention by undergraduate teachers, none was mentioned more often than his treatment of love and sexuality. Of the book-length studies of the subject, the most highly praised is Nathaniel Brown's *Sexuality and Feminism in Shelley*. A controversial 1986 study by Nora Crook and Derek Guiton, *Shelley's Venomed Melody*, relates the sexually resonant imagery of disease and health in the poetry to an alleged early case of venereal disease.

Shelley's use of science is also a topic frequently raised in the undergraduate classroom. The recommended studies include Carl Grabo's book *A Newton among Poets*, which focuses on the use of science in *Prometheus Unbound*; Lloyd Jeffrey's study *Shelley's Knowledge and Use of Natural History*; and Desmond King-Hele's *Shelley: His Thought and Work*, which clearly demonstrates the extensiveness of the poet's acquaintance with the science of his day.

Current critical interest in literary influence has made Shelley's relationship to his Romantic contemporaries a concern in the classroom. The most often cited influence, that of Wordsworth, has been the subject of numerous articles. The first of what one expects will be several contemporary book-length studies devoted completely to that relationship is G. Kim Blank's work *Wordsworth's Influence on Shelley*. The complex relationship with Byron has been studied from a primarily biographical perspective in John Buxton's *Byron and Shelley: The History of a Friendship*, and Charles E. Robinson combines biographical evidence with literary analysis in the often recommended *Shelley and Byron: The Snake and Eagle Wreathed in Fight*.

Shelley's responsiveness to the contemporary Gothic revival is the subject of John Murphy's *Dark Angel*. Roland A. Duerksen's *Shelleyan Ideas in Victorian Literature* examines the considerable influence exerted by the poet on the later nineteenth century, and George Bornstein's *Yeats and Shelley* works out in detail Yeats's complicated, often self-reflexive responses to his Romantic precursor.

In addition to citing the works by Reiman, Webb, Chernaik, and Baker referred to in "Recommended Readings," the respondents named the studies by Butter and King-Hele noted earlier in this section as good general introductions to Shelley's thought and poetry for undergraduate students. Patricia Hodgart's *Preface to Shelley* in the Longman Preface Book series can also be mentioned here, if not recommended. Stuart Sperry's 1988 book

Shelley's Major Verse, which links the poetry to the poet's life, may well become a widely used critical and biographical introduction.

Several monographs and book-length studies devoted entirely to or focusing on single poems by Shelley were also mentioned in the survey. They include four extended analyses of *Prometheus Unbound* by Earl Wasserman (included and expanded in his *Shelley: A Critical Reading*), Carl Grabo, Bennett Weaver, and William Hildebrand; Carl Grabo's Neoplatonic exegesis *The Meaning of "The Witch of Atlas"*; two monographs on *Alastor*, William Hildebrand's *Study of Alastor* and Harold Hoffman's *Odyssey of the Soul*; Edwin Silverman's *Poetic Synthesis in Shelley's Adonais*; Donald H. Reiman's book *Shelley's "The Triumph of Life"*; and Stuart Curran's book *Shelley's Cenci: Scorpions Ringed with Fire*. The most recent book-length analysis of an individual poem is Ann Shealy's 1985 critical study of *Epipsychidion*.

Respondents noted several collections of critical essays on Shelley that they recommend to students and place on library reserve. Two collections from the 1960s, George Ridenour's *Shelley: A Collection of Critical Essays* in the Twentieth Century Views series and R. B. Woodings's *Shelley* in the Modern Judgments series, both remain valuable resources despite the fact that they are somewhat dated.

The burst of recent critical interest in Shelley is evidenced by the appearance of at least three collections in the 1980s. Miriam Allott's *Essays on Shelley* in the Liverpool English Texts and Studies series collects original essays, by members of the department of English at Liverpool University, that focus on the modernity and the craft of Shelley's poetry. A more varied and more impressive collection is Kelvin Everest's *Shelley Revalued*; the volume includes a wide range of original essays written by participants at the two international Shelley conferences held at Gregynog, Wales, in 1978 and 1980. Harold Bloom's *Percy Bysshe Shelley* in the Chelsea House Modern Critical Views series includes published essays and excerpts from critical studies. Finally, *Studies in Romanticism* devoted its Fall 1984 issue to Shelley, with the focus on *Adonais* and *Prometheus Unbound*.

Aids to Teaching

According to the survey, relatively few teachers use audiovisual materials in their undergraduate classes on Shelley, although a growing number are incorporating examples of Romantic art in their survey courses to illustrate the change from a neoclassic to a Romantic aesthetic. The artist most frequently compared with Shelley, because of his dynamic impressions of landscape and light, is Turner. *William Wordsworth and the Age of English Romanticism*, the catalog compiled by Jonathan Wordsworth, Michael C. Jaye, and Robert Woof, from the recent exhibition, reproduces a number of paintings and drawings relevant to the study of Shelley's poetry. Similarly, John Purkis's *World of the English Romantic Poets* presents pictorial representations of dominant images in Romantic poetry, central among them being the figure of Prometheus. Peter Quennell's *Romantic England: Writing and Painting, 1717–1851* also reproduces relevant sketches and paintings.

Some teachers bring in portraits of Shelley, either on slides and postcards or reproduced in such volumes as the biographies by Newan Ivey White and Richard Holmes. Teachers also reported using picture postcards or their own slides and photographs of places and artifacts associated with Shelley's life and work: for example, the Keats-Shelley memorial in Westminster Abbey; the Protestant Cemetery and the Baths of Caracalla in Rome; the Casa Magni in Lerici; Mont Blanc; Guido Reni's portrait of Beatrice Cenci; and the *Trionfo della Morte* fresco in the Campo Santo, Pisa. There is also a small but growing interest in the sketches scattered throughout the pages of Shelley's working notebooks. Neville Rogers reproduces and comments on some of the sketches in *Shelley at Work*.

Professionally produced 16-millimeter educational films, 35-millimeter sound filmstrips, and videocassettes on Romantic poetry are plentiful, although the producers tend to bring them in and out of distribution, switch distributors, and change titles with an abandon that makes accurate bibliographic citation difficult. Among the currently available films, sound filmstrips, and videocassettes that treat Shelley at least in passing are *The Romantic Age; The Romantic Era; The Romantic Protest; Romanticism: The Revolt of the Spirit; The Rise of Romanticism*, which relates poetry to painting; and *The Spirit of Romanticism*, which presents the central political and cultural episodes of the period. In *The Glorious Romantics, Pt. 3: Percy Bysshe Shelley*, Jean Marsh and John Neville-Andrews dramatize incidents from Shelley's life and poetry. *Romantic Poetry* presents the classical themes in Shelley's work, and *The Younger Romantics* focuses on Shelley's conception of the poet as rebel and martyr.

A 16-millimeter film, *English Literature: The Romantic Period*, dramatizes selections from the great Romantic writers. One respondent called Ken Russell's feature film *Altered States* the visual equivalent of act 4 of *Prometheus Unbound*. Another Russell film, although certainly not for the squeamish, is *Gothic*, his almost X-rated, highly impressionistic telling of the genesis of *Frankenstein*. Professorial discretion is strongly advised.

Few teachers reported using recordings of Shelley's poetry, although a number are available on records and audiotapes. Vincent Price's readings of several lyrics and parts of *Adonais* in *Poetry of Percy Bysshe Shelley* is a classic. Other recordings of selected poems and passages include those by Robert Speaight and Robert Eddison in *Treasury of Percy Bysshe Shelley*; Hilton Edwards in *Golden Treasury of Milton, Keats, and Shelley*; Bramwell Fletcher in *English Romantic Poets*; and Claire Bloom, Anthony Quayle, Frederick Worlock, and Ralph Richardson in *English Romantic Poetry*.

Finally, a growing number of audiocassette programs provide critical, historical, and biographical information aimed at the beginning undergraduate student. Currently available cassettes include *Shelley, Percy Bysshe*, a critical analysis of five poems by John Holloway; *The Romantics*, a discussion of critical problems and poetic techniques in Shelley and others by Christopher Salvensen and William Walsh; *Poetry of Percy Shelley, Pts. 1 and 2*, including oral interpretations and discussions of selected poems; *Percy Bysshe Shelley*, a commentary on both the life and the work; *"Ozymandias" by Percy Bysshe Shelley*, a general critical discussion of the poem; and *English Romantics and the French Revolution*, featuring Shelley in its assessment of the effects of the French Revolution on Romantic writers.

Part Two

APPROACHES

INTRODUCTION

The next thirty-two essays, written by contributors to the survey that preceded the preparation of this volume, reflect a wide range of subjects and concerns identified by teachers of Shelley's poetry—historical backgrounds, literary relations, theoretical and critical perspectives, pedagogical strategies, analyses of individual texts, and so on. The collection as a whole attempts to be representative, expressing the interests of a variety of teachers in a variety of teaching situations. It includes essays by well-known scholars who teach Shelley on the graduate level and in specialized undergraduate seminars and by teachers who approach Shelley exclusively in lower-division literary surveys. It includes essays by men and by women. Different institutions with different student populations in different geographical areas are represented. What brings all thirty-two essayists together here is a common commitment as teachers and, in their own ways, as students of Shelley's poetry.

The essays vary in length, style, and content. Within the limits imposed by space and by editorial policy for the series, I have tried to allow each essay to develop its own voice. Some are pedagogical, focusing on such topics as the choice and the arrangement of texts, course development, and teaching methods. Others are more informational, analytical, and theoretical and do not present ready-made classroom models or procedures. Some are critical and scholarly in orientation, others more anecdotal. Readers will find it necessary to interpret and adapt the contributor's experiences and ideas to their own teaching situations. Whether directly or indirectly, however, all the essays in the collection offer valuable insights and stimulate productive questions for the teacher of undergraduates. I hope that even specialists in the field, as well as nonspecialists and beginning teachers, will find things in the volume to engage their interest.

SELECTED PEDAGOGICAL APPROACHES

Shelley's Grasp upon the Actual

Stuart Curran

F. R. Leavis's infamous critique of Shelley may now, some fifty years after its initial publication, be construed, in the terms with which Leavis dismissed Shelley, as "almost unreadable . . . to the mature" mind (211). And yet it is comparatively easy, perhaps it is almost instinctive, for students to share Leavis's sense that Shelley had "a weak grasp upon the actual" (206). That notion stems partly from the undergraduate's inexperience with the conventions and even the nature of poetry. The typical student brings to poetry expectations honed by Hallmark cards and advertising jingles, confuses metaphors with messages, and is prone to allegorize away from the actual as quickly as possible. The student, then, is all too ready to adopt Leavis's Shelley, the poet of feeling, if given half a chance. The problem, of course, is that Shelley's mind is always in the way. So, if they would but realize it, are the minds of our students. The challenge in teaching Shelley to undergraduates is to reinforce the common bond of thought.

As might be expected from someone who appears to have spent half his life worrying over the text, I begin with *The Cenci* (which, by the way, since a few students are bound to get it wrong, is authoritatively pronounced "*Chen*-chi"). I have never known a student who did not respond with some degree of excitement to this drama; and even its echoes of Shakespeare, however fussed about in the critical literature, offer a sense of comfortable bearings, at least for a time.

The feminist awareness in the past decade has brought the social and political dynamics of Shelley's drama into everyday life—so much so, indeed, that I no longer find it easy to stimulate the gendered conflict of perspectives between men and women that used to erupt as the discussion continued. If, however, you are particularly adept as a teacher at leading students down the garden path in the manner of Socrates, *The Cenci* is certainly the text for a virtuoso performance. Once you have produced general acquiescence on the guilt of Beatrice, it may be followed by a quick scrawl on the blackboard—*Women Against Rape*—which ought to bring the house of cards down in a flash.

However you get there, the valuable point of the discussion ought to be to derive from the authentic experience of the students themselves a sense of the profound moral casuistry of Shelley's drama. You may even ask them how as a jury they would cast a vote—on everyone, from the Pope on down—and in what order of culpability. From that you can progress to how justice is perceived by the principals: what ends it serves, on what premises it rests, on what contingencies it depends. When everyone is indictable, who is to judge and on what grounds? Every student in your class—and it doesn't take a Socrates to prove it—is at base a moral casuist—everywhere, that is, except in an English literature classroom. To elicit that awareness is, simply speaking, to confirm their own—and Shelley's—grasp upon the actual.

For me, the essential value of beginning with so accessible and seemingly so traditional a work as *The Cenci* is that the easily disconnected but inter-woven threads of Shelley's thought—political, religious, philosophical, psy-chological, aesthetic—are all present together. In the midst of the tragedy's moral ambiguity, the underlying coherence of Shelley's thoughts, even if represented within a deconstructive cul-de-sac, is accentuated for the stu-dent. From that base I turn to "Mont Blanc" and "Hymn to Intellectual Beauty" and find the students prepared, particularly in the case of "Mont Blanc," to recognize their own mental processes mirrored in Shelley's. (It is, I think, much harder to gain that sense of identification through a normal chronological sequence.)

Much earlier in the course, we will have confronted the basic philosophical dichotomy between Locke and Berkeley, materialist and idealist; but "Mont Blanc" is invariably where the essential truth of Berkeleian idealism—that the actual is a mental phenomenon—hits home. The continual round robin of Shelley's meditation is little more, but nothing less, than a representation of how we all purchase our grasp of the actual. That it is also a self-reflexive exercise in empowering a metaphor leads students to recognize how de-pendent are processes of thought on its instruments, which are both nec-essary and dangerously restrictive. The "vacancy" that is the last word and last image of "Mont Blanc," enabled by the ultimate irresolution of its concluding question mark, is rather neatly balanced by the mirrored nonmeaning of the final line of *The Cenci*, Beatrice's "Well, 'tis very well." That, then, may be the point to introduce a note of skepticism into the discussion.

To get to that level of competence and comfort with Shelley's characteristic poetic mode takes about two 1-hour-and-20-minute periods or three 50-minute periods. The students should by that point feel comfortable with the notion that reality is always a mental construct negotiated between self and not-self (Fichte's premise), that metaphors are at once the means to that ongoing process and inhibitors of it, that social institutions are metaphors writ large and codified, and that we have no guarantee that either metaphors or institutions have any authority independent from that invested in them by the mind.

After that, as you can discern, *Prometheus Unbound* will be, if not exactly a piece of cake, certainly palatable. How long you keep Prometheus banging his head against the Phantasm of Jupiter depends on your Socratic patience; it also depends initially on your students' capacity for keeping afloat on this great sea of diction. It may help, without reducing the discourse to comic-book proportions, to offer the students, preliminary to their reading, an unelaborated, sequential exposition of the plot of act 1—what actually happens. In that way, when they break through during the class discussion into the actuality of what has happened—with Prometheus progressively deconstructing his own metaphor, which is Jupiter—they will be primed to see it mirrored in their own reading or their own considerable difficulty with reading. That is to say, to revert to my governing rubric, the elusiveness of the students' grasp upon the actual in *Prometheus Unbound* recapitulates the problem confronting Prometheus and Asia for some three thousand years; it also illustrates, when they come to it, the chanciness of the act 4 utopia and why Demogorgon in the end all but predicts its collapse.

Given that interest in not just making Shelley accessible to undergraduates but also enforcing the extent to which the linked processes of thought and institutionalization on which he concentrates are embedded in the quotidian experiences of us all, I find much of the academic discourse on *Prometheus Unbound* unhelpful in the classroom. To construe Prometheus as the One Mind (Wasserman, *Shelley*), or to identify Demogorgon as Necessity or Eternity is to forge distinctions without a difference, mechanisms to abstract Shelley's sharply specific symbolic import and to distance it from its applications to his world and ours. On the other hand, to reduce his symbolic universe to the expectations of realism (which also, against all odds of common sense, continues to figure in the critical literature) is to falsify its nature, leading one to wonder if it is really proper for this bourgeois couple, Prometheus and Asia, to lock the doors to the cave so early in act 3. In both cases the hard questions and the awesome poetic genius implicit in *Prometheus Unbound* are removed from the discourse. To draw them directly to the fore, we may ask, among other pointed questions, whether any student in the class is prepared to argue against the case put by the Furies in act 1; why music is the underlying metaphor and the metaphoric dynamic of act 2; just what are "those foul shapes . . . / Which under many a name and many a form . . . Were Jupiter" (3.4.180–84)—and let us not, please, forget to observe that the teacher constitutes one of those forms; and whether any of our students or universities would be prepared to exist in Shelley's fourth act?

At this point—with side excursions intervening to that deeply political document, *A Defence of Poetry*, and whichever of the canonical poems there is time for—we are ready to confront the triumph of metaphor over life in which we all seem doomed to lose our grasp upon the actual, in which not once but in three overlapping sequences (which might have been compounded many times over had Shelley lived) innocent Beatrice Cenci is ravaged and beheaded. Since by this point "The Triumph of Life" teaches itself, I have no more advice to offer. Except, perhaps, to observe that the "shape all light" is not some distant cousin of the One Mind and the unique problem of poor Rousseau but what we all most dearly desire, what drives us to metaphor and then inexorably traps us in it—Dante, Shelley, you, me, all of us.

"The Mind in Creation":
Life as Metaphor

Ross Woodman

In his *Defence of Poetry* Shelley affirms his poetic faith (often clothed in the borrowed apparel of religion) in the power of the imagination to penetrate, however briefly, a transcendental realm "beyond and above consciousness" (Reiman and Powers 486). The exercise of that power, however, is subject to two radical limitations. The first and more serious limitation is the reification of the power of imagination into a fixed system that constitutes tyranny, particularly the tyranny of religious faith that Blake calls "Priesthood" or the turning of "poetical tales" into "forms of worship" (*The Marriage of Heaven and Hell*, pl. 11). The second limitation is the fading of the power during the act of composition, so that what finally emerges as a text is "a feeble shadow of the original conception of the poet" (504). The two limitations are intimately connected: the "feeble shadow" becomes through reification the fixed system. If, therefore, poets are, as Shelley argues, "the unacknowledged legislators of the World" (508), they are also in danger of becoming through the reification that attends acknowledgement the tyrants of the world. How to prevent that reification (prophet becoming priest) is for Shelley crucial if poetry is to act as the liberator of both the individual and society.

My approach, therefore, focuses on Shelley's account of "the mind in creation" (503–04) in his *Defence of Poetry* and the dangers of arresting its "transitory brightness" (504) into a fixed system of belief. I invite my students to look initially at some of Shelley's images (in "Hymn to Intellectual Beauty," for example) and to comment on the importance of their "transitory brightness" as a way of avoiding the dangers of a religious system. I invite them to question, from this perspective, the accusations of vagueness and imprecision so often leveled at his poetry. I then begin my reading of actual poems by juxtaposing the early *Alastor* and the final fragment, "The Triumph of Life."

In my examination of *Alastor*, I focus on the vision of the veiled maid as it suddenly dissolves into nothingness. I compare that experience to Rousseau's encounter with the "shape all light" (line 353) in "The Triumph of Life." Rousseau's regret is that "the spark with which Heaven lit my spirit" had not been "with purer nutriment supplied" (201, 202). The insistence of both Rousseau and the Visionary on a "purer nutriment" than the imagination can provide finally reduces their visions to the "dust of death" (388), to vacancy or nothing at all. The question I pose to the students is whether in Shelley's view that nothingness is preferable to the tyranny that arises from the hardening, rather than the dissolving, of vision. It is a question to which I keep returning.

Lacking in both the Visionary and Rousseau (neither of whom should be identified with Shelley himself) is an understanding of the vitally metaphoric nature of language, which has the power to bring together what Shelley in his *Defence* calls "the before unapprehended relations of things" (482). Those "before unapprehended relations" constitute a re-creation of what would otherwise be a universe "annihilated in our minds by the recurrence of impressions blunted by reiteration" (506), "pictures of integral thoughts" becoming "signs for portions or classes of thought" (482). That annihilated universe is the "dust of death" to which both the Visionary and Rousseau are reduced through their desire for a "purer nutriment" that would allow them to unite with a source or origin that for Shelley remains inaccessible. To have access to it (assuming that it does in fact exist) is to lay claim to a delusive omnipotence that is, for Shelley, alien to the spirit of poetic faith, as opposed to religious faith. What does exist for Shelley is not the source but the poet's vanishing apparitions of it that are and must remain "frail spells" ("Hymn to Intellectual Beauty" 29). The source is but an "impulse" of an otherwise "vacant brain" (*Alastor* 191). To arrest that "impulse" into a fetish is to be seduced by the winged joy into a fatal entrapment.

The examination of *Alastor* and "The Triumph of Life" as explorations of the fatal desire for omnipotence that destroys the life of metaphor prepares the way for a close reading of *Prometheus Unbound*. I begin with the figure of Jupiter, whom I present, in the context of Shelley's Gnostic rejection of the Christian doctrine of the Incarnation, as a demonic parody of "the mind in creation" understood as a "fading coal" (504) awakened by an "invisible influence" (504) to a "transitory brightness" (504). Thus, when Jupiter cries "Rejoice! henceforth I am omnipotent" (3.1.3), I invite students to apply that rejoicing to Shelley's "Man were immortal, and omnipotent" in "Hymn to Intellectual Beauty" (39) and to compare the dream vision in *Alastor* to the union of Jupiter and Thetis, from which "mingling" of "two mighty spirits" emerged, according to Jupiter,

> a third
> Mightier than either-which unbodied now
> Between us, floats, felt, although unbeheld,
> Waiting the incarnation. . . .   (3.1.44–47)

Students quickly learn to distinguish between the imagery of Incarnation and an "unbodied" imagery that "floats," is "felt," and is finally in its dissolution "unbeheld."

In turning from the Jupiter of act 3 to Prometheus addressing him in the opening lines of act 1, I ask the students to consider the relationship between them. The Jupiter who inhabits the mind of the bound Prometheus reflects the mind of a poet who has become the victim of his vision by allowing it to harden into a system of belief. Jupiter is the poet's shadow or specter who is ready to assume control whenever "a poet becomes a man, and is abandoned to the sudden reflux of the influences under which others habitually live." Jupiter inhabits "the [poet's] intervals of inspiration," which, Shelley asserts, "may be frequent without being durable" (507). Prometheus in the first act is, in the absence of Asia, struggling, essentially in vain, to release himself from the Jupiter within. In that struggle Shelley, like Blake before him, is offering his own reading of the struggle between God and Satan in Milton's *Paradise Lost*. Partly for that reason, I invite the students to point out the echoes of Milton, particularly the speeches of Satan, in the opening speech of Prometheus.

The ways in which both the presentation of Asia and the lyrics that invoke and enact her presence keep Shelley's drama from hardening into a system of belief become a focus for class discussion of the second act. The process of unveiling is endless. "Veil after veil may be undrawn," Shelley writes in his *Defence*, "and the inmost naked beauty of the meaning never exposed" (500). I invite the students to explore the first act in relation to the second; the unbinding of Prometheus by the action of the will finds its true or poetic ground in the unveiling of Asia.

In reading the drama as an enactment of "the mind in creation," making use of Shelley's account in his *Defence of Poetry* of his own radically subversive way of reading, I encourage the students to think of themselves as belonging to what Shelley in the preface calls "the more select classes of poetical readers" (135). I want them, that is, to see in the drama a mirror of their own minds in the act of reading. Only when the mind becomes conscious of its own activity and assumes full responsibility for its own actions by bringing what is initially beyond and above consciousness into the orbit of human awareness can we, according to Shelley, be free. Rather than treat those actions in a dogmatic or philosophical manner, he chooses to treat them as spells. Demogorgon, for example, assumes, as a magician, a role like Prospero's in *The Tempest*. Summing up the action of the psychodrama enacted on a stage that is a mirror of the mind, Demogorgon at the conclusion directly addresses, as does Prospero, the audience of readers:

> These are the spells by which to reassume
> An empire o'er the disentangled doom.   (4.568–69)

The "mind in creation" is what Keats calls "Soul-making or spirit creation" (21 April 1819), understood as a process in which the soul imagines itself, rather than defines itself. By means of metaphor, the soul transposes questions about its nature to a mythopoesis of actual imagining, which is what Shelley means by "spells." That metaphoric perspective, as James Hillman points out in *Archetypal Psychology*, "darkens with a deeper light" (21). It also "brings about the death of naive realism, naturalism, and literal understanding" (21). In *Suicide and the Soul*, Hillman argues that the proper metaphoric action of soul-making is suicide, an action with which *Adonais* figuratively concludes. Metaphor as life thus contains within it a vision of the literal as death, a vision that Shelley explores in considerable depth in "The Triumph of Life."

Shelley's Workmanship of Style

William Keach

William Wordsworth, despite deep personal and political reservations, called Shelley "one of the best artists of us all: I mean in workmanship of style" (qtd. in N. I. White, *Shelley* 2: 637). Helping students understand the force of Wordsworth's judgment isn't easy. They may be inclined either to assume that the emotive intensity of Shelley's poetry has nothing to do with "workmanship of style" or to take such workmanship for granted (as an obvious characteristic of all the writers they are asked to read) and wonder why it should ever be at issue. The perspective I want to sketch out here is meant to challenge such attitudes by readings of two contrasting yet intricately connected texts—one predictable and familiar in undergraduate courses, the other much less so.

Chronologically, just four or five months separate "Ode to the West Wind," begun in late October 1819, when Shelley was living in Florence, from "The Sensitive-Plant," written in March 1820, after he had moved to Pisa. Both were among the "Other Poems" included in the *Prometheus Unbound* volume published in August 1820, and they represent distinctively inflected explorations of a question that also pervades Shelley's lyrical drama: how will the mind respond and articulate its relation to power and temporal change in the world?

Poetically, the two poems explore that question in radically divergent keys. Yet the keys can and do converge. "And the leaves, brown, yellow, and grey, and red, / And white, with the whiteness of what is dead, / Like troops of ghosts on the dry wind past" (3.34–36)—this reprise of the opening of the "Ode" in part 3 of "The Sensitive-Plant" indicates that both poems construct their imaginative perspectives in relation to seasonal changes from growth to decay, from birth to death—changes that may or may not resolve themselves into a conventional, harmonious, ultimately optimistic cycle. What I most want to emphasize here is Shelley's versatile workmanship of style as the articulation of his necessarily vexed relation to the power of temporality.

"Ode to the West Wind" is an apostrophe, a direct personifying address to a natural phenomenon that becomes, from the first line, a figure for the power of change and transformation (Culler 62–67). The apostrophic rhetoric of the poem is so intense that the conventions on which it depends are put under unusual pressure. The speaker's desire that the wind "hear" the articulations of his breath even as he hears and feels the "breath of Autumn's being" is more demand than prayer or request. Nowhere in Romantic writing is the trope of the "correspondent breeze" (Abrams, *Correspondent*) so fiercely and riskily amplified. The amplification is carefully structured, though, by figurative transformations of the wind itself and, more significantly for the first four stanzas, of the objects of the wind's destructive and preservative power. "If I were a dead leaf . . . ; / If I were a swift cloud . . . ; / A wave . . .": the speaker's conditional projective identifications at the beginning of stanza 4 recapitulate the figurative development in each of the preceding stanzas. The identifications also precipitate a crisis. The notorious expression of defeat and despair that embarrasses most readers—"I fall upon the thorns of life! I bleed!"—follows inevitably from the speaker's identifying himself with passive objects of the wind's power: "Oh, lift me as a wave, a leaf, a cloud!" Even as he has rhetorically "striven . . . with" the wind, he has figuratively placed himself "beneath thy power."

It is the work of the fourth stanza of the "Ode" to make painfully evident a contradiction in the speaker's previous imaginative relation to the power of the wind and the power of his own writing. The fifth stanza pushes beyond that contradiction—not toward a reductive or arrested reconciliation but through a movement that remains open to and that appropriates change and difference. Here the speaker runs the risk of insisting on a direct identification with the wind itself ("Be thou me, impetuous one!"). But on either side of the gesture are complex revisions of the figures by which he sought to locate himself in objects of the wind's force. A "lyre" (57), understood as an eolian harp, is in one sense yet another passive object for the wind. But it is also a human construct that gives new articulation, at once natural and artificial, to the wind's mighty breath. It is, in other words, a figure for the constructed incantatory power of the verse itself. But it is not the final such figure. In commanding the wind to "Be through my lips to unawakened earth / The trumpet of a prophecy!" (68–69), Shelley reworks his own earlier figure of spring's awakening "clarion" (10) and makes himself both a militantly prophetic wind instrument and the wind that blows it. The west wind may take a "deep autumnal tone" from a lyre but not from a trumpet, which requires the focusing, articulating agency of human breath, inspired by a power to which it contributes its own purposive energy.

The elaborate figurative network of Shelley's "Ode" (students should be encouraged to extend and refine the broad lines of development) elicits an experience of change and temporal movement that is never completely reducible to an experience of natural order, progression, cyclical recurrence. Political readings of the poem that assert an easy analogy or congruity between historical change and the natural seasonal cycle overlook the ways in which the "Ode" questions such analogy and congruity; the poem suggests, instead, that politics, like poetry, depends on a productive transformation of nature through individual and collective human agencies.

The poem's figurative sequences evoke disruption and discontinuity, as well as continual, followable connection. This is also true of the astonishing merger of terza rima and sonnet structure in the versification of the "Ode."

These two formal traditions themselves suggest historical continuity, yet Shelley's bringing them together makes such changes as have yet found no succession. The tumbling, linked, ever-changing rhymes of Shelley's terza rima have appeared to some readers to be an analog for the images of blowing leaves, swirling clouds, and churning waves (Wimsatt 115–16). Shelley's syntax and grammar accentuate the effects that the rhyme pattern itself evokes; not only single lines but entire tercets are left radically open. Shelley's writing articulates an experience of changing sequential power by simultaneously violating and affirming the organizing force of terza rima conventions.

Shelley achieves related effects by enclosing his terza rima tercets in fourteen-line stanzas. The opening stanza of the "Ode" makes its sonnetlike turn from present autumnal decay and dissemination to future springtime rebirth and reconstitution on the temporal conjunction "until." That turn comes at the end of line 8 and thus prematurely from the point of view of sonnet convention, as if to enforce the speaker's impatient anticipation of a future that will reveal autumnal dying ("Each like a corpse within its grave") as a simile after all, a transitory passage, rather than a fixed extinction. The grammatical pause after "grave," followed by the swift enjambments at "until" and "blow," take the reader momentarily into an imagined future on the energy of desire. Shelly's writing style acknowledges temporal change not by denying or merely submitting to it but by advancing it while asserting its own real though incomplete power of ordering articulation.

"Ode to the West Wind" ends with a famous question about time that is usually taken to be rhetorical: "If Winter comes, can Spring be far behind?" "The Sensitive-Plant" shows that this is a real question, not by rendering it unrhetorical (whatever that may mean) but by taking us through the darker possibilities of that conditional "If" and of our assumption that temporal existence can be truly cyclical, that spring will necessarily return as its idealized former self.

Nature in the first two parts of "The Sensitive-Plant" is overtly represented as a paradisiacal springtime order, a garden of the idealizing, desiring imagination that becomes, as Earl Wasserman has shown (*Shelley* 154–79), the figurative counterpart of heavenly perfection. Temporal sequence, desire, and death enter that world only to be transfigured for a while in the lilting fantasy of Shelley's quatrains:

> Then the pied wind-flowers and the tulip tall,
> And narcissi, the fairest among them all,
> Who gaze on their eyes in the stream's recess
> Till they die of their own dear loveliness. (1.17–20)

Do the narcissi actually die, or is that just an autoerotic swoon? The question is held in suspension by writing that may seem more like self-indulgent play than workmanship.

Even in the early sections, however—sometimes when we least expect it—we can feel the pressure of an alert purposiveness. At night the garden becomes "an ocean of dreams," as well as a starry heaven:

> And the beasts, and the birds, and the insects were drowned
> In an ocean of dreams without a sound
> Whose waves never mark, though they ever impress
> The light sand which paves it—Consciousness.   (1.102–05)

The difference between "never mark" and "ever impress" here marks the difference between our conscious access to waking and to dreaming experience (Davie 153). Shelley's style asks us to be awake, even as we read about what it's like to be asleep.

The temporality and death that have so far been held in transfigured suspension enter the poem with shocking abruptness at the end of part 2, when the Lady who tends the garden, nurturing and sustaining its perfection, suddenly dies. That she dies "ere the first leaf looked brown" (2.60) suggests that her death is a cause, rather than an effect, of the seasonal sequence that follows; her funeral takes place before "Swift summer into the autumn flowed" (3.22). It is as if the "azure sister of the spring" from stanza 1 of the "Ode," having been present in nature continuously, rather than intermittently, were to become "a corpse within its grave."

That autumn and winter now spoil the garden of its previous loveliness is less disturbing than that the spoliation is represented through figurative transformations as conspicuous as those in parts 1 and 2. The garden continues to grow, along with the imagination that creates it in writing: "And plants, at whose names the verse feels loath, . . ." (3.58–61). The verse takes on an explicitly self-conscious life of its own now, a sign that the poet-speaker's imagination, far from being dead, is grotesquely alive. The very figures that linked the garden to heavenly perfection earlier in the poem— "The beams which dart from many a star / Of the flowers," (1.80–81)—now return as signs of its corruption—"starred with a lurid dew." And when spring does return at the end of part 3, it comes as a hideous parody of its regenerative identity earlier in this poem and in the "Ode" (3.112–13). "When Winter had gone and Spring came back" (3.110) echoes with ironic dismay "If Winter comes, can Spring be far behind?" The deep question that the poems pose is not whether there will be future change but whether that change can be made to conform to the desiring imagination.

Neither the "Ode" nor "The Sensitive-Plant" is explicitly political; even the prophecy that the speaker longs to trumpet at the end of the "Ode" remains unspecified. But the poems carry crucial and divergent implications for the possibilities and the limits of radical change at every level of experience. The militantly prophetic anticipation at the end of the "Ode" finds a less arousing but historically telling alternative in the conclusion to "The Sensitive-Plant," where death and decay are countered by a gently skeptical surmise:

> It is a modest creed, and yet
> Pleasant if one considers it,
> To own that death itself must be,
> Like all the rest,—a mockery.   (13–16)

In the perspective of Shelley's entire career, that colloquial urbanity, so reflective of his class background and education (Davie 133–59), is not the prevailing response. Neither is the subsequent claim that "For love, and beauty, and delight / There is no death nor change" (21–22). What prevails, instead, is a recognition that resists both idealist surmise and apocalyptic prophecy: for everything—including love and beauty and delight—there is death and change. That is the fierce triumph of temporal life to which imagination and desire and will themselves belong; that is what Shelley's style works persistently and brilliantly to realize.

Shelley for Sophomores

Nancy Moore Goslee

If we were skylarks, we could gain a visionary perspective by soaring upward, out of time, but if we are teaching sophomore survey courses, we necessarily look before and after, finding ways in which history may interpret poems or poems may order history. For teaching Shelley in a sophomore British literature survey, I propose a thematic pattern that is broadly political: the theme of revolutionary hope—for the individual, as well as for society—and the repeated disappointments of that hope. To show the interplay between Shelley's revolutionary hopes and his recognition of their limits, I have mapped out three groups of poems, easily accessible in an anthology such as the Norton. Each group or a poem from it may work as one class assignment. To clarify the contexts of philosophical and political thinking from which the briefer lyrics spring toward vision, the assignments include some larger works.

After a glance at a few incendiary passages from *Queen Mab* (on monarchy, marriage, organized religion, and Shelley's millennial vision of the future), I follow Shelley's turn away from overt political criticism to quests for more private vision in *Alastor*, "The Hymn to Intellectual Beauty," and "Mont Blanc" (1814–16). Mary Shelley's *Frankenstein* acts as a bridge to the second group of poems, the public, prophetic works of the early years in Italy (1818–21): selections from *Prometheus Unbound*, "Song to the Men of England," "England in 1819," "Ode to the West Wind," "To a Sky-Lark," and the prose essay *A Defence of Poetry*. My final group of poems includes the two deeply pessimistic redefinitions of life in *Adonais* and "The Triumph of Life." After giving a few brief suggestions for the first and third groups, I offer a fuller set of suggestions for the central group.

The first group of poems or any one of them may be discussed as attempts to test Wordsworth's postrevolutionary hopes: to see what salvation can emerge from individual searches for relationship, whether with other people or with nature. Margaret's ennobling but destructive hope in Wordsworth's "Ruined Cottage," framed by the Pedlar's search for consolation in nature, leads both to *Alastor* and to the 1816 poems. "The Hymn" tests both the *Alastor* visionary's ideal and Margaret's in an increasingly less human form; "Mont Blanc" tests the ideal of the Pedlar and of the *Alastor* narrator, natural consolation. Are such visions enabling or crippling? Narcissistic, transcendent, or prophetic? How do they differ from traditional religious or romantic quests for vision? (See Schapiro; Wasserman, *Shelley*; Chernaik.)

In the third group of poems, both *Adonais* and "The Triumph" propose radical redefinitions of what we can hope for from life in this world. Both use public, ceremonial processions to dramatize their criticisms and to illustrate the conflicts between a poet's or prophet's vision and the fate of that vision in the public world. Asking students to catalog the groups of mourners or to draw the chariot and its cohorts can help them clarify the conflicts. For *Adonais*, discussing the pastoral elegy as a version—if often a self-praising version—of mourning conventions may bring the poem closer to home. For "The Triumph of Life," a range of visual and social analogies may be helpful—from Blake's illustration for Beatrice's chariot in *The Purgatorio* (not to mention the Dantean allusion in the terza rima) through the film *Cleopatra*, with its Roman triumph, to the homecoming parade outside the classroom window, with its floats and campus politics. Election-year politics and spectacles offer further possibilities. Deconstructionist readings of "The Triumph of Life" undoubtedly increase our skepticism about the possibility of truth, but discussing the difficult relationship between skepticism and ethics should receive the primary emphasis in a sophomore class.

My second major group of poems—the political sonnets and songs of 1819, "Ode to the West Wind," *A Defence of Poetry*, and excerpts from *Prometheus Unbound*—illustrates Shelley's renewed commitment to a prophecy of outward social change. With that renewed commitment comes the confidence to draw on and revise some magisterial precursors: Aeschylus, Dante, Milton. "Song to the Men of England" and the sonnet "England in 1819" make his political commitment obvious. "England in 1819," in particular, transforms the Miltonic political sonnet into a compact model of Revelation's claim that the worst conditions must signal a rebirth to come. Although the same politicized religious model appears in "Ode to the West Wind," the ode cannot be limited to political rebirth. Students should be asked how the wind resembles those possibly natural, possibly transcendent forces moving through "Hymn to Intellectual Beauty" and "Mont Blanc," as through Wordsworth's and Coleridge's earlier poems. The west wind's role in rebirth echoes Chaucer's General Prologue. The simile of the autumn leaves carries even older echoes: from Vergil, then Dante and Milton, and later Eliot. We can speculate about how Shelley's lyric, like those epics, asks what can be salvaged from fragments of the past. Shelley's oblique use of the mythic nightingale who falls on thorns to sing also recalls Milton's sense of isolation and despair before completing his prophetic epic.

Questions about the sources of inspiration and about the function of literary works in preserving or renewing culture lead to the *Defence* and *Prometheus Unbound*. With its humor a catalyst, Peacock's "Four Ages of Poetry" can provoke a debate about the interdependence of poetry and society or the irrelevance of poetry to society. The ambiguous sources of inspiration proposed in the *Defence* also define a range of significance for the mythic figure of Prometheus in the play. Shelley's analysis of the multiple arts of Athenian drama in the essay points toward his choice of genre for *Prometheus Unbound*; analogies to film suggest the drama's social functions, as well as its cinematic effects.

From the opening hopelessness of the static hero to the exultant but cautionary final speech of Demogorgon, the play works out a pattern of re-created and re-creating hope. Other epic and dramatic parallels to the hero chained by his mind-forged manacles can be drawn from world and British literature: the epic figures Odysseus, Aeneas, and Satan and the dramatic personages Aeschylus's Prometheus and Milton's Samson. Around that central figure, students can observe the landscapes and the figures through which his change of heart appears. From the tableaux illustrating the failures of Christianity and the French Revolution and the final fury's temptation to despair in act 1, students can trace the visionary encounters that ultimately lead to recognizing Jupiter as only a vision or phantasm and thus to the empty, abandoned thrones and altars after his fall in act 3—a scene recalling the Roman settings where Shelley wrote but ironically not yet true of post-1815 Europe, its thrones again full.

Northrop Frye's hypothesis that the Romantic quest for meaning is downward and inward (*Study*) and Frederick Pottle's essay on Asia as a theological quester can draw together parallels with earlier symbolism of height, depth, and gender, not only in "Mont Blanc," but in, for example, *The Prelude*, "Kubla Khan," and *The Marriage of Heaven and Hell*. To turn from the regeneration of act 3 to that of act 4, we may ask students about science-fiction versions of utopian future societies in which most physical limits have been overcome. The most effective visual equivalent for the fourth act may be simply a sketch or two from some of Shelley's notebook pages: the recurrent motif of burgeoning or explosive trees, linked to his revisions of the lyrics of Earth and Moon spirits, shows the creative energy—sexual and cosmic—in process.

At least two motifs point toward the Victorian and modern eras. An assessment of Shelley's muse-woman—from the dream-woman in *Alastor* through Asia and Urania to the "shape all light" and Life in his final poem—can lead to comparisons first with the women in Keats's poems and then with those in the Victorian and modern novel. Finally, trivial as it sounds, an almost paradigmatic comparison for sophomores is the bird question: tracing the changes in the symbol of the bird from Shelley and Keats through Darwin, Hopkins, Hardy, and Yeats. Though Hardy's "darkling" bird—carrying its burden of somber meaning from Milton, Keats, and Arnold—may appeal more to modernists, the right context for Shelley's skylark may make even those readers appreciate its soaring once more.

Knowing a Romantic Poem:
A Sequenced Research Project

Mary A. Quinn

Three years ago I introduced an extended research project into a British Romanticism course to counteract students' superficial reading, uninformed discussion, and boring writing. I knew that most students did not want to be superficial, uninformed, or boring, but strategies for reading and re-reading a poem, for thinking and rethinking it from many perspectives, were anathema to most of them. Few had known the excitement of studying a single literary work for many weeks, of living with a poem entwined in their daily experiences because of their continual engagement with it. I narrow my students' choice of poems to selected works by Shelley because, at the moment, my interest, expertise, and reference resources center on his work. But the project is useful for students' extended, independent study of any substantial poet or poem. It is particularly effective in guiding students to a full understanding of difficult poems while broadening their general knowledge of a period. Collaborative work among students, a key aspect of the project, is made easier if all students work on one author, with at least three or four students writing about a single poem. In a class of thirty, the students choose from five or six poems.

Sequenced reading and writing assignments constitute the core of the project, around which I schedule periodic, in-class, peer-group collaboration involving the reading of and responses to selected parts of the project as they are completed. The project entails extensive reading in a range of literary, historical, philosophical, and other relevant supporting materials, which I place on library reserve (see below). In conjunction with the readings, the students write in various modes: an ongoing research journal, four short idea papers, a prospectus for the culminating formal paper, a 10–15-page formal paper. At first, the project may seem daunting to both student and teacher; but in practice the progressive, interlocking assignments guide the students into the complexity of productive research and help them write effectively about what they discover. They pace their work during the semester, a practice that eliminates last-minute, half-baked thinking and writing and enlivens class discussions in surprising, gratifying ways. Although we do not study Shelley's works as a class until after we have read Blake, Wordsworth, Coleridge, and Byron, I encourage students whenever possible to bring information from their research into class discussions. I emphasize the importance of reading all the Romantic writers in relation to one another.

The project demands considerable preparation time before the term begins, but, once the assignments have been delineated and the reference materials assembled, the hard labor is over for the teacher. Details of the project are explained in the assignment reproduced here except for the lists of reference materials on library reserve. Those materials include reading list 1—background reference materials (primary sources, such as letters, journals, memoirs, and other writings by Shelley and his circle, and secondary sources, such as several biographies, for comparison, and historical, philosophical, literary, and other relevant reading); reading list 2—critical backgrounds and general reference materials (including background readings related specifically to Shelley); reading list 3—critical views of *Alastor* or whatever poem is being studied (specific responses to the selected poem ranging from criticism contemporary with Shelley to the present).

British Romanticism Research Project
Student Assignment

Throughout the semester you will be working on a single poem by Percy Bysshe Shelley, reading diverse materials to extend your knowledge of the poem, and writing a research journal and four short idea papers. The writing will help you organize and process the readings in preparation for a culminating formal paper. Several times during the term you will exchange your writings with other students working on the same poem to give one another collaborative support and responses as your work progresses. I, too, shall read and respond to your work each time you complete a journal segment and idea paper (as explained below).

Within the next week, read the following poems by Shelley and choose one that interests you: *Alastor,* "Mont Blanc," *Epipsychidion, Peter Bell the Third, Adonais,* "The Triumph of Life." The reading is tough, probably the most difficult of the semester. Choose the poem that snags your attention, gets under your skin, confuses you utterly. Do not choose the easiest poem. (Don't be fooled; none is easy. Remember, you *will* master one poem by the semester's end.) I ask you to narrow your choice because they are interesting, representative poems by Shelley, poems that other students have found worth their extended attention; because our library has sufficient reference materials for the poems; and because several students must be studying the same poem in order to collaborate.

The Research Journal

During the first ten weeks of the term, keep a research journal as you read in preparation for writing the formal paper late in the semester. Please write the journal in an 8½ by 11 inch loose-leaf notebook. (You will give me sections of the journal on the due dates listed below.) Date each entry; note the time and the place you worked, as well as your initial research objectives; record complete, accurate citations of the materials consulted. You should be taking good notes during each research session; however, I am concerned primarily not with your note-taking skills but, rather, with what sense you can make of Shelley, his era, and his poetry as a result of your research. Therefore, at the end of each research session and at intervals during the session, if you choose, take 10–15 minutes to write an entry based on what you have read and thought about during the session. Summarize, consolidate, speculate, question, establish new research objectives. Over a 10-week reading period you will gather an overwhelming body of information. You need to establish a method for regularly reflecting on, culling, and giving some shape, however tentative, to what you discover. When reviewing your journal segments, I shall look closely at your consolidating comments. Please mark them with an asterisk. If you are unsure how to proceed with any part of the research project, feel free to read copies of successful projects in my office.

Idea Papers

While keeping the research journal, you will also write four idea papers: 2–4-page typewritten informal papers focusing on aspects of particular interest to you. General topics and the due dates are listed below. By "informal" I mean that the papers need not be tightly argued essays; rather, they should be speculations about pertinent aspects of the poem and the supporting materials you read.

Prospectus and Formal Paper

As you work through the progressive assignments for the research journal and idea papers, develop your topic. During the last four weeks of the semester you will write a formal paper based on the research, thinking, and writing you have been doing. To narrow your focus, to frame and refine your ideas, first write a prospectus, a formal overview of your paper. All your research and writing will come to fruition in the paper you create from your knowledge and particular interest. (The final paper should not be a rehash of what you have written in your journal and idea papers.) I expect that you will write 10–15 pages, although that length is not a hard-and-fast requirement. Please include notes and a bibliography, following *The MLA Style Manual*.

Collaboration

You can learn from and assist one another with the project by periodically reading and responding to one another's work. Every time you turn in a journal segment or idea paper, you will spend the class period reading the papers of your peers who are writing on "your" poem and writing a detailed response to two of those papers—asking questions, offering suggestions. (I shall provide suggested response guidelines.) Our last class meeting is devoted to your reading and responding in writing to four students' formal papers—two on "your" poem, two on other poems.

Evaluation and Grading

Your performance on the project will be progressive and cumulative; therefore, I shall not grade individual journal segments or idea papers. I shall, however, comment on your journal and idea papers each time I review them. At midterm, I shall review all your work to date and assign a provisional grade. You are welcome to discuss your progress with me at any time. Your command of your subject will grow as the semester proceeds; your progress throughout the semester will reflect your growing knowledge. The research project accounts for 60% of your final grade (journal = 20%, idea papers = 20%, prospectus and formal paper = 20%). Class participation, both discussion and collaborative work, accounts for 30% and the final exam 10% of your course grade.

Schedule of Due Dates: Journal, Idea Papers, Prospectus, Formal Paper

Week 2 [date]: *idea paper 1*. Your own close reading of the poem (do not consult outside sources yet), including some selective stylistic analysis based on your review of library-reserve materials on prosody.

Week 4 [date]: *journal segment 1 and idea paper 2*. Background information (biographical, historical, literary, intellectual). See reading list 1: background reference materials.

Week 6 [date]: *journal segment 2 and idea paper 3*. Critical views, 1816–1960. See reading list 2: critical background and general reference materials. Read and summarize at least five critical views. Read across the entire period, if possible, to get a sense of the changing critical temper. Note critics' assumptions about Shelley, literature, and life, as revealed by their commentaries. Note the points of agreement and disagreement among the critics, as well as when, how, and why one critic works with another's ideas.

Week 8 [date]: *journal segment 3 and idea paper 4*. Critical views, 1960–present.

See reading list 3: critical views on (your poem). Follow the same procedure as for journal segment 2 and idea paper 3.

Week 11 [date]: *prospectus* (2 or more pages).

Week 14 [date]: *formal paper* (10–15 or more pages), accompanied by your research journal, idea papers, and prospectus.

Writing-across-the-Curriculum Techniques for Teaching Shelley

Art Young

Writing in the Fall 1987 *MLA Newsletter*, Phyllis Franklin stated that one important recommendation of the English Coalition, representatives of eight national English associations convened to consider directions for the profession of English, was "linking of the study of writing and the study of literature at all levels" (5). When we teach Shelley with writing-across-the-curriculum techniques, we demonstrate one way to turn that lofty recommendation into a reality. Although most writing-across-the-curriculum techniques can be used to teach Shelley at any level and with various student populations, this essay envisions a generalist teacher who teaches Shelley to mostly non-English majors in a sophomore survey course of British literature.

Most traditional writing assignments—critical essays, term papers—play a role in writing-across-the-curriculum courses, but they are not handled in traditional ways. Writing across the curriculum seeks to avoid assignments like critical essays that are produced in one draft the night before the assignment is due; are read only by the teacher, who looks for errors and suggests how the paper could have been written better; are kept totally separate from the daily classroom activity of lectures and discussions; and are rarely valued by the writer or the reader. Such writing is often unwittingly assigned not to engender communication (let's argue about why we disagree on the central theme of "Ode to the West Wind") but, rather, to fulfill some ancient ritual of noncommunication (show me you can write an essay on Shelley without making too many spelling and grammar mistakes). But if that is what the writing-across-the-curriculum classroom seeks to avoid in writing assignments, what does it seek to embrace?

Writing-across-the-curriculum teachers assign writing frequently, often daily, and integrate the writing into other classroom activities—reading, listening, talking, thinking. Writing is assigned to assist students in reading a difficult text—"Mont Blanc," for instance. The purpose of such writing-to-learn assignments is not to communicate what has been learned about Shelley's poem but, rather, to assist the learner in acquiring the knowledge necessary to fulfill the task. When the teachers make writing-to-communicate assignments—such as formal essays, in which the writers are expected to represent their best thinking to a reader—it is done in the context of substantial critical reading and discussion. The revision of ideas and of prose is an expected and nurtured aspect of the process.

Writing-across-the-curriculum teachers are concerned with the social context for language and learning, and they seek to make their classrooms into communities in which the knowledge of particular texts is developed interactively and collaboratively and in which student writing plays an important role in the development of communal knowledge. Students write to each other and *to* the teacher (not *for* the teacher), and the teacher writes to the students. For some student writing the teacher plays the role of one sympathetic reader and writer listening and responding to another; for other writing the teacher plays the role of critical reader and editor. Such considerations do not negate the teacher's authority as an experienced reader of poetry and knower of Shelley; rather, those considerations create an environment in which the teacher can use that experience and knowledge to empower students to contribute to the development of knowledge about reading Shelley's poetry. Thus, the writing-across-the-curriculum teacher's goal is to use student writing and talking about Shelley's poetry as a tool for developing the students' confidence and competence in their experiences with language and literature.

Writing-to-Learn Assignments

Most writing-to-learn assignments are brief, and several may be assigned for one homework session. Because their main purpose is for students to learn about Shelley, rather than to communicate to others what they have learned about Shelley, the students need not be concerned with spelling and correctness. The students write as they read the homework assignment, and they keep their writing in a journal or folder. Typical assignments include list making, questions, paraphrases, journal entries, summaries, reader responses, essay questions, letters to classmates, free-writes, and focused writes. Some topics are assigned by the teacher, and others are self-selected. Some assignments are given in a sequence to develop an understanding of a specific issue, and others develop out of the discussions in a particular class session. Students need to know who will read their informal writing; often such writing is read by the teacher and by fellow students. Students need to do the writing and the reading when assigned, for class activities need their informed participation. After the students have been assigned to read particular poems by Shelley for homework, the following writing-to-learn assignments may be completed before particular poems are discussed in class:

> Make lists of the similarities and the differences in the poetry of Wordsworth and Shelley.
> Write a stanza-by-stanza paraphrase of "Hymn to Intellectual Beauty."
> After listening to the instructor's lecture on Shelley's use of the sonnet form, take five minutes in class to summarize the three most important concepts presented; be prepared to read your summary to the class at the beginning of the next class period.
> Write a double-sided journal entry on "Ode to the West Wind." Draw a

line down the middle of the page; on the left side of the page, paraphrase each stanza in succession, and, on the right side of the page, make interpretive suggestions and note the connections between the stanzas. Write a double-sided entry on a scholar's interpretation of the poem from one of the books on reserve in the library; on the left side of the page, paraphrase the scholar's argument, and, on the right side, make speculative comments.

Write a free-write in which you comment on personification and symbolism in the characters Anarchy and Hope in "The Mask of Anarchy"; after the poem is discussed in class, write a letter to classmates on the poem's portrayal of civil disobedience and nonviolent protest as a means to resolve conflicts and achieve social justice.

Take thirty minutes to answer the following essay question for homework: (Provide a question from a previous year's exam.)

After you have read *Alastor*, write a journal entry in which you describe your reading process as you read the poem. What problems did you face? How did you solve them?

Write two hundred words on whatever aspect of Shelley's work interests you most. Consider what works or themes of Shelley's you may want to learn more about.

Write a letter to your parents in which you quote your favorite poem by Shelley, and explain to them what it means to you and why you like it.

Write a poem as a homework assignment. You may imitate Shelley's style, choose a Shelleyan theme, or describe your opinion of Shelley (as Shelley wrote of Wordsworth) or your experience in reading Shelley (as Keats described his experience in reading Chapman's Homer).

Working together in groups of four, prepare a brief position paper and a fifteen-minute oral report on the concept of love in Shelley's poetry.

Read the letter that the teacher has written to you and your classmates on the perceptions of the role of women depicted in the poetry of Shelley and Byron. Write a letter of response.

Review your writing on Shelley. What does your writing tell you about yourself as a writer and reader? What values have you expressed in your writing? In what ways have your values been in conflict with the values expressed by Shelley?

Such student writing should operate in an interactive context. The writing may be read by the teacher, by fellow students, aloud in class, or by readers beyond the classroom. The teacher responds to such writing as a mentor assisting novices who are unfamiliar with Shelley and Romantic poetry. Fellow students use what they feel is valuable in their classmates' writing to build their own understanding of Shelley's poetry. Because such writing is exploratory and collaborative, individual pieces of writing should not be graded. Teachers often acknowledge the importance of all writing-to-learn pieces collectively by assigning such writing a percentage of the final grade. The writing can be evaluated on completeness, commitment, and the growing understanding of course material exhibited in the writing and may count anywhere from 25% to 75% of the final grade.

Writing-to-Communicate Assignments

Students continue to learn about Shelley, of course, as they struggle with the process of communicating what they know to others. Students seek to make a contribution to the knowledge about Shelley and to develop an increased competence in academic discourse by a continual negotiation with their existing knowledge of Shelley and by the writing of academic prose within the supportive environment of interested listeners and readers who form the classroom community. Formal assignments often use traditional academic forms—such as the critical essay, the book review, and the term paper—and they frequently integrate writing-to-learn exercises as one way to develop intention and purpose in such writing. However, other forms of communication are also possible, such as a scholarly letter to a literary critic or a journal editor, a collaborative report presented to students and teachers in other classes, and a report prepared for students at a high school and sent by a computer network.

A teacher may integrate into the goals of the course opportunities for collaborative interaction in developing a topic and a purpose for the writing, as well as for revising, editing, and evaluating the writing. Such interaction may occur between teacher and student or student and student(s) or a combination of both. To write a successful piece of communication, the writer must possess information or an interpretation that is not known by the other members of the class and that will be of interest to them. Thus, the process and the context for developing an interpretation of a Shelley poem and the means to effectively express that interpretation become one. It often involves reading and rereading Shelley and works about Shelley, developing a sense of the audience for the piece of writing, and drafting and revising in response to the emerging sense of purpose and audience.

Students can work at developing a piece of formal prose for the class through group work with fellow students and conferences with the instructor. Such activities work best when the students make a self-evaluation, either orally or in writing, of the draft or the ideas that they are submitting for consideration. For students to maintain ownership of their writing, their voices need to be listened to—about the purpose of the writing, about its strengths and weaknesses, about the problems yet to be solved, about the areas in which assistance or critical commentary is needed and would be appreciated. Teachers respond to work in draft form as sympathetic but experienced colleagues, pointing out what is strong or original, suggesting claims that need to be supported better, noting places of confusion in thought and syntax, suggesting possible approaches to revision. A formal essay should be graded only after the process of development is completed and the essay is submitted for evaluation. Teachers may want to consider grading on a portfolio system, so that, rather than grading each writing assignment individually, the entire term's formal assignments are assessed, taking into consideration the student's developing achievement and contribution.

TEACHING INDIVIDUAL TEXTS

Two Voices:
Narrator and Poet in *Alastor*

Stephen C. Behrendt

One of the difficulties that students at all levels encounter in dealing with Shelley's poetry involves the presence there of strategies and techniques that reflect the poet's interest in the intellectual tradition of skepticism and the rhetorical form of the skeptical debate. *Alastor* affords an excellent opportunity to introduce students to that skeptical element in Shelley's poetry.

I like to begin with some discussion of skepticism in general and of the keynote ideas of the unattainability of absolute knowledge or Truth and the concomitant necessity of subjecting every hypothesis to continual testing. C. E. Pulos's synopsis of the tradition is particularly helpful here (ch. 2). I then briefly outline the principal suggestions about the identities of the poem's central figures: (1) the narrator as a Wordsworthian naturalist and the visionary as a pursuer of an unattainable ideal (Wasserman, *Shelley* 15–16), (2) the narrator as Shelley and the *Alastor* poet as a figure unaware of a universal collective unconscious (Abbey 20, 28), and (3) the wandering poet as "the projection of a submerged impulse in the narrator's mind," "the narrator's deeper self projected as spectral other" (Keach 87). In suggesting that we attempt to discover more about both figures by looking closely at the clues the text offers, I remind the students that the entire poem is cast within the point of view of the narrator; even when the visionary poet speaks (lines 280–90, 366–69, 502–14), we must trust the narrator to be a reliable recorder.

We begin in earnest by developing a profile of the narrator from what he reveals about himself in the invocation, the first forty-nine lines. By supplying components that the narrator leaves out of his formulations in the first sentence (1–17), we learn that he apparently identifies himself with fire (element, 1), afternoon (time of day, 5–7), summer (season, 8–12), and human being ("life form," 13). He aligns himself, in short, with images and symbols traditionally associated with creativity and productivity and with a relative externality that contrasts with the internality of the imagery he associates with the visionary. "This boast" (16) can be seen to be the narrator's claim not to have injured but ever to have loved and cherished all creatures, a claim that reflects the mutual interchange governing his relations with the entire natural universe. That he calls his song "solemn" (19) indicates his seriousness not only of purpose but also of mind in addressing his invocation to Nature as Mother. That such declarations of seriousness of mind and purpose traditionally preface works to which their narrators attribute considerable moral import significantly signals the narrator's attitude toward the tale he will tell, a tale whose plot, substance, and resolution he, of course, already knows.

At this point I like to stress that, knowing how his story will turn out, in nevertheless addressing the "Mother of this unfathomable world" (18) the narrator reveals virtually from the outset an inherent skepticism (though he is apparently quite content not to know or understand fully the world in which he moves), and I suggest that the students be alert to subsequent indications of the narrator's inability to fully comprehend exactly what has occurred or what its real significance may be. That point lends additional weight to his subsequent identification of himself with an eolian harp (42–49) on which and through which he expects his "Great Parent" to participate in the making and the meaning of his song.

After that initial exploration of the narrator's character, we move on to consider what his subsequent narrative reveals about the judgments he makes about the visionary poet, his values, his ideals, his aspirations, and his life choices. To better clarify those judgments, I ask students to demonstrate from the textual evidence what appear to be the narrator's corresponding values, ideals, and choices. Students generally agree that the narrator's orientation is significantly different from that of the young poet whose history he records. But they typically fail to recognize the extent to which the meaning of the tale—to which the narrator attributes moral significance, even if he cannot entirely identify or comprehend what that significance is

—is determined by the narrator's own mental set. Much of our discussion, therefore, centers on the question of how one tells a story that one understands only partially at best.

I find that approach to *Alastor* particularly productive—and the students engage with increasing eagerness in discovering evidence of narrative editorializing—because it gives us some reasonable mechanism by which to begin resolving some of the problems and seeming contradictions in the poem that otherwise prove frustrating. That approach is not to excuse or rationalize the problems inherent in a poem that is not entirely successful from a technical standpoint (Abbey 11–12). But what may strike readers initially as carelessness or contradiction may be shown, on closer examination, to be Shelley's calculated emphasis on the mutually subversive nature of the elements in a skeptical debate. Hence, I point out that in the rhetorical form of the skeptical debate, which form Shelley already knew well enough to have used skillfully in *A Refutation of Deism* (1813–14), both sides argue their positions so effectively that each is rendered untenable, and the audience is forced by default to construct a new, third position out of the ruins.

That point becomes particularly important in *Alastor* when we begin to contrast the narrator's obvious conviction that the poet's renunciation of life has been a great loss to the world with the equally obvious fact that the poet himself placed relatively little value on mortal existence as he knew it. Likewise, the point affects our response to the narrator's agonized record of the poet's transformation after his first abortive dream encounter with the veiled maiden (207–22). It is the *narrator*—not the poet himself—who concludes that in his pursuit of the ideal the poet "overleaps the bounds" (207) and is, consequently, cast into a vacant universe of eternal and comfortless wandering that reflects or externalizes the state of his own "vacant brain" (191). Ironically, the narrator, whose voice is heavily freighted with deliberate echoes of the Wordsworth whose doctrine of Nature he embodies and epitomizes, forgets or does not know that it is precisely in such states of mental vacancy that the opportunity for spontaneous renovation particularly inheres, as it does most specifically in the "vacant" mood (20) in which the memory of the daffodils flashes on Wordsworth's "inward eye" (21) in "I Wandered Lonely as a Cloud."

At that point I like to call attention to the poet's three speeches, each of which turns on irony. In the first he claims estrangement from the swan and hence from Nature in egotistically lamenting that Nature "echoes not my thoughts" (290). Here and in his third speech the visionary suffers from a *lack* of vision, an inability to see how profoundly true is his pronouncement to the stream: "thou imagest my life" (500). He draws near—but his words imply he never fully comprehends—the dynamic position he occupies as a sentient human being within the individual mind's and person's "unremitting interchange / With the clear universe of things around" ("Mont Blanc" 39–40). The narrator, who expresses clear awareness of such an unremitting interchange in the poem's first seventeen lines, is, in fact, better suited to recognize the error of the visionary's faulty notion, articulated in his second speech, that "Vision and Love" are divided from his mortal existence (366–69), rather than being an encompassing, interpenetrating, and vitalizing part of it.

I find it most useful next to have students consider whether the narrator remains at the end of the poem what he had been at the outset or whether any changes may be said to have occurred. He is significantly altered through the telling of his tale, it appears from the conclusion—his easy confidence in the apparently supportive and nurturant mutual interchange of Nature and humanity at least temporarily shaken. That his confidence appears intact at the beginning of the poem—when, as we know, he already knows how the poet's story ends—suggests that, like Coleridge's mariner, in telling his tale he undergoes a temporary alteration of consciousness, but that alteration is not permanent. It is important to remind students of that point, since the narrator's prior familiarity with the tale facilitates his ability to lace its recounting with moral judgments. Indeed, that he is so strongly affected, even if only temporarily, by the poet's fate is an indication of the degree to which the narrator is susceptible to sympathy, which the skeptical tradition—particularly Hume, whose works Shelley especially admired—designated as "the chief source of moral distinctions" (Pulos 23). That sympathy is akin to "the great secret of morals," Love, which Shelley describes later in *A Defence of Poetry* as "a going out of our own nature, and an identification of ourselves with the beautiful which exists in thought, action, or person, not our own" (487), a response capable of producing profound transformations within a person.

So intense is the narrator's experience in relating his tale, in fact, that at the end he undergoes an experience similar to that of the visionary in his relation to external Nature. Even as the visionary had perceived a vacant Nature that reflected his own "vacant brain" (191), rather than appreciating that it was not the external universe but he who had changed, so does the narrator conclude that with the poet's death all is altered, that "Nature's vast frame, the web of human things, / Birth and the grave" are now "not as they were" (719–20). As the conclusion of "The Sensitive-Plant" (written in 1820) later attests, it is not in Nature but in ourselves and in our own obscure organs of perception that the alteration inheres. When students recognize that significant paralleling of experiences, they are quick to point out that the alteration devastates the visionary, but the narrator is apparently soon able to resume the mental set we see in the invocation that sufficiently sustains him and his needs.

Once we have examined the complexity created by the presence in the poem of the two voices, one actual (the narrator's) and one virtual and essentially projected (the visionary's), and once the students have volunteered the perception, as they generally do, that neither voice has exclusive claim to an absolutely accurate or truthful view of affairs, I direct our attention to the preface. The voice we encounter there begins by counseling a Shelleyan universal benevolence but concludes with remarkable intolerance, effectively condemning all those who choose to reject the position that the preface's speaker advocates and doing so, most ironically of all, by invoking the presumed exemplar of tolerance and charity, Wordsworth. That phenomenon produces a good deal of discussion, partly because the students ordinarily and reasonably assume that the speaker here is Shelley himself and partly because the preface seems to embody the same sort of troubling contradictions that vex the poem.

I encourage the students to consider whether Shelley created here yet another nonauthorial or pseudoauthorial voice in order to intentionally inject the destabilizing consequences of the skeptical debate even into his preface. For all the critical acuity it advertises in its role as preface, the preface oversimplifies the gist of the poem that follows, encasing it in a relatively inflexible dualism that traps characters and readers alike in an either-or distinction that neglects the extent to which both right and wrong are necessarily relative. Like the poem that follows, the preface forces the reader into a strenuous activity that exercises reason and imagination alike in formulating informed judgments. Once the students understand that the activity is part of Shelley's design and that the design stems from an important and well-established philosophical tradition, they become more discerning and generally more appreciative readers of Shelley's poetry.

Contrasting Styles:
Teaching "Mont Blanc" with Coleridge's "Hymn before Sun-Rise"

Adam J. Frisch

Shelley's "Mont Blanc" is a difficult work to teach, perhaps because it seems to reward those students who tend to skim poems by offering them several awesome lines about the metaphysics of the cosmos that they don't really understand while apparently punishing good students who work hard for close readings by perplexing them with an entire poem that they don't understand. Yet "Mont Blanc" is an important work, for it directly confronts that tension between empiricism and idealism, between the wish for a liberal egalitarianism and the desire for a poetic priesthood that continually challenged both Shelley and the Romantic movement. I have found that by contrasting "Mont Blanc" with other local meditational Romantic poems—in particular, Coleridge's poem on Mont Blanc, "Hymn before Sun-Rise, in the Vale of Chamouni"—the instructor not only clarifies the dilemma of authority issue but also suggests some reasons why Shelley chose to use a deliberately perplexing style to address that tension.

"Mont Blanc" seems, on initial reading, more like five stanzas of cipher in search of a key than like a lyric addressed to a receptive audience. Most readers find, however, that, even though they cannot resolve many of the poem's mechanical and syntactical ambiguities, several important images and ideas emerge. The speaker of the poem clearly sees Mont Blanc as an appropriate symbol for the power underlying and animating his objective and subjective experiences. Like the Arve River, which flows down from Mont Blanc's glaciers, the universe of things seems to flow through human minds in a powerful but apparently random and indifferent fashion—sometimes destructive, sometimes life-sustaining. Like the glacial snows at Mont Blanc's top, the sources of that power seem to the speaker to lie hidden from human view, silent and cold, beyond the reach of earth-confined senses. At one point in the poem, the speaker asserts that, whether persons come away from Mont Blanc with faith or in doubt, the mountain, if understood, can help human beings "repeal / Large codes of fraud and woe" (lines 80–81). But even after that assertion, especially in the poem's last stanza, Shelley's emphasis remains on the mountain's and the power's silent, cold invisibility.

In keeping with its skeptical, uncertain vision of power are the poem's associative leaps, ambiguities, fragmented and run-on sentence structures, and variant punctuations. For example, in the opening lines Shelley's speaker moves from an image of the material universe as a mighty river through a series of antithetical descriptions of that river's qualities to a metaphor of the human mind as a tributary stream of that river—all within the stanza's first half sentence. The remainder of the stanza develops the tributary metaphor—or possibly the universal river metaphor if the pronoun "its" in line 6 refers back to lines 1–2—by means of another simile comparing the sound made by that feeder stream with the sound assumed by a feeble brook in a wilderness setting. However tenors and vehicles align, the ensuing description is still ambiguous. For example, is the "vast river" of line 10 producing noise by raging over its own rocks somewhere nearby the feeble brook? Has that river somehow managed to invade the rocks of the brook itself? Or are the river and the brook now conjoined?

Few students possess the talent and the inclination to work through poems such as Shelley's, where images and ideas are juxtaposed in layered metaphors, rather than logically connected. Yet a close comparison of "Mont Blanc" with apparently clearer poems, such as Coleridge's "Hymn before Sun-Rise," can usually convince students of Shelley's artistic accomplishment. Coleridge's "Hymn" is not a simple poem to read, but most students with a little work can manage to outline, stanza by stanza, the speaker's development from an initial passive awe at Mont Blanc's majesty to a final call for active praise of God by all parts of Nature. Students sharing Coleridge's general religious attitudes appreciate the poem's biblical tone and musical language (it is, after all, a hymn), whereas students of more skeptical persuasions usually complain that the speaker tells, rather than shows, that reverence is due. The skeptical students are often amused to find out that Coleridge never visited Mont Blanc but plagiarized many of the poem's details from a German poem by Frederike Brun (Parker 144–45).

The tell-versus-show argument is important, since Coleridge must carefully orchestrate the natural imagery presented by his speaker in order to achieve a series of awakenings in both the speaker and the reader. For example, by setting the poem in the darkness before dawn (sunrise occurring in the penultimate line), Coleridge allows his speaker to notice or remember natural details at moments appropriate for the poem's theme of a universal communion. Coleridge also structures the poem as a series of continual up-and-down visual shifts, displaying a concern for verticality of imagery that marks many Romantic transcendence pieces. The speaker begins by looking up to a star—actually, a planet—and from then on continually moves the reader's vision up and down the mountain, from its forest, base or even, at one point, its "sunless pillars deep in Earth" back up again past the frost line to its glacial peak. In effect, Coleridge repeatedly bows the readers' heads in adoration and then lifts them up in choral praise of the divine.

One difficulty with Coleridge as choir director is that he has also dramatized himself as a member of the choir. His speaker leads himself and his audience on an apparently sincere quest through a probing series of "Who caused?" questions to a final awareness of Nature's unity under God. The speaker eventually rejects the possibility raised by his own opening question—namely, that some entities, such as Mont Blanc, have by right a magic domination over other objects, such as the morning star. Yet the mountain could not have awakened the speaker or his audience in the first place had it not overwhelmed his vision almost completely; sublimity demands dominance. Given his theme, Coleridge would prefer simply to show his audience the communion of Nature, yet, to do that, he must create a persona who, like the mountain before him, almost literally connects Earth to Heaven.

Shelley does not need to assume control in that way, because the point of "Mont Blanc" is that only something far removed from the speaker possesses the power to harmonize the chaotic tumult of the details that his eyes perceive. If Shelley's readers get lost trying to thread their way through the multiplicity and fragmentation before them, so does Shelley's dramatized speaker (as in the second stanza, where, after a series of attempts at orderly description, he gives up trying with the exclamation, "Dizzy Ravine!" [34]). Getting lost becomes the point of a poem that sees all things in the subalpine universe as incomplete and mutable:

> All things that move and breathe with toil and sound
>   [speaker and poem included]
> Are born and die; revolve, subside, and swell.
> Power dwells apart in its tranquility,
> Remote, serene, and inaccessible.   (94–97)

In such a cosmos Shelley can assume only the reflective power of "the wise, and great, and good / [to] Interpret, or make felt, or deeply feel" (82–83). He knows by the final lines of the poem that his mind and his imagination play pivotal roles in the scheme of things, but he lacks Coleridge's certainty about the precise nature of that scheme and of that role. Shelley, while composing "Mont Blanc," signed himself into a visitors' guest book near Chamouni as: "Democrat, Philanthropist and Atheist" (Bloom, *Mythmaking* 11). In the introductory note to the first printing of his poem on the vale of Chamouni, Coleridge asked rhetorically: "Who *would* be, who *could* be an Atheist in this valley of wonders!" (qtd. in Perkins, *English* 434). It is appropriate that Coleridge's lyric begins with a question and ends in an authoritative assertion, whereas Shelley's poem starts with a challenging vision but ends only with a question.

Myths of Power and the Poet:
Teaching "Hymn to Intellectual Beauty"

Spencer Hall

My first objective in teaching Shelley's "Hymn to Intellectual Beauty" to undergraduates is to get them to read closely, by which I mean primarily to pay careful attention to the words on the page. Students tend to respond carelessly, whether positively or negatively, to the rhetoricity of Shelley's lyrics, and one needs, first of all, to make students see the significant choices of diction, image, and figure that underlie and usually complicate the seemingly "spontaneous overflow of powerful emotion." I try to organize the close reading around the central mythmaking impulses in Shelley's poetry, specifically around what I call his myths of power and the poet. (See my "Power and the Poet" for a full reading of the "Hymn" in this context.)

Specific study questions in advance of class discussions are useful. I often have the students write for five minutes on one of the questions at the beginning of the hour; that exercise usually leads to a much more focused discussion. A good place to start with the "Hymn" is at the beginning. Here is a sample question about stanza 1: "The first stanza consists of two sentences. What claim does the poet make in the first sentence (lines 1–4)? How does the second sentence (5–12) amplify or add to that claim?"

The obvious response is that Shelley (I shall use "Shelley" synonymously with "the speaker of the poem" here, something about which I always warn my students) seems to declare his belief in an ultimate "Power," one that students are usually prepared to accept, rather uncritically, in traditional religious terms: "The awful shadow of some unseen Power / Floats though unseen amongst us" (1–2). The real point of the discussion, however, is to bring out the tentativeness and the skepticism that qualify what seems to be, at first glance, a clear-cut metaphysical or religious proposition. The indeterminant "some" (a favorite Shelleyan adjective); the repetition of "unseen"; the inconstancy connoted by "floats"; the fact that not only the "Power" but also its "shadow," which is its only manifestation "amongst us," is unseen, thus putting the Power itself at three removes from human perception—all that needs to be opened up.

The sense of inconstancy and ephemerality already present in the first sentence is reinforced by the multiple similes in the second, and one can profitably explore the problematical imagery of light in darkness that permeates them and the rest of the poem. On a deeper level the thematic function of the similes as similes should be raised. Do they tell us more about the nature of the unseen and unknown Power or, as occurs so often in Shelley's work, about the nature and the power of the poet himself, struggling in and through metaphorical language to fashion his fleeting perceptions into a coherent, if always provisional, mythopoeic form?

My bias, then, is to teach the poem as an example of and frequently as an introduction to Shelley's Romantic mythmaking, with the result that I see the Intellectual Beauty of the title as a fictional construct (in Wallace Stevens's phrase, "a necessary fiction") or transcendental hypothesis, rather than as an antecedent metaphysical reality. It is important to make clear some of the implications of that view, especially in upper-division classes on Romantic literature. For one thing, such a view rejects the once popular interpretation of Shelley as Platonist, and that rejection is particularly relevant because the "Hymn," along with *Adonais* has long been the cornerstone of Platonic readings of his poetry.

A central interpretative question with which students should come to grips is the relation between that kind of secular Romantic mythmaking and Christianity, the primary source of prophetic mythology in Shelley's culture. Here is another study question: "The poem, beginning with its title, uses many religious, specifically Christian, forms of thought and expression. Give some examples. Does Shelley use Christian ideas and terms to express non-Christian points of view?" Students should have no problem in coming up with examples of the poem's pervasive theological and biblical vocabulary. "Hymn," after all, is in the form not only of a hymn but of a prayer, and it records something like a religious conversion experience in stanza 5.

The non-Christian points of view are best elucidated by a close reading of stanzas 3 and 4. The skeptical core of the poem and of Shelley's mythmaking is clearly stated in lines 25–31. "No voice" from on high has ever given "to sage or poet" the ultimate answers that traditional religion promises. As Demogorgon puts it in *Prometheus Unbound*, "a voice / Is wanting, the deep truth is imageless" (2.4.115–16). The Christian myth in particular, "the name of God and ghosts and Heaven," is singled out as a "frail spell" that cannot "sever" from the experiential world ("all we hear and all we see") the existential evils of "Doubt, chance, and mutability." In stanza 4 the traditional Christian virtues of faith, hope, and charity are systematically transvalued from transcendental, God-centered imperatives to humanistic and psychological goods. Love of God becomes the erotic "sympathies" in "lovers' eyes"; Hope in the afterlife becomes hope for "This world" (70); Faith in God becomes "Self-esteem."

Teachers need to carefully sort out the levels of anti-Christian discourse in the poem, an activity much enhanced by reading the "Hymn" in conjunction with Shelley's "Essay on Christianity," which was probably written at about the same time. On the one hand, the poem uses Christian forms of perception and expression ironically to subvert Christian supernaturalism and, for Shelley, its attendant moral and social evils in this world. Even more fundamentally, perhaps, Christianity is Shelley's and his culture's prime example of a mythmaking that forgets to be skeptical of itself and thus reifies into dogma—a fate against which the mythmaking poet also needs to guard.

A final study question can ask students to identify the ways in which Shelley dramatizes or represents himself in the poem. The major structural division in the "Hymn" is between stanzas 1–4 and 5–7, the last three stanzas switching focus from the hypothetical Power to the poet who perceives, expresses, and, in an important sense, creates it. As in "Mont Blanc," "To a Sky-Lark," "Ode to the West Wind," "Lines Written among the Euganean Hills," and other lyrics that can be taught as part of a unit on Shelley's mythmaking, the poet, as well as the Power, becomes a mythopoeic figure. In the "Hymn" important comparisons and contrasts can be made with Wordsworth's stories of poetic- and self-maturation in "Tintern Abbey" and "Intimations of Immortality." Shelley, too, portrays himself as advancing through various stages of awareness, although he characteristically emphasizes a particular moment of sudden epiphany, rather than an integrated continuum of subjective and objective experience reaching back to childhood.

The main point, however, is that by the end of the "Hymn" the poet and his words, not the Power, have taken center stage. In and through the poet's "onward life" (80), the inconstant, unknown, and unseen Power—identified in the course of the poem with the "Spirit of Beauty" (13)—will find a local habitation and a home. As so often occurs elsewhere in his poetry, Shelley's myth of Power in "Hymn to Intellectual Beauty" becomes as well a myth of poetic self-creation and empowerment.

Look on My Words, Ye Mighty, but Don't Despair: Teaching "Ozymandias"

Gyde Christine Martin

Many students feel that poetry is not a very efficient way of expressing ideas. To help them overcome their prejudice and impatience, I like to introduce "Ozymandias" at the beginning of undergraduate courses for non-English-majors. Although most students feel that it is a poem they understand after a single reading, what most of them understand is only the poem's simple irony of situation that arises from the empty threat of the tumbled tyrant. That the tyrant's words ring fearfully true if we read them in a different context and that the poem is a reflection on art and truth is something that they rarely recognize.

I begin by drawing out some of the facts of the poem that demonstrate that Shelley had a foot in the real world. If the students' anthology does not explain in a footnote that the "antique land" (line 1) refers to Egypt and Ozymandias to the Egyptian king Rameses II, I provide those details and add that Rameses II, succeeded to the throne in 1304 BC, that he belonged to the nineteenth dynasty, and that the first dynasty began in 3100 BC. That last piece of trivia leads to my next question: Why did Shelley choose Egypt as the setting, rather than ancient Greece or Italy? The hoped-for answer is, of course, that the Egyptian culture is much older. I also ask the class about the peculiarity of the desert as a place of decay. Since many of my students are from the Southwest, I don't have to wait for a biology or geology major to point out that the processes of decay and erosion in an arid climate are extremely slow.

Once the students realize the distances in time and space that separate us from the scene of the tumbled statue, they can easily point out those words and phrases that suggest distance and infinity, such as "traveller," "antique land," "boundless," and "level sands stretch far away." If I read the poem aloud, slowly and with a little exaggeration, it becomes apparent that the sounds of those long last syllables of the last four lines—"despair," "decay," "bare," "away"—are partly responsible for the sense of distance and duration.

Next, I draw attention to the second line of the inscription, "Look on my works, ye Mighty, and despair" (11), and to the many mouths and hands through which those words have passed before reaching us, the readers. The first in the chain is Ozymandias, who dictated that challenge or threat to the sculptor, who chiseled it into the pedestal and thus preserved it for the traveler, who related it to the speaker of the poem, who is now passing it on to us. The irony that struck the students during their first reading is, of course, that Ozymandias's challenge has become ridiculous; even though the exact words have been transmitted intact through the ages, time and change have annihilated their claim to truth. What the students still need to realize is that time and change have created a new context and thus a new meaning for the words. To make the new context apparent, I tell the students to ask themselves if the words are ringing fearfully true in a different sense—as the words of the force that conquered Ozymandias.

At that point the students usually begin to ask the questions: Does that mean that we should despair in the face of time and change? Can anything withstand those forces? What did Shelley think? Did Shelley as a poet believe that nothing can outlast time and change, that all art is temporary? For answers we turn once more to the poem. The internal evidence the students discover is not encouraging at first; Ozymandias's words didn't survive, nor did the sculptor's statue. But then they consider the poem itself as an artifact. Here the disagreement begins. Some students think that Shelley's poem has survived; after all, we are reading it right now, more than 170 years after it was written, and we are understanding it. Others argue that very point: How do we know that we really understand what Shelley meant? Maybe we are seeing the poem in a new context that wasn't intended at all—similar to what happened to Ozymandias's words. Maybe Shelley didn't have an opinion and just wanted us to think about the problem.

I use the impasse we have reached in our interpretation of "Ozymandias" as an opportunity to point to other sources. For the next class meeting I assign *A Defence of Poetry* and tell my students to search it for an answer to the question that left us divided. The passage in *Defence* most frequently cited is the one in which Shelley contrasts poetry with prose fiction, the eternal with the topical and temporal: "A poem is the very image of life expressed in its eternal truth . . ." (485).

In an upper-level course I also send my students to secondary sources, so that they can find out how other critics have interpreted the poem, but only after they have grappled with it themselves. In a sophomore survey course I use the *Defence* as a springboard for further explorations of Shelley's poetry and concerns. Whatever the scope of the course, "Ozymandias" has proved itself helpful both as a plea for greater open-mindedness toward the Romantics and poetry in general and as a way to alert students to the preoccupation with art and the imagination that is pivotal in Romantic poetry.

Julian and Maddalo:
An Introduction to Shelley

Charles Rzepka

Although not finished until some months after the event, *Julian and Maddalo* builds on an actual conversation that took place between Shelley and Byron during a ride along the Lido on the afternoon of 23 August 1818, the day that Shelley first arrived in Venice. The two poets had not seen each other since their summer as neighbors on Lake Geneva, some two years earlier, when their friendship was first formed. In the interim both had become self-exiles, ostracized by English society. It is in the light of their expatriation that the ironic comparison of the two poets' conversation in Italy, the "Paradise of exiles," to the "forlorn" debates of the devils in Milton's Hell (lines 39–59) is to be understood.

Quite aside from biographical curiosities that make good classroom theater, like Maddalo-Byron's prescient warning to the infidel Julian-Shelley to beware of Providence "if you can't swim" (117–18), I find the poem useful in two ways: first, as an introduction to Shelley himself, his personality, ideas, and stylistic variety; second, as a species of conversation poem linking Shelley to and distinguishing him from his less skeptical first-generation precursors.

Julian and Maddalo presents the reader with two portraits of Shelley himself, showing two contrary sides of his personality. There is, first of all, his ostensible surrogate, Julian, whom Shelley, in his preface, introduces in a manner that is irresistably engaging, objective, even humorous. Julian, of course, takes himself quite seriously, "forever speculating how good may be made superior" to evil, but Shelley's own deadpan statement "Julian is rather serious" cautions us against seeing Julian as a mirror image of his creator. In this way, the preface not only inoculates students against the rather painful self-characterizations of "Ode to the West Wind" and *Adonais* but also serves as an essential countervailing piece of evidence in assigned papers on Shelley's authorial self-presentations.

Shelley's distancing of himself from Julian does not reduce the power and seriousness of Julian's declarations of revolutionary optimism (170–76). Indeed, in *Julian and Madallo* Shelley ponders many of the theological and epistemological questions that fascinated him throughout his life, but in a manner more accessible and concrete to undergraduates than that found in poems like "Mont Blanc" and "Hymn to Intellectual Beauty," simply because the questions are applied to the immediate problems of madness and despondency. Having my students follow the logical consequences and contradictions of searching for the "love, beauty and truth" that are already "in our mind" (175–76) prepares them for a more challenging major work like *Prometheus Unbound* and enables them to better understand the precarious balance that Shelley himself maintained between revolutionary faith and epistemological skepticism.

Shelley's second self-portrait, the Maniac, embodies his state of depression soon after his visit to Byron, an affliction that severely tested his faith in human will. Specifically, the Maniac's speech, expressive of the torments of lost love, reflects the poet's reaction to Mary's withdrawal of affection after the death of the Shelleys' daughter, Clara, which Mary felt had been precipitated partly by Shelley's insistence that his family join him immediately in Venice, even though Clara was ill. Simply asking my students to consider the many personal affinities between Julian and the Maniac (14–15, 247–49, 237, 541–46) usually helps them appreciate the difficulty Shelley had in maintaining his revolutionary optimism and his faith in the infinite freedom of the will while fighting against despair and unreason.

Even so, Julian's optimistic attitude toward this tormented soul is not entirely unwarranted. The enigmatic fate of the Maniac, who recovers his wits (but for how long and with what result?) when his beloved returns, leaves room for speculation that Julian's prescription, "To love and be beloved with gentleness" (208), can indeed restore one from the "living death" of his "own willful ill" (210–11), if only temporarily. Maddalo-Byron, of course, a man "capable, *if he would* direct his energies to such an end, of becoming the redeemer of his degraded country" (preface; my emphasis), provides the perfect lightning rod for darker reflections. Indeed, some of my best classroom discussions have begun with a consideration of the relative merits of Julian's and Maddalo's contrasting and complicated responses to the Maniac's plight.

Byron's presence is also felt stylistically, both as a direct, almost Horatian influence on the verse style of the framing narrative—"a certain familiar style of language to express the actual way in which people talk with each other," as Shelley described it in a letter to Hunt (F. L. Jones 2: 108)—and as a counterpoint to the Maniac's "wild language," "such as in measure were called poetry" (541–42). The differences between these two Shelleyan voices is marked enough to be noticed by most undergraduates reading the poem for the first time. The conversations and the narration are easy for them to follow, but the Maniac's conspicuously "unconnected exclamations" (preface) are relatively opaque, and not only because the man is "mad": the syntax is often as tortured as the thought and pocked with archaisms (439–58). Wrestling with fragments of the Maniac's "wild talk" (200) not only increases students' syntactic and conceptual agility, limbering up the uninitiated for the "intense inane" (*Prometheus* 3.4.204) of Shelley's more recondite works, but leads them to consider how a poet's stylistic choices can promote a point of view, enhance or complicate a character's personality, advance an implied argument, or develop a particular theme. (A paper on Shelley's style may compare and contrast the Maniac's speeches with Beatrice Cenci's, which they anticipate.)

Julian and Maddalo's complex narrative structure offers the teacher of a Romantic survey course an excellent starting point for placing Shelley and his generation in the context of English Romanticism. *Julian and Maddalo* is, clearly, a conversation poem but a revisionist one. In contrast with the monologic first-generation examples of Wordsworth's "Tintern Abbey" and Coleridge's "This Lime-Tree Bower My Prison," "Frost at Midnight," and "Dejection: An Ode," Shelley's poem embraces both real dialogue (Julian's reported conversations with Maddalo) and monologue (the Maniac's soliloquies) in order to show the limits of and obstacles to a complete communion of minds.

It is an irony seldom noted that in "Tintern Abbey" and in Coleridge's typical conversation poem the poet's interlocutor is silent or absent, not an active participant in the purported conversation. (Coleridge's "Eolian Harp," interrupted by the darting of Sara Fricker's "more serious eye," is the exception that proves the rule.) In *Julian and Maddalo*, the monologic conversationalist becomes a maniac—solipsistic, isolated, self-communing (270). Like a diabolic version of Shelley's own nightingale-poet in *A Defence of Poetry*, the Maniac is a frenzied bird in a cage gilded by Maddalo (252–58), singing in the darkness of his own soul to torment, not delight, himself. Meanwhile, the Maniac's listeners, counterparts to the nightingale-poet's eavesdropping audience in the *Defence*, stand aside, entranced by the jarring discord but helpless to confront and engage the Maniac in a true conversation.

That Julian can be so moved by the Maniac's disjointed talk as to declare, in a poem celebrating his friendship with Maddalo, "Never saw I one whom I could call / More willingly my friend" (576–77), demonstrates Shelley's recognition that to some extent feelings of sympathy and friendship remain presumptuous until tested in the crucible of real discussion, with its give-and-take, its resistance to strictly private interpretive appropriations. However, real dialogue, such as that between Julian and Maddalo in the opening scene of the poem, while beginning in the exhilaration of a presumed communion of minds—"the swift thought, / Winging itself with laughter . . . [flying] from brain to brain" (28–30)—leads ultimately to disunion and distinction, the heightening of contrasts in personality and outlook. Neither the overheard monologs of poetry nor the shared dialog of conversation can overcome the obstacle that language poses to a true communion of souls: the one makes communion illusory, a willful self-projection; the other makes it, finally, impossible. Shelley's linguistic skepticism, I tell my students, characterizes the ironic disillusionment and detachment of the second-generation Romantics as a whole.

Aggression and Regression in
Prometheus Unbound

Thomas R. Frosch

Although students in my undergraduate Romantics course at first tend to respond negatively to *Prometheus Unbound,* it often turns out to be their favorite among all our readings. I find it necessary to go over the text sequentially in as much detail as time allows; I spend two weeks or even more on the play, even if we then have no time for any other Shelley readings. I also find it best to give the students an organized view of how the play's overwhelming multitude of complicated details work together. The view that I suggest makes use of certain basic psychoanalytic concepts, especially aggression and regression. Both terms usually have negative connotations for students, but I describe them neutrally as basic emotional tendencies that can have both constructive and harmful effects.

By aggression I mean attitudes or acts not only of anger and destructiveness but also of protest, ambition, mastery, and detachment. Indeed, aggressive energy plays a role in any assertion of the self to change things. By regression I mean ultimately an inner return to the mother and to what Freud at the beginning of *Civilization and Its Discontents* calls the oceanic feeling, the sense of oneness that the infant knows at the breast and, even more strongly, in the womb. As such, regressive energy plays a role in any sense of connection or unity. The play as a whole I present in terms of the adventure of an ego, the partly conscious organizing capacity of the self, working out its aggressive and regressive impulses on the way from enslavement to an ideal freedom and fulfillment.

I begin with two statements in Shelley's preface: his explanation that, in his revision of the original story, the world's "Champion" will not surrender to its "Oppressor" and his assertion that Prometheus is free from the vengeance and personal ambition that mar another wronged and courageous opponent of tyranny, Milton's Satan. The problem Shelley sets for himself in the preface, then, is to purify aggression.

The play itself begins with Prometheus, in effect, blinded by his own aggression, "eyeless in hate" (line 9), but in his opening speech he undergoes a change. First, he expresses the conviction that he will one day triumph; that belief leads him to a fantasy of revenge against Jupiter, which is followed by a sudden renunciation of hatred. I suggest that the reason for his change lies in the development of his aggression itself. Shelley begins the play by gathering aggression to a climax, and then, just as vengeance becomes a real possibility, he jumps to an opposite extreme, from blind hatred to "I hate no more" (57). That is an example of what Freud called reaction formation; Shelley is defending against the extremity of his own rage. The same pattern of building up aggression to the point of violence and then sacrificing it can be observed elsewhere in Shelley—for example in "The Mask of Anarchy."

But a reaction formation is not a purification; in order to truly master his aggression, Prometheus has to go back to its roots in his original cursing of Jupiter. He finds the words of the curse in a deep double-world of phantasms, a Shelleyan unconscious; but he refuses to have his own phantasm repeat the curse, for he has reacted so strongly against his own aggression that he cannot bear seeing it associated with anything resembling himself. Instead, he orders the Phantasm of Jupiter to repeat the curse; in so doing, he projects his own aggression onto Jupiter, a repetition of what he did in uttering the curse in the first place. As Prometheus's words are delivered by the Phantasm to Prometheus himself, we see that he, in effect, has legislated his own suffering and that of humanity and Nature as well; indeed, in the words of the curse, Prometheus tells Jupiter exactly what punishments to inflict. After hearing the curse repeated in that way, Prometheus acknowledges his own aggression and is able to master it: "Were these my words, O Parent?" he asks the Earth. "I wish no living thing to suffer pain" (302, 305).

Earth mistakenly thinks that Prometheus has surrendered; but as Prometheus's resistance to Mercury in the next episode makes clear, to master aggression is not to eradicate it. In cleansing his opposition to Jupiter of its self-defeating components, he has actually strengthened it, for the Prometheus who now faces Mercury has a new confidence and quiet firmness. As Mercury unleashes the Furies against him, Prometheus, in his new sense of self-mastery—"Yet am I king over myself" (492)—is confident that he can withstand any physical and emotional torment they can inflict. But they succeed in reducing him nearly to despair by torturing him morally with the possibility that all his struggles for the world will only lead to an increase in human suffering. The Phantasm of Jupiter embodied the dark side of a good man, but the Furies suggest something even more deeply disturbing: the dark side of his goodness itself. Prometheus is able to free himself from the Furies by accepting the painful awareness they inflict on him as part of the necessary burden of a realistic, rather than naive, reformer: he pities those whose hearts have become so hardened that they are not tortured by the Furies' words.

Prometheus is now soothed by the Spirits of consolation, who, above all, bring him news of love, present but embattled in Jupiter's world. In response, his thoughts turn in longing to his own love, Asia, and, when they do, the drama reaches a turning point. The whole course of act 1 has been a process of education to bring Prometheus to the naming of Asia. At the beginning he focused on what he hated and wished to destroy, and he got in return a world ruled by Jupiter, a principle of pure aggression; now he focuses on what he desires, and in return Asia enters the play.

Asia is an object of desire, but she is also a subject in her own right and must undergo her own process of change. She is a "transforming presence" (832), but at the beginning of act 2 she is weak and restricted, able to transform only the vale of her own exile. Act 2 begins with a vague sense of expectation and a conversation about dreams. In such flickerings on the margins of consciousness, the process of renovation in its positive phase of desire, rather than its negative phase of protest, begins; act 2 tells of the gradual materialization of those imaginings. Indeed, a dream that both Asia and Panthea have had appears outside them, calling "Follow, follow!" (1.131). The sisters begin a journey in pursuit of their dream; they follow echoes and songs; they pass through a musical forest of nightingales; they are following beauty. All the songs and echoes are leading to a primal realm of being, in the same way "As inland boats are driven to Ocean" (1.46). I compare that Ocean with one that appears in a previous reading in the course, Wordsworth's "Intimations of Immortality": "that Immortal sea / Which brought us hither" (163–64), the world of glory we knew before birth. Asia's journey is regressive, a return to the mother and to an original sense of oneness. Beauty for Shelley is a revolutionary force in the world of the father because it brings us back to a different, earlier world from which we feel we have fallen, the archaic world of the mother.

The regressive journey takes Asia into a cave, where she faces the "mighty Darkness" of Demogorgon (2.4.2). Demogorgon is necessity, the order of things, the connection between acts and consequences. In *Queen Mab* Shelley called necessity the "mother of the world" (6.198); what regression brings us to is the mother as a tremendous and mysterious might. Demogorgon suggests the infant's sense of the mother not as a source of nourishment and love but as the absolute power of his universe for both good and ill. We see now that, like aggression, regression must be mastered and purified, for the primal mother has a dark side: before her overwhelming dominance, the infant is passive and helpless, and she also has a potentiality for inflicting harm. It is suggestive that Demogorgon is dark and "shapeless" (2.4.4) just like the Furies (1.1.472) and that the original Furies, who did not appear in Aeschylus's *Prometheus Bound*, were terrible avengers of offenses against the mother.

In the scene in the cave, Asia, the good mother of gentleness and love, achieves precedence over the mother as sheer impersonal might. In that scene, too, Asia undergoes a certain education: in act 1 Prometheus, who is associated with thought, received an education in feeling; in act 2 Asia, who is associated with feeling, receives an intellectual education. Before the two can be brought together, each must be inwardly integrated. Approaching Demogorgon as an absolute authority, Asia asks a series of questions to discover the source of the world's suffering. The unsatisfying answers force her to refine her questions. Finally, as if in frustration, she tries to figure out for herself how the world reached its present state, and in telling that story, Asia articulates for herself that Jupiter cannot be an absolute power.

At that point, she begins to question the words in which the discourse has been conducted: "Whom calledst thou God?" Demogorgon's answer—"I spoke but as ye speak" (4.112)—reveals not only that she has been confined within a traditional and futile concept of authority but also that she has all along been playing the dominant role in the interview.

Demogorgon then tells her that there is no competent authority to whom she can ever appeal for help; "Fate, Time, Occasion, Chance, and Change" all facets of Demogorgon's own impersonal power, cannot answer her questions: "To these / All things are subject but eternal Love" (119–20). But if there is no authority that can help Asia, there is also no authority that can limit her own power. Demogorgon's final refusal to answer confirms what she has previously felt. Her intellectual education is complete; she has learned that the real authority is within herself—"Each to itself must be the oracle" (123)—and she has learned to believe in the flickerings, intuitions, and imaginings that have been guiding her all along but that she has never before thought of as forces. She still has one question to ask; it is the right question to which the entire interview has brought her. She says that she knows that Prometheus will arise; the question is when. And Demogorgon's answer is "Behold!" (128).

Thus, just as Prometheus, embodying an active principle, had to learn a wise passiveness, a restraint from violence and hate, to become effective, so Asia, embodying a passive principle, learns to be active. Now the power of Demogorgon, the primal maternal might, is placed at the disposal of the good, loving mother. As Asia ascends to rejoin Prometheus, she is transfigured into a new Venus; she has been strengthened into a universal power. The love she embodies has a regressive character: to know her radiant presence, as we see in the song of the Voice in the Air, is to dissolve into a primal oneness. The act ends with Asia's journeying back through the stages of human life, through infancy to a "diviner day" (5.103), to Wordsworth's immortal sea. In that ecstatic vision, regression has been not only strengthened into a redemptive and life-giving force but also purified. Asia's womblike paradise is "Peopled" by figures "Which walk upon the sea" (108, 110). In that vision of the oceanic feeling, we can know oneness without losing our human identity; we can enter the immortal sea without drowning.

It is important not to rush through acts 3 and 4. At first they seem to students much less vital and much more difficult than acts 1 and 2, but without them the play's problems are not fully resolved, and we miss much of its originality, its truly Shelleyan character.

In contrast to the close of act 2, act 3 opens on a note of aggression: Jupiter rapes Thetis, and Demogorgon, Jupiter's "child" (3.1.54), the revolutionary consequence of his tyrannical acts, arrives to drag him from his throne. The play thus far has tried to answer the question of how to get rid of Jupiter;

the rest of the play tries to answer the equally ambitious question of what the world will be like without him. More deeply, it tries to answer a question posed by Asia's song. The power of the mother has saved us from the evil father, but, once its regressive energy has been released, the danger arises that it may sweep us away to oblivion. Can we have what, in effect, is a return to the womb and still have a world in which the ego is independent and capable, a ruler in its own realm? Shelley has thus far only asserted, however powerfully, that we need not fear drowning in the Immortal Sea. The rest of the play tries to handle the problem by placing the regressive or transcendental impulse, the passive impulse toward oneness, into a dialectic with a progressive impulse toward a recognizable earthly and human world, toward the active and mastering individual ego—that is, toward aggression in the large sense. To read the last two acts is to follow a rhythm in which those two impulses answer each other back and forth.

The remainder of act 3, with its series of perspectives on the new world, stresses the progressive impulse. The Spirit of the Earth, for example, reports in surprisingly casual terms the great renovation that has taken place: people will wake from their sleep, see that they have all "somewhat changed" (4.71), and go back to sleep again. With that drastic understatement, Shelley is trying to keep his own apocalyptic and regressive tendencies under control, trying to keep his paradisiacal vision within the range of human possibility. The Spirit of the Hour, beginning in the same understated vein, is "disappointed not to see / Such mighty change as I had felt within / Expressed in outward things" (4.128–30). But as his report continues, it becomes rapturous; the veil of life is torn aside, and a totally new existence is revealed. Reaching that climax, however, the Spirit then insists that human beings will remain recognizably human, creatures not "exempt, though ruling them like slaves, / From chance and death and mutability," which remain as "clogs of that which else might oversoar / The loftiest star of unascended Heaven, / Pinnacled dim in the intense inane" (200–04). Shelley asserts the continued existence of such clogs just as the paradisiacal vision is about to carry us away into nothingness. Act 3 ends on a note of mastery, not only of chance and death but also of the regressive impulse. Aggression here takes the form of imposing limits on the self's own Dionysian impulses.

But Shelley could not end the drama of human liberation on a note of limitation. If act 3 stresses the mastering ego, act 4 pulls out the clogs, as it were, and gives full expression to Dionysian yearnings. Yet Shelley keeps the ego in view. In the play's final ecstasies the only recognizable presences are Panthea and Ione; as common observers, they serve as our guides to the celebration, as links between this new and rapturous state of being and our human world. They become especially important as the celebration climaxes in two visions that strain our senses and our imagination to the dissolving point. In those visions, derived from the chariot visions of God in the Bible, the Moon and the Earth appear as chariot-borne, rejuvenated spirits. In place of the father-god of the Bible, the new divine powers are infants—even, in their chariots, infants in the womb. Here are the play's culminating emblems of regression. And within them is something dangerous: the "thousand sightless axles" of the Earth's chariot spin with a "self-destroying swiftness" (248–49). In addition, the child-Earth has a beam of light on its forehead that pierces into the ground to reveal buried secrets, monsters of aggression. Here, the dream of regression brings us to a nightmare of archaic violence.

As if in reaction, love takes over, and it is mature, sexual love, not regressive. The Earth and the Moon begin a mating dance; the cold and barren Moon, fertilized, bursts forth with new life; and on the Earth humanity progresses as an autonomous and capable power: "All things confess his strength"; "The Lightning is his slave"; his language becomes an "Orphic song" able to rule otherwise "senseless and shapeless" thoughts (412–18). But as the love dialogue continues, the rapture intensifies; the Earth speeds around the sun; the Moon moves "Maniac-like" around him "Like a Maenad" (470, 473). The regressive impulse takes over again and turns dangerous; Dionysian ecstasy leads to images of destruction by the mother. At that point the Earth and the Moon disappear from the perception of Panthea and Ione; the regressive impulse has gone too far, into an oceanic dissolution; the vision of renovation has gone beyond an identifiable human reality.

Now in reaction we move from the heights to the depths. Demogorgon returns to call the roll of the universe; and as the elements of the universe are named and affirm their presence, distinct identities return; we move from oceanic oneness back to the differentiated world of the ego. Having called the elements back within the range of our perception, Demogorgon closes with a sermon, in which we are warned that Jupiter may return again; aggression has been not eradicated but tamed; our potentiality for sheer destructiveness and for projecting our aggression always remains. But Demogorgon reminds us of the Promethean virtues with which we can control "Destruction's strength" (564), should it emerge again. The play thus ends on the theme of mastery, in this case not as limitation but as capability.

Aggressive and regressive tendencies were both vital elements of Shelley's imagination, but he regarded both with great ambivalence. In *Alastor* he showed regression leading to a tragic death. In *The Cenci*, he showed aggression also leading to a tragic death. In *Prometheus Unbound* he brought those forces together, imagining a purification of their dangers, engaging them in a creative interplay in which each saves us from the negative side of the other, achieving a vision in which the impulse toward oceanic oneness and the impulse toward mastery and the autonomous ego both find fulfillment.

Love and Egocentricity:
Teaching *Alastor* and *Prometheus Unbound* with Mary Shelley's *Frankenstein*

Betty T. Bennett

Frankenstein has been read as a counterargument to *Alastor*; *Prometheus Unbound*, as a counterargument to *Frankenstein*. Those works, however, are far more consistent with the Shelleys' philosophic perspectives when they are viewed as variations on the same theme: the necessity for a value system based on universal, selfless love.

I begin my discussion of *Alastor* with two guiding questions: What is the relationship of the frame poet of the first and last forty-nine lines of the poem (the invocation and the close) to the central Poet? How closely can either poet be identified with Shelley's philosophy, as expressed in the preface? Shelley uses his preface to direct the reading of the poem. The Poet of his story was "morally dead" because of his "self-centred seclusion," which led to his actual death by the furies (Alastor) of his "irresistible passion." The reader is to understand that the Poet's sensitivity and his remarkable intelligence, however sympathetic, are in themselves insufficient and inevitably destructive.

From the preface, one might expect *Alastor*'s frame poet to express Shelley's own perspective. Instead, the invocation introduces a poet driven to extremes (charnels and coffins), obsessively seeking answers to his own "obstinate questionings" (24) about nature, and out of touch with humanity. Self-centered and passive, he prays for the "Great Parent" (45) to speak through his own voice. The invocation, in establishing a compulsive link between the frame poet and nature, is a précis of the main story.

That poet and the Poet of the central poem have much in common. A Faustian figure, the Poet dedicates his life to the search for nature's secrets. Untouched by human love, he falls in love with a vision he creates, "the voice of his own soul" (153). The embodiment of Narcissus, the Poet wanders the earth searching for his other self. Instead, he finds only his own shriveling image and, though ever in "mystic sympathy" (652) with nature, the Poet dies alone and unmourned. The lines describing his death as "A fragile lute, on whose harmonious strings / The breath of heaven did wander" (667–68) recall the frame poet's passive self-description. In closing, the frame poet mourns the dead Poet as brave, gentle, and beautiful, but, quoting Wordsworth, he says the loss is too "deep for tears" (713) and that Nature, human things, birth, and the grave "are not as they were" (720).

Ironically, according to the poem, all things are exactly as they were. Because the Poet was apart from humanity, his existence, however idealized, made no difference. The concluding quotations from Wordsworth recall the invocation's allusions to Wordsworth. And that, in turn, suggests that *Alastor* is about three poets or poet types: the central Poet, narcissistically caught up in self; the frame poet, who admires and echoes the central Poet but does not understand his essential failure; and Shelley, who, in telling the story of both, points out that their value system can lead only to a meaningless, solitary death.

From that discussion I turn to Mary Shelley's *Frankenstein* as an extended, complex exploration of egocentricity and, implicitly, of systemic social failure. First, I ask the class to consider the similarities between *Frankenstein* and *Alastor*, to examine (1) the scientist's obsessiveness compared with the poet's; (2) the creation of another being—the Poet's creation in his own dream, the scientist's creation in his laboratory, both representative of egocentric control; (3) the use of frame narrators who reflect the obsessions of the main figures; (4) the Poet's engagement with nature but not with humanity; the scientist's relation to nature and humanity, fluctuating in converse proportion to his involvement with his power quest; (5) travel, exotic versus geographically familiar; (6) intellectual exploration of secret knowledge (charnels and coffins in both); (7) the role of mythological and literary allusions, particularly Greek mythology and Milton's *Paradise Lost*.

Discussing the similarities leads naturally to a discussion of the differences between the two works. First, we discuss the most obvious difference, form. The poem—with its richer, metaphoric language—is unquestionably more difficult than the prose story for most students. The novel, despite its occasional stiffness and unfamiliar language, easily carries its readers along through its increasingly complex, surprising story. An exercise I find useful here is to select some relatively brief Nature passages from both works and to analyze them with the class, so that the students can compare their effects.

Next, I note that in *Alastor* social failure is characterized through the Poet's self-destructive egocentricity. In *Frankenstein*, by contrast, the scientist and the creature represent conflicting value systems: the scientist's values are based on power indifferent to social responsibility; the creature's values are based on love and community. For Mary Shelley the scientist's irresponsible abandonment of his creature represents her view of traditional sociopolitical authority. (The creature, from that perspective, symbolizes any socially rejected person or group, and that symbolism lends itself to a discussion of contemporary interpretations of the outcast.) Frankenstein's failed values lock him and his creature in symbiotic hatred, which leads to their mutual moral and physical destruction (see William Godwin's *Caleb Williams*, an important model for *Frankenstein*). However admirable the alternative system exemplified in the values of the creature, it cannot succeed in a world governed by egocentricity. Though it explores potential choices, *Frankenstein*, like *Alastor*, ends in destruction.

For a positive resolution to the problem of egocentric power, we turn to *Prometheus Unbound*. I find it helpful to remind the students that the two works we have already considered prepare their readers initially to expect the Poet and the scientist to represent good and the creature to represent evil and that the subtitle of *Frankenstein, The Modern Prometheus*, is an ironic description of Frankenstein's failure to care for his creature. Unexpected reversals are even more integral to understanding *Prometheus Unbound*. I ask the students to consider how the reversals in all three works cause readers to question their own assumptions, opening their minds to reassessments of values and perspectives.

Reversing the Aeschylus play, Shelley's Prometheus refuses to reveal his secret knowledge of Jupiter's demise in exchange for an end to his suffering. Instead, in an act that empowers good over evil, Prometheus recants his terrible curse on Jupiter, unknowingly setting necessity in motion that results in his own and universal freedom. Thus, he exemplifies Shelley's belief that evil is not inherent in the system of creation, that it can be overcome. In Prometheus's recantation of his curse, we can also see the *Frankenstein* creature's capacity for love carried to its moral consummation.

Prometheus Unbound is Shelley's idealized working out of a new order of harmony and freedom that springs from Prometheus's universal love. As in the two earlier works, the action describes spiritual development; scientific, mythological, and literary allusions; and extensive geographic travel. The Adam of American literature, having reached the limits of the physical frontier, is said to have turned inward. In *Prometheus Unbound* Shelley uses limitless travel—inner and extraterrestrial—to symbolize humanity's ability to determine the character of its own universe.

In *Alastor* Shelley depicts the egocentricity that he judged to be the source of his contemporary antithetically grounded sociopolitical system. In *Frankenstein* the interaction of Mary Shelley's two main characters symbolizes that same destructive system, but she offers an alternative. In *Prometheus Unbound*, through Prometheus's expulsion of his evil aspect—his hatred of Jupiter—Shelley showed how that alternative could be achieved. In a world already in flux—social, political, industrial—he envisioned the possibility and the necessity of a new social system in which, through will and commitment, as Mary Shelley says in her note on the poem, "Love, untainted by any evil, becomes the law of the world" (Hutchinson 273).

Windows of Meaning in
"Ode to the West Wind"

Seraphia D. Leyda

Taken out of context, the last lines of "Ode to the West Wind"—"O Wind, / If Winter comes, can Spring be far behind?"—appear simpleminded. That Shelley considered an even more blatant commonplace for his conclusion —"When Winter comes Spring lags not far behind" (Chernaik 204)—only confirms the point. The discrepancy between the prosaic content of those lines and their powerful effect on a reader provides a good starting point for classroom discussion. By beginning at the conclusion and drawing students into an exploration of the process that transforms a cliché into a powerful poetic statement, I find that they better understand how poetry works and better appreciate Shelley's art and intellect.

After a brief introduction and an overview of the poem, I tell students we are going to walk through the poem, giving particular attention to several "windows" as we move toward its conclusion. Those windows open up the text, taking us far beyond Shelley's encounter with the "tempestuous wind" in Florence (221). Being more than literary allusions, they construct the poem's meaning. In an advanced class I may justify the approach by citing Shelley's claim in *A Defence of Poetry* that poetry "acts in a divine and unapprehended manner, beyond and above consciousness," and "awakens and enlarges the mind itself by rendering it the receptacle of a thousand unapprehended combinations of thought" (486–87).

We warm up with "Pestilence-stricken multitudes" (line 5). When students look hard at the metaphor, they see hordes of diseased, dying human beings. When pressed to explain why, they realize that "ghosts" (3) slants their reading of "multitudes" away from things and toward people. They notice that "Pestilence-stricken" goes well beyond a description of natural seasonal change. The "polluting multitude" in "Lines Written among the Euganean Hills" (352–73) reinforces Shelley's subtle introduction of humankind in the opening lines of "Ode to the West Wind."

Students quickly discover the human dimension in the next window: "The wingèd seeds, where they lie cold and low, / Each like a corpse within its grave . . ." (7–8), but they may need prompting to make the connection with the New Testament. "Verily, verily, I say unto you, Except a corn of wheat fall into the ground and die, it abideth alone; but if it die, it bringeth forth much fruit" (John 12.24) and "Thou fool, that which thou sowest is not quickened, except it die . . ." (1 Cor. 15.36). Both Jesus and Paul use metaphors to describe the resurrection of the human body. With a little encouragement, the students also hear in the succeeding lines an echo of Paul's, "In a moment, in the twinkling of an eye, at the last trump: for the trumpet shall sound, and the dead shall be raised incorruptible, and we shall be changed" (1 Cor. 15.52). The winged seeds have directed our view toward Christianity, which posits death and rebirth at the core of its doctrine, the figure of Christ crucified, and the empty sepulcher.

"Destroyer and Preserver" (14) opens the window on Hinduism and Eastern religions. Students are fascinated by Siva and Vishnu and Brahman the Absolute; in fact, it is often difficult to move them away from the window of transmigrating souls, the illusions of maya, and the oneness of all. I make them realize that Hinduism is the oldest of the great world religions, and I encourage them to do some independent reading.

"Angels of rain and lightning" (18) is glossed as "Literally, 'messengers' " (222), but students look through that window and see Judaism and Christianity—from the angel with a flaming sword guarding the gates of Eden to the guardian angels hovering above meek children. (A question or two helps them see that the metaphor reinforces the angelic quality of Spring with her clarion just as it prepares for the Gabriel trumpet of the conclusion.) Occasionally, a student knows that angels play important roles in Islam.

The clouds shift and reshape themselves, and we are suddenly looking through a different window. The angels of rain and lightning have become the locks of the approaching storm, the bright hair of "some fierce Maenad" (21). The students associate the orgiastic dancer with Bacchus, whom they think of primarily as a drunken reveler. With a little prompting, they recall the god's Greek name, Dionysus. (They may need to be reminded that Greek mythology, now a "creed outworn," was once a living religion.) The Maenad worshiping the god of the vine summons to view not only Dionysus but Orpheus, Pentheus, Actaeon, Adonis, Attis, and Osiris. My students are eager to learn more about the dying and reviving vegetation gods introduced to my generation through Jessie L. Weston's From Ritual to Romance and James G. Frazer's Golden Bough. Joseph Raben's observations on the Dionysian substrata in Shelley's poetry are also helpful.

The "pumice isle" (32) opens another window. It is an easy step from pumice to lava to volcanoes. With luck, a student recalls Vesuvius and the destruction of Pompeii. I suggest that Shelley has directed our attention to the potential for radical, destructive change that lies deep in the heart of the earth. After a little more time the students realize that the dark side of natural change is a preserver, as well as a destroyer, and that the flow of burning lava created a new land mass (and preserved Pompeii). G. M. Matthews ("Volcano's Voice") is invaluable background. Volcanic eruption as a Shelleyan metaphor for revolutionary social change is reinforced by the view from the next window.

Looking at the "old palaces and towers" (33) in the sea's dream, we see imperial Rome. When asked about other great civilizations that have fallen, students compile an impressive list. I may turn to *Hellas* and read a bit of "Worlds on worlds are rolling ever / From creation to decay . . ." (197–238). Shelley's letters to Peacock describing his excursions to Baiae and Vesuvius and his detailed account of a visit to Pompeii (F. L. Jones 2: 61–63, 71–75) are useful. If the class thinks that I am reading too much into the text, I quote Shelley at Pompeii: "O, but for that series of wretched wars which terminated in the Roman conquest of the world, but for the Christian religion which put a finishing stroke to the ancient system; but for those changes which conducted Athens to its ruin, to what an eminence might not humanity have arrived!" (F. L. Jones 2: 75). The pumice isle and underwater ruins have revealed that change in the natural world is paralleled by revolution in the social and political worlds. The vista is a long one.

Students open the window of "the thorns of life" (54) directly on the passion and death of Christ. They may need help to realize that Shelley's Jesus Christ is a human hero who metaphorically embodies the dying-resurrecting god, but they are quick to note that Shelley prefigures his poet's destruction and transfiguration by drawing the suffering Christ into the person of the poet. At that point, I suggest that all the views from all the previous windows have begun to converge: the pestilence-stricken multitudes, the winged seeds, the angels, the Maenad, the pumice isle, and the ruined towers and palaces. As the students consider the correspondences in those previously "unapprehended combinations of thought," they notice that the wind's force has been shifted away from the unfeeling world of nature toward the suffering world of humanity.

Now the students better understand the funneling action of the last two stanzas. They see that the poet, functioning as a conductor, gathers and channels the extraordinary power of natural change and channels it into the human sphere. Through Shelley's windows we have caught sight of India, Egypt, Greece, Rome, and Renaissance Italy; we have watched the dying and the rebirth of Dionysus, Adonis, Osiris, and Christ; we have witnessed the emergence of Hinduism, Judaism, Christianity, Islam—the quickening of new life out of death. The Italian West Wind has become the power of change flowing through the natural world, through history, through civilizations, through religions, through all human life. The students are ready for the rising intensity and passion of the ode's last stanza.

Standing before the last window, the "unextinguished hearth" (66), the students see that Shelley has turned away from the vegetation metaphor toward the fire of the volcano, humanizing and civilizing it into the image of the hearth. We talk about hearths, domestic and metallurgical. I ask what happens when one scatters "ashes and sparks" (67). Students see the apocalyptic conflagration that Shelley intended. Touched by the burning coal of prophecy (here, if not earlier, I read Isaiah 6.6–8 to the class), the words of the poet become the ashes and the sparks, the death of the old and the birth of the new, destroying and preserving. Now the students realize that "Winter" (70) is not only the last phase in Earth's vegetation cycle but also the death of gods and religions and civilizations and political institutions and individual human beings. "Spring" promises renewal but not only of Earth's vegetation. It heralds the rebirth of the individual person, the human imagination, the social and political order. It announces Shelley's Promethean age.

Although to do so may seem a bit melodramatic, I conclude the class with a reading of the whole poem. As I read the ode aloud, the students integrate all their insights and comments into an immediate experience. The reading of the text becomes an incantation, focusing the power of the poem on each student, and the last lines explode with the passionate meaning that Shelley carefully created for them.

Teaching "To a Sky-Lark"
in Relation to Shelley's *Defence*

John L. Mahoney

Like many teachers of Shelley, I enjoy teaching his short lyrics as a welcome interlude between longer, often ponderous pieces like *Alastor* and "The Triumph of Life." We talk and write about those lyrics on their own terms, but teaching Shelley's only major critical treatise, A *Defence of Poetry*, in conjunction with a lyric like "To a Sky-Lark" can also generate a stimulating discussion of his theory and practice of art.

I have found it helpful at the beginning to pass out to the class a one-page handout of negative critical comments on the poem. We read T. S. Eliot's comment that "To a Sky-Lark" lacks "brainwork" and is "sound . . . without sense" (*Lancelot* 135). And then there is F. R. Leavis leading an anti-Shelley charge, calling the poem "a mere tumbled out spate ('spontaneous overflow') of poeticalities, the place of each one of which Shelley could have filled with another without the least difficulty" (215). We note that even Shelley's recent biographer Richard Holmes regards "To a Sky-Lark" and other late Italian lyrics as "of no serious concern to Shelley . . . haphazard acts of inattention" (ix). Such a quick overview provides a context for seeing how charges of carelessness, vagueness, and uninformed enthusiasm have been a continuing phenomenon among Shelley's readers and critics. I often assign a short paper at that point, asking students to compare their own first reactions to the lyric with those critiques.

After that brief background we read A *Defence of Poetry* because it seems to advance some of the theoretical underpinnings of Shelley's lyricism. I stress the Platonism of the *Defence* (see J. E. Baker) to illuminate the two worlds of "To a Sky-Lark." Shelley elevates poets to the role of inspired bards, priests who range beyond mere versifiers, writing in both verse and prose as lawyers, statesmen, and teachers. Poets are those who see and dramatize the distinctions between the One and the Many, the transcendent and the real; they "draw into a certain propinquity with the beautiful and true, those partial agencies of the invisible world which is called religion" (482). How nicely that image of poets and their recognition of the gap between the real and the ideal highlights the predicament of the speaker of the poem. From the opening lines he is located squarely on this "earth" (7), and that positioning is reinforced throughout. He knows "languor" (77), "annoyance" (78), "love's sad satiety" (80), "death" (82), "pain" (89), "Hate, and pride, and fear" (92). Still, like the poet in the *Defence*, he aspires to the transcendent as he hears the music of the skylark soaring "Higher still and higher / From the earth" (6–7) and pleads to know "What sweet thoughts are thine" (62).

From there I try to suggest the logic or the rhetoric of emotion in the poem that gives it structure and pattern, making it more than a mere gush of emotion. And I invite students to write short papers about its structure and organizing principles. I use the memorable lines of the *Defence* as a point of departure: "Poetry, as has been said, in this respect differs from logic, that it is not subject to the control of the active powers of the mind, and that its birth and recurrence has no necessary connexion with consciousness or will" (506).

For teaching purposes, I divide the poem into three parts. I see stanzas 1–6, triggered by the speaker's emotional greeting, "Hail to thee, blithe spirit," as a celebration of the bird and its song. No one image seems adequate to capture the brief glimpses of the skylark's world, hardly seen but deeply felt. Rather, what we notice is something like a collage, a scattering of similes, arrows launched toward a target, each one suggesting the speaker's struggle to describe the bird. The *Defence* is most helpful as we study the imagery, especially its explanation of how "a word, a trait in the representation of a scene or a passion, will touch the enchanted chord, and reanimate, in those who have ever experienced these emotions, the sleeping, the cold, the buried image of the past" (505). That collage of similes, like the intricate variations in a piece of music, is closed with a crescendolike, "All the earth and air / With thy voice is loud" (26–27).

Stanzas 7–12 develop the opening invocation to the skylark in an excited but carefully constructed unit of questioning. The speaker concedes, "What thou art we know not" (31), yet will not resist the temptation to question the nature of the bird and its world. Again, similes are clustered "as if description is inadequate to convey the intense quality of the experience" (Chernaik 127). Words will not do, yet words are our only resource; as Angela Leighton puts it, "if original power is imageless, it is nothing if not images and words" (104). Working with that dimension of the poem can provide a teachable moment with undergraduates, and I often pause to raise questions about the kinds of figurative language—simile, metaphor, symbol—the students are encountering and to provide suggestions for a vocabulary that will allow them to discuss the figures. On occasion I compare Shelley's strong orientation toward simile with, for example, Keats's orientation toward metaphor and symbol.

Stanzas 13–21 take a final step in the developing emotional rhetoric of the poem: from address to the bird to questioning of its origins and essence to a final prayer for inspiration. The skylark continues to be "Sprite or Bird" (61), part of another and better world yet heard in this world, and the speaker pleads to learn the source of "the flood of rapture so divine" (65), a song greater than any "Chorus Hymeneal" or "triumphal chant" (66–67). While the first two sections of the poem afford fine opportunities for teaching the workings of figures of speech, the final section can be used to teach the compression of poetry, the power of verbal repetition and questioning. The repetition of "What" underscores the insistency of the poet's questions: "What objects" "What fields . . . waves . . . mountains . . . sky . . . plain . . . love of thine own kind . . . ignorance of pain" (71–75). Reading aloud enlivens the process and prepares the way for the power of the closing. Here, returning again to the Platonic motifs of the *Defence*, we see the skylark as "scorner of the ground" (100), dreamer of "Things more true and deep" (83), and those images dramatize the plight of the speaker even more vividly. His is a world—emphasized by the repetition of "we," as well as "I"—where "Our sweetest songs are those that tell of saddest thought" (90), where "I know not how thy joy we ever should come near" (95).

And then there is the question of how to read the ending: Hopeful? Despairing? Ambiguous? Again, I try to bring in the *Defence*; as a result, I see the ending as hopeful. The speaker and the skylark are clearly separated as the argument of the last stanzas builds, and we are reminded of the plight of human beings described in the *Defence*, unable to see beyond, "a slave" to "facts and calculating practices" and unable to find "the poetry of life" (502–03). Yet if the speaker, now emerging as the poet-priest-advocate of humankind, could learn "half the gladness" (101) of the bird, he would achieve the "harmonious madness" (103) of inspiration. He would preach spontaneously, ecstatically to a world of "saddest thought" (90), and "the world should listen then," as he is "listening now" (105). That is, he would achieve both for himself and for his auditor that enlargement of the imagination, that "identification of ourselves with the beautiful" that the *Defence* calls "the great secret of morals" and the special gift of inspired poetry (487).

Shelley as Poet and
Dramatist in *The Cenci*

Vincent F. Petronella

Exploring the way a historical event becomes a dramatic and poetic event is important to the teaching of Shelley's representation of a grim narrative in his verse play *The Cenci*. The teacher should devote the first of three or four class meetings to Shelley's main source, "The Relation of the Death of the Family of the Cenci." Four interrelated questions need to be considered: What does Shelley take unchanged from his source? What does he add? What is condensed? What artistic or dramatic features result from his use of the source material? In advance of the class meeting dealing with those matters, the students should know the questions and have access to copies of "The Relation."

From "The Relation" Shelley derives the basic narrative (Cenci's hatreds, his wish to burn his wealth before death, Beatrice's undelivered petition to the Pope, her resistance to Cenci, and her subsequent victimization, for example), but he adds other details, such as the act of incest itself (committed offstage and never referred to specifically); the creation of the self-centered, sly Orsino, who suggests that Cenci be murdered (Beatrice makes the proposal in "The Relation"); the arrival (shortly after the murder) of the papal legate Savella, who carries an order for Cenci's immediate execution; and Beatrice's determination to argue her cause and maintain her faith in God. Those additions intensify the power of dramatic irony. The treachery and the cowardice of Orsino, for example, make Beatrice look all the more sympathetic and heroic, thus complicating our response to her role as an accomplice in a murder. But the additions to the source, as Robert F. Whitman explains, do more than underscore the dramatic irony: Beatrice's hasty plotting, the unexpected appearance of the perspicacious Savella, and Beatrice's early faith and later sense of being abandoned by her God accentuate the hopelessness of her situation and generate powerful pity and fear in a tragedy that is centered on character and personal responsibility (253).

To intensify the tragic energy, Shelley condenses the legal discussion of the innocence or guilt of Beatrice, Giacomo, and Lucretia. The result is a classic conception of tragic inevitability, which is developed by focusing on the consequences of choosing to kill Cenci. What in the historical account is spread out over more than a year is reduced to slightly less than a week in Shelley's play. The tendency is toward a unity of time. That, along with offstage violence and a *mythos*, enhances the classic quality of the play.

Rather than add to or subtract from his source, Shelley attempts to transform "The Relation." His Cenci is both a criminal and, in contrast with the source, a theist who specifically invokes God and who often associates himself with God's paternal image. But the play never mentions his many sexual crimes. Even the word *incest* is never used. Shelley's concern about audience sensibilities prompted those omissions, but the wary reader or viewer realizes in time that incest is at the core of Beatrice's crumbling world. Shelley plots his play so that an incompletely concealed and expanding terror is gradually disclosed. That terror is potentially melodramatic, but Shelley uses artistic control: terror is set up in relation to a strong sense of pity, but that pity is offset by the hubris welling up within Beatrice, all of which is given enhanced tragic value by Shelley's poetry.

In a well-known letter to Shelley (16 Aug. 1820), John Keats comments on the drama and poetry of *The Cenci*. He urges Shelley to " 'load every rift' of [his] subject with ore" (2: 323), so as to temper the usual crusading ingredient in his work with a poetic art more painstakingly fashioned. In fact, Shelley is nowhere more controlled as a propagandizing artist than he is in *The Cenci*. He does manifest negative capability. As we expect, Shelley speaks out against the horrors of tyranny and the abuse of the individual, but he does so through a dramatic poetry that reveals a disciplined mastery of the Shakespearean tradition, as Stuart Curran clearly demonstrates in his book-length study of *The Cenci* (97–128).

Students should analyze one or two samples of Shelley's blank-verse technique. Here are some lines of Lucretia:

> If, for the very reasons which should make
> Redress most swift and sure, our injurer triumphs?
> And we, the victims, bear worse punishment
> Than that appointed for their torturer?   (3.1.190–93)

Set off by a spondee, the entire first line runs on into the next, which is made up of twelve syllables that end in a proselike rhythm: ". . . our injurer triumphs." Line 192 has the ten syllables expected of iambic pentameter, but the phrase "worse punishment," which leads in enjambment to line 193, begins with a spondaic foot, as does line 190. Rhythmically the effect is natural. Add the forthright, nonfigurative diction, and we see that Shelley, keeping the Wordsworthian promise stated in the preface to his play, creates a poetic line that reflects "the real language of men" and avoids "mere poetry" (241). Another example comes in Cenci's threat to burn his property before death:

> When all is done, out in the wide Campagna,
> I will pile up my silver and my gold;
> My costly robes, paintings and tapestries;
> My parchments and all records of my wealth,
> And make a bonfire in my joy, and leave
> Of my possessions nothing but my name.   (4.1.55–60)

"Out" in the first line, "I" in the second, "paintings" in the third, and "nothing" in the last offer enough variation of the regular iambic pentameter foundation to place emphasis on *where* things are to be burned, *who* will burn them, *what* kinds of things will be burned, and *how* they will end up. The position of those four words in proximate lines results in naturalness by altering the iambic pattern; the four words act in counterpoint against the regularity established by the eight phrases initiated by the dramatically important possessive pronoun "my," a word often on the lips of the self-absorbed Cenci.

At other times, regular lines occurring at moments of tension suggest powerful forces erupting through surface calm, as when the ravished, frantic Beatrice enters crying at the beginning of act 3: "Reach me that handkerchief!—My brain is hurt; / My eyes are full of blood. . . ." We again hear the repeated possessives, but now they direct us toward Beatrice struggling within a circle of terror. The handkerchief is wanted to encircle her head and provide soothing pressure. It is a dramatic emblem related to Giacomo's metaphor depicting Cenci's victims as "scorpions ringed with fire" (2.2.70). Both circles (handkerchief and fire) apply pressure to those who have felt either the threat or the reality of Cenci's violence.

By play's end Beatrice's request for assistance with the girdle that encircles her becomes a thoroughly ironic gesture of entrapment:

> Here, Mother, tie
> My girdle for me, and bind up this hair
> In any simple knot; ay, that does well.
> And yours I see is coming down. How often
> Have we done this for one another; now
> We shall not do it any more. My Lord,
> We are quite ready. Well, "tis very well.
> (5.4.159–65)

The collected, resigned Beatrice says her last lines and presumably starts to walk toward the scaffold. She closes the play on a note of domestic simplicity; in fact, her entire parting speech (beginning at line 141) has a poignant clarity, a classic simplicity of line and diction. Shelley even does some Shakespearean punning and internal rhyming with "farewell" and "well," portraying Beatrice as one engaged in *ars moriendi*; poetically, she bids farewell to life and loved ones, and she enacts the drama, to use her phrase, "very well."

A fusion of poetry and drama is crystallized in her art of dying. With a relatively placid rhythm and uncluttered, literal images Shelley creates the calm and the lucidity of Hamlet's "the readiness is all" (5.2.222) in Beatrice's more direct "We are quite ready" (5.4.165). She asks for the tying of her girdle and the binding up of her hair—gestures that suggest order, form, and the bond between people: "How often / Have we done this for one another." The bond is in striking contrast to the bondage that became her life. To be sure, Beatrice has been trapped from the outside by both father and church fathers; but, ironically, she contributes to her own entrapment from within. Herein lies her tragedy: she meets Cenci's willful action with a Cenci-like reaction and, consequently, is caught within a ring of fire, a vicious circle that has grown out of herself and out of her own family circle.

Teaching Shelley's Anatomy of Anarchy

Stuart Peterfreund

Shelley's letter of 6 September 1819 to Charles Ollier offers a clue to the genesis of "The Mask of Anarchy": "The same day that your letter came, came the news of the Manchester work, & the torrent of my indignation has not yet done boiling in my veins. I wait anxiously [to] hear how the country will express its sense of this bloody murderous oppression of its destroyers" (Jones 2: 117 and n.). Shelley suggests that, while he is waiting for England's expression of outrage, he will frame his own. He draws on *The Cenci*, recently completed, and quotes the speech of Beatrice (3.1.86–87) as she contemplates vengeance to repay the Count's incestuous violence: "Something must be done . . . What yet I know not." The implications are that "The Mask" is Shelley's expression of outrage—the "something" that "must be done"—and that the expression is at once historically grounded and a transformation of history, much as *The Cenci* is at once grounded in the history of late-sixteenth-century Rome and a transformation of it.

The genetic reading of the poem is common enough. (See King-Hele.) And, to be sure, had the murder of innocent protesters by drunken guardsmen at Saint Peter's Field, near Manchester, not taken place, Shelley would not have written "The Mask." But to say that the poem is the result of the Peterloo massacre is not to say that "The Mask" is exclusively about that unfortunate event, any more than to say that Blake's *Marriage of Heaven and Hell* (1790–93), which resulted from the American and French revolutions, is about those revolutions or to say that Byron's *Vision of Judgment* (1821), which resulted from the death of George III, is about the death of that monarch. Those satires by Blake and Byron are not chosen at random: both are variants of Menippean satire, the subgenre that Northrop Frye categorizes as the "anatomy" (*Anatomy* 308–12). One way to teach "The Mask," especially in an upper-level undergraduate or a graduate course, is as an anatomy.

Of primary importance among the generic elements is the focus of the anatomy. It "deals," as Frye observes, "less with people as such than with mental attitudes. Pedants, bigots, cranks, parvenus, virtuosi, enthusiasts, rapacious and incompetent professional men of all kinds, are handled in terms of their occupational approach to life as distinct from their social behavior" (*Anatomy* 309). That focus is apparent in Blake's *Marriage*, which purports to demonstrate the necessity of "Contraries" such as "Attraction and Repulsion, Reason and Energy, Love and Hate" (pl. 3) by pitting the angelic state of mind against the diabolic. The same (arch-)angelic-diabolic opposition is apparent in Byron's *Vision*, which pits Michael against Satan in an "occupational approach"—the litigation of a capital crime in "neutral space" (33.1)—to question what state of mind to assume in response to established power: Michael serves it, while Satan opposes it.

That "The Mask" "deals less with people as such than with mental attitudes" is evident from the beginning of the speaker's visions: persons are likened and subordinated to mental attitudes. Murder "had a mask like Castlereagh"; Fraud is gowned like Eldon; Hypocrisy rides a crocodile, like Sidmouth; and Anarchy is pale, like the subject of Benjamin West's painting *Death on a Pale Horse* (lines 4–33). The emphasis on the occupational approach to life is taken up by the mercenaries, lawyers, and priests, who proclaim Anarchy their sovereign hoping that he has work for them (58–73).

The oppositional dynamic in "The Mask," although not so evenly matched as in *The Marriage* and *The Vision*, still scrutinizes orthodox notions of good and evil, order and disorder, by pitting them against each other. Orthodox notions of divine-right kingship and of the king as God's vice-gerent are pitted against the unorthodox notions of popular sovereignty and full equality. Anarchy's opponent is "a maniac maid" named Hope (86–87). Transfigured by an act of passive resistance—she lies down in the path of Anarchy's procession (98–101)—Hope arises to vanquish Anarchy and his followers (130–34) and to instruct others opposing tyrants to do so by passive resistance. "Stand ye calm and resolute, / Like a forest close and mute," she subsequently enjoins, and "Look upon them as they slay / Till their rage has died away" (319–47).

Frye observes that the anatomy form "is not primarily concerned with the exploits of heroes, but relies on the free play of intellectual fancy and the kind of humorous observation that produces caricature. It differs also from the picaresque form, which has the novel's interest in the actual structure of society" (*Anatomy* 309–10). "The Mask" is by turns antiheroic—there is nothing heroic or even admirable about Anarchy's band—and supportive of a common and popular heroism that rescinds any notion of heroic uniqueness or privilege. Notwithstanding Shelley's outrage at a government that condones, let alone tolerates, the events in Saint Peter's Field, the poem has to it a definite element of political lampoon, as Stuart Curran (*Annus* 181–86) and Michael Scrivener (200) have noted. Far from observing the structure of society, "The Mask" presents a Utopian vision of the English people freed from the chains of custom, privilege, and hierarchy that constituted the structure of English society before reform.

"The Mask" is also an anatomy on rhetorical grounds. "The short form of the Menippean satire is usually a dialogue or colloquy, in which the dramatic interest is in a conflict of ideas rather than of character" (Frye, *Anatomy* 310). The first part of the poem, before the entrance of Hope, rings ironic changes on the notion of dialogue, at least in the Socratic sense of dialogue as dialectic. Dialogue, when it does exist, takes the form of repetition. The mark on Anarchy's brow proclaims "I AM GOD, AND KING, AND LAW!" (37), and it elicits two responses: the awed silence of "the adoring multitude" that Anarchy and his train trample "to a mire of blood" (40–41), and the repetition, with variations, of the message on Anarchy's brow by those who would serve him and, in so doing, serve themselves. One conclusion about the political reality of Anarchy's world is that meaningful dialogue is impossible, as is suggested by a number of prosecutions for seditious libel, including that of Leigh Hunt, in England. Hunt's imprisonment on that charge (1813–15) may have had something to do with the decision to defer publication of "The Mask" until 1832, thirteen years after its composition.

But Hope's appearance transforms the second part of the poem; it sets forth the conditions under which extended colloquy—speaking together in the several senses of the phrase—will be made possible. She enjoins the multitude to begin by refusing to speak the language of the oppressor. "Stand ye calm and resolute, / Like a forest close and mute . . ." (319–20). In the silence that follows, "The old laws of England" will supplant the laws of the tyrant Anarchy and replace his voice with a "solemn voice [that] must be / Thine own echo—Liberty!" (331–35). At that time, a second transfiguration will take place, one that will usher in a millennial age in which the multitude speak with one mighty voice that offsets and reverses the univocality of Anarchy and his minions (364–67).

Teaching "The Mask" and The Marriage and The Vision as types of the anatomy adds the element of design to the element of occasion. Moreover, the design, drawn from classical literature, establishes a continuity between Romantic satire and the satire of the eighteenth century with this important distinction: Eighteenth-century satire reduces the occasion to the classical background; it finds new ways to state old truths. Romantic satire, at least in those three poems, uses the classical element of design to make the occasion cohere; it finds old ways to state new truths. Ultimately, the distinction is one between wit and vision (Peterfreund 14). That distinction leads to a useful essay topic focusing on "The Mask" either by itself or in comparison with one of the other anatomies: how do the the generic norms of the anatomy help the reader organize the historical moment depicted in the poem and view that moment from the perspective of a higher truth or justice?

Shelley and Androgyny:
Teaching "The Witch of Atlas"

Diane Long Hoeveler

I have taught "The Witch of Atlas" on both the graduate and the under-graduate levels as an interesting variant on Shelley's mythic quest for union with the ideal; however, in that poem the Shelleyan hero has been replaced by a woman, a Witch, and her ironically ideal creation takes the form of a hermaphrodite. Shelley seems to be gently poking fun at himself, his poetic obsessions, his idealizations, and his failures to achieve erotic apotheosis. Or perhaps he is suggesting that any attempt to make external what must be internal is doomed to fail, his own ideals notwithstanding. He sought a selfless self on the one hand; on the other hand, he idealized the notion of merger with a feminine other who would complete his identity. He knew on a deep and intuitive level that his personal and poetic quests were bound up with the permutations and limitations of sexual identity; neither sex can escape its gendered consciousness long enough to accept the other as a complement to the self, rather than as a threat.

I have developed a method of teaching "The Witch" through a series of heuristics. Rather than present my theory on the meanings of the poem and the androgynous, I present the pieces of evidence that I have used as a scholar to interpret the poem and then ask the students to interpret, sup-plement, and in various ways respond to the data.

The first piece of evidence I present is the general notion of androgyny as distinctly different from hermaphroditism, a distinction that Shelley un-derstood and accepted (see Brown; Veeder). The androgynous union of mas-culine and feminine principles in a psyche has long been confused with the presence of male and female sexual organs in one person. Hermaphroditism produces a physical monstrosity that merely accentuates the differences between the sexes. Androgyny, by contrast, is a merger of psychic charac-teristics within the imagination. The image of the androgyne expresses the restoration of the psyche to its original, asexual wholeness, while the her-maphrodite represents an earthly and physical parody of that state.

The second large category of evidence I present is the mass of contradictory critical discussions of the poem by various literary critics. (The critics I cite include Knight 228–29; Grabo, *Witch* 22; Baker, *Shelley's Poetry* 211; Holmes, *Pursuit* 605; Bloom, *Mythmaking* 100, 197; Rubin 223; Reiman, *Shelley* 118–19; and Rosenbaum 40.) Students see from those varying interpretations that criticism of "The Witch" is divided; some see Shelley's hermaphrodite as an ideal spirit, and others see it as an attack on that ideal. The exercise also helps students realize that there is no one right interpretation. At the same time, the nature of textual and extratextual evidence or the lack of it becomes a crucial topic of class discussion.

The third piece of evidence I present to the students is a picture of the visual source for the Witch's creation, the statue of the sleeping hermaphrodite that Shelley saw in the Borghese Palace in Rome, where he wrote short pieces on several classical subjects. Supplementing the illustration is his response to the hermaphrodite as recorded in the rejected fragments of *Epipsychidion*; he compares Emily to a hermaphrodite: "Like that sweet marble monster of both sexes, / Which looks so sweet and gentle that it vexes, / The very soul" (Ingpen and Peck 6: 378). Similar in tone is Shelley's most serious charge against Elizabeth Hitchener—that she was "a hermaphroditical beast of a woman" (F. L. Jones, *Letters* 1: 336). On the basis of these two statements, Shelley's translation of Aristophanes's speech in Plato's *Symposium* (also given to the students as another piece of evidence) and Shelley's familiarity with the classical tradition, the students generally conclude that Shelley's use of the hermaphrodite has been misread; he was using a pagan image with a negative meaning, but contemporary literary critics have been inclined to interpret the image as its opposite, a Platonic ideal.

We now have our first premise, and the students are ready to extrapolate from it to interpret the two major poetic personae in the poem, the Witch and her creation, the hermaphrodite. At that point I introduce the notion of true and false copies of love objects, imagery that Shelley drew from Spenser's *Faerie Queene*. I contend that it is most plausible that Shelley intended the Witch to be an androgynous foil to the hermaphrodite she created. The Witch is Shelley's True Florimell, the true love object who is androgynous and immortal, while the hermaphrodite is the false copy, a purely physical love who lures the poet into the limiting realms of self.

"The Witch of Atlas," we conclude, contrasts the two forms that love and women have assumed throughout Shelley's poetry. The Witch, in the tradition of Asia and Cythna, is an idealized anima figure who holds the promise of androgynous reintegration. Like them, the Witch lives for a time "Within a cavern by a secret fountain" (56) to gain the wisdom necessary for her redemptive activities. Like Asia, she is also veiled and brilliantly beautiful (151). Like Spenser's Una, the Witch can tame the savage, although the source of her power seems to be both her intellect and her spirit (104, 89–91). She is similar to the poet described in the preface to *Alastor*, who unified the wonderful, wise, and beautiful, the functions of the imagination, the mind, and the heart. But, like the hero of *Alastor* and like Shelley himself, the Witch is not content with her own self-integration; she must have a double to reflect her own integration.

The Witch's creation of the hermaphrodite (321–36) is closely examined in class as a piece of textual duplicity and self-irony by Shelley the poet. On the surface (which is how students initially tend to read), we have an idealized portrait, but the tone and the action or lack of action make it clear that the hermaphrodite is a parody, a sterile "Image" and "shape," a physical anomaly, a "sexless thing" (326,327,329). The Witch was earlier described as the embodiment of "gentleness and power" (96); so now is the hermaphrodite described (332). The immediate allusion is to the creation of the False Florimell, for the creation of the hermaphrodite stands as a mockery of the Witch's androgynous perfection. Further, the hermaphrodite's qualities are phrased in tentative terms: "It *seemed* to have developed no defect" (330; my italics), but the poet implies some uncertainty on the point. Finally, the superficially ideal hermaphrodite exists in a perpetual state of lethargy, spending most of its time reclining in the Witch's boat "with folded wings and unawakened eyes" (362). It unfurls its wings only once, causing the boat to journey upstream against the current, a suitably ambiguous gesture, because the journey upstream can lead nowhere.

Only when the hermaphrodite disappears from the poem—its exit marked with considerably less ceremony than was its entrance—does the Witch begin to use her powers seriously. After the hermaphrodite's departure, the Witch, like a poet, uses her eyes to see the "naked beauty of the soul," and she is able through "a charm of strange device" to "Make that spirit mingle with her own" (571–76). That achievement resembles the goal of the alchemist, who seeks the essential form in an attempt to rejoin it and thereby redeem himself and his world. The Witch's power ultimately has poetic and spiritual implications, for she attempts to rejuvenate a dead man by transforming his lifeless, mortal body into a body that is "Mute, breathing, beating, warm and undecaying . . . And living in its dreams beyond the rage / Of death or life" (610–14). Of course, the Witch cannot return the man to life, but she can instill the dreams of imagination that have their own immortality. The poet can hope for no more from his art.

Epipsychidion and
Romantic Passion Love

Jeffrey C. Robinson

From the traditional point of view, Romantic poetry captures the essence of poetry—meditative, lyric, pure—and transcends the world. Of Shelley's 604-line lyric *Epipsychidion*, we can say that its transcendence takes the form of extravagance: extravagant and excessive metaphor, extravagant fantasies, impossible love. In the recent spirit of refining an ideological and cultural consciousness for Romantic poetry, I have devised a course in which *Epipsychidion* makes sense not only in that tradition of the Romantic poem (transcendent of politics and changing social culture) but also in the tradition of what Stendhal calls *l'amour passion*. The literature of passion love constitutes a major effort by post-Enlightenment writers to portray passionate love as a threat to a social order defined by domestic stability and to join in the challenge to the repressive elements of that stability. My course challenges the rigidity of the view that Romanticism *is* poetry, and it affirms Marilyn Butler's notion that what we call Romanticism is only one counter-revolutionary moment in the literature of the post-Enlightenment period (*Romantics*). Here I show how I place *Epipsychidion* in that setting.

In defining passion love, I begin with what it is not. In the tradition of the Romantic lyric, passion love is not the domestic form of intimate communion found in many poems by Wordsworth and Coleridge. It is not Coleridge's love for his infant son Hartley in "Frost at Midnight," for Charles Lamb in "This Lime-Tree Bower My Prison," or for Sarah Hutchinson in "Dejection." It is not Wordsworth's love for his sister, Dorothy, in "Tintern Abbey" or for his wife, Mary, in "She Was a Phantom of Delight." Those are not poems of erotic desire; they are poems of self-preservation, not self-annihilation.

If the younger Romantic poets are to enter the tradition of passion love, they cannot model themselves on the major poetry of Wordsworth and Coleridge. Rather, to the degree that such poetry hovers in their consciousness, they must subvert it.

I often begin my course in Romantic passion love by contrasting Wordsworth's "She Was a Phantom of Delight" with Keats's sonnet "Bright Star." Wordsworth's poem is a celebration of his wife. It is written as an autobiography of their relationship—more precisely, as an autobiography of his changing view of her. In the poem passion love gives way to domestic love, which leads to a permanent spiritual love. Furthermore, the poem records the "maturation" of the poet-husband, the "maturation" of his gaze on the woman. It is the autobiography of his transcendence of passion for the sake of his entrance into domestic and spiritual and, underneath it all, social stability.

If Wordsworth's "She Was a Phantom of Delight" records the successful passing of the crisis of passion love, Keats's "Bright Star" records the crisis itself with no promise of resolution. In passion love the male speaker has no distance on himself; he is all fantasy and desire. Giving shape to the self, which male Romantic autobiographic writing tries to do, is the story of "how I recovered from strange fits of passion." In "Bright Star" such recovery would be death and such stability would deny the overwhelming reason for staying alive, passionate love of the woman, even though the loss of self in love also implies death to the poet. However, that trap of feeling is, as a poem, a liberation; "She Was a Phantom of Delight" buries the feeling and the fantasy of love by rationalizing them as a stage of experience.

The poetry of passion love subverts the poetry of domestic love by joining the tradition of sentimental love and passional love in fiction. In his first love letter to Fanny Brawne, Keats claims to have torn up a previous letter that he found too Rousseauistic. Keats immediately recognized that his way of entering the experience of love was literary and that Rousseau was his model. In my course we do not get to Keats and Shelley until we have read Rousseau's *Nouvelle Héloise*, Goethe's *Sorrows of Young Werther*, Mary Wollstonecraft's *Maria: Or, The Wrongs of Woman*, Constant's *Adolphe*, and Stendhal's *De l'amour*. Also on the list are sections of Byron's *Don Juan* and Hazlitt's *Liber Amoris*. Clearly, other works could appear as well. But in spite of the range of convictions and nationalities and genres, all those works speak to the power of passion love and erotic fantasy to unsettle the organization of middle-class society; they speak to the lover as a heroic type, one whose intensity of living and fullness of fantasy signify a grappling with the modern world.

In 1821, in the age of Keats and Shelley and in the year of *Epipsychidion*, Stendhal published *De l'amour*, that strange, anecdotal treatise on the dominant literary preoccupation of the preceding fifty years. Students are mesmerized by Stendhal's book, particularly if it is read late in the course, since it creates a critical or technical vocabulary and an analysis of the writing with which they have just become familiar. It is a superb, if quirky, piece of cultural criticism. The key term is "crystallization," a metaphor for an early stage of falling in love. If a tree branch is dropped into a supersaturated salt solution, such as one finds around salt mines, and is left there for some time, on removal it will look not like a branch but like a glittering array of crystals. That phenomenon is equivalent to the initial idealization of the beloved by the lover. The lover then projects everything onto the beloved, including jealousy.

The paradox of Stendhal's love is that love results from the intensity of the narcissistic projection. More surprising, at one point he shows that the projections have more to do with the reality of the other person than one might suppose. Indeed, the more real, independent, and subjective the object of love is, the more intensely life-giving is the love itself. That idea has powerful implications for the independent life of women. (Simone de Beauvoir calls Stendhal a feminist.) The fuller the life the woman leads, the better is love.

That setting is a good one into which to introduce Shelley's *Epipsychidion.* You have at once a technical vocabulary with which to explore the extravagances of the poem, a literary tradition in which to place it, and a historically sound tradition in which to explore its cultural and political resonances. That is not to say that other influences are less valuable—influences such as the rest of Shelley's poetry, Dante's *Vita nuova,* and the reemergence in Shelley's time of the Psyche myth. But the passion love theme removes *Epipsychidion* from the periphery of Shelley and Romanticism and restores it to a center. Shelley wanted the poem published anonymously; according to Charles Ollier, Shelley's publisher, Shelley wished that the poem "should not be considered as my own" (Perkins, *English* 1038). Since the poem is about his falling in love with another woman, one can understand his wishes, but one can understand them even more if it is realized that he has tapped into a potent, often unsettling literary preoccupation.

In a variation on the drama of the love triangle in passion love, the father (representing social power and order) wishes his daughter, in whom he invests much of his libidinal energy, to marry someone whose background will reinforce the aristocratic order. The daughter, however, falls in love with someone outside that order, and the unaccepting father eventually kills the daughter to prevent the anticipated social upheaval of what he regards as an inappropriate marriage. That is the story of Lessing's *Emilia Galotti.*

The speaker in *Epipsychidion* is equivalent to the lover in Lessing's play: Emilia Viviani's father has imprisoned her in a convent, and Shelley's poem rages at that tyranny in the language of extravagant love and desire. But just as the lover cannot penetrate the shield of aristocratic order in the play, so Shelley cannot reach Emilia through the lyric brilliance of his language:

> Woe is me!
> The winged words on which my soul would pierce
> Into the height of love's rare Universe,
> Are chains of lead around its flight of fire.—
> I pant, I sink, I tremble, I expire!   (587–91)

Shelley's Emilia, far more than Lessing's, inspires a vision of transcendent love, of something reaching both beyond and within ordinary reality to a golden-age essence of communion and intensity. Poetic language is the vehicle of the transcendence, poetic language energized by that special love.

In the language of Stendhal, it is a poem of crystallization: "I never thought before my death to see / Youth's vision thus made perfect" (41–42). The profusion of metaphoric language for which the poem is famous suggests the glittering crystals, the idealizing projections of love onto the object. Shelley marvelously abuts his acute sense of personal frailty on his erected wall of love's language; how fragile is the daring commitment to passion love!

Romantic literature of passion love, written almost completely by male authors, raises the question of the portrayal of women. At first glance, a woman is always the object of the man's fantasy. Does that literature simply portray yet one more version of the woman as object of erotic desire? The politics of most of the male writers of passion love suggests their commitment, to some extent, to the independent life of the woman. The life of the fantasy of love increases as the life of the object of love increases. In *Epipsychidion* the issue grows complex, since Emilia has been immobilized by her father in a convent. Shelley's ambivalence about women and free love surfaces dramatically in the context of the passion-love theme.

The density of language, the excessive imagery, and the sheer length of a poem essentially in the lyric mode have traditionally made *Epipsychidion* one of Shelley's most difficult poems for students. Perhaps more to the point, for many readers the theme does not seem to warrant the length. But placing the poem in the context of a theme historically, culturally, and politically central to the Romantic period allows it to emerge as a beautiful and challenging artifact for student and teacher alike.

Teaching *Adonais* as Pastoral Elegy

Judith W. Page

Soon after I began teaching at Millsaps College, I discovered that one of the most popular courses was a sociology class entitled Death and Grief. Students, I learned, were attracted to the way in which the instructor fostered openness in discussing the process of working through profound loss. After some failed attempts at teaching such pastoral elegies as "Lycidas," *Adonais*, and "Thyrsis" in various courses to students who would have agreed with Dr. Johnson's stern assessment that pastoral conventions are "vulgar, and therefore disgusting" (1: 163), I decided to introduce the genre in terms of the social and psychological processes of grieving. I found that my students could appreciate the conventions of the pastoral elegy more fully when they first discovered the naturalness of the conventions in relation to grief and mourning.

For the course in which I teach *Adonais* (a two-semester advanced course on nineteenth-century poetry and prose, with the second semester beginning with Keats and Shelley), I have found that the approach leads to rewarding discussions of the many-layered complexity of Shelley's poem. Without using any particular psychological model or specialized language, we talk about the anger and the questioning that precede consolation or, sometimes, its failure. A student familiar with Freud's distinction between melancholia and the work of mourning may introduce those concepts; another student may mention Elisabeth Kubler-Ross's *On Death and Dying*. Still others speak of their own experiences of loss. Because I am trying to guide the discussion toward the poetry and its conventions, I emphasize how grief is channeled into the formal and ceremonial elements in mourning: the eulogy, the memorial service, the rites of burial.

After a ten- or fifteen-minute discussion (out of an hour and fifteen minutes), I turn to the assigned reading, which for the first class is "Lycidas." I begin with Milton for several reasons: I want the students to see the elegy tradition, with its continuities and discontinuities, and I find that the transition from the previous discussion works better with "Lycidas" than with *Adonais*—in some ways "Lycidas" is a more compact and approachable poem. We discuss the formalized representations of the mourner and the subject as shepherds, and we analyze the stages through which the mourner proceeds, from the lament for lost youth to the questioning of providence to the final Christian consolation.

A complaint about the number of footnotes in the text can be turned into a minilecture on Milton's imagination of the classics; the origins of the pastoral elegy in Theocritus, Bion, Moschus, and Vergil; and its later development in the Renaissance by Spenser in "Astrophel." By understanding that Christianity alters the genre in the Renaissance, students are prepared for Shelley's further transformation. When I mention and sometimes read from Bion's "Lament for Adonis" or the *Lament for Bion*, attributed to Moschus (both of which Shelley translated), or Spenser's elegy for Sidney, I introduce the elegist's concern for his own fate, which we see worked into the fabric of "Lycidas" from the passage on fame to the speaker's final declaration that he is on "to fresh Woods, and Pastures new" (line 193).

Admittedly, that is not a close analysis of "Lycidas." But the discussion at least introduces the students to the work's incredible richness, leaves them with questions to pursue, and makes them eager to discover what Shelley does with the form. The students see from the preface to *Adonais* that Shelley places his elegy in the context of the contemporary politics of reviewing, in which valuable works like Keats's and his own were scorned in favor of the "meanest" productions. Shelley establishes the strong connection between the elegist and the subject from the outset, even before explicitly identifying himself as one "Who in another's fate now wept his own" (line 300). Because we have discussed that identification in mourning and the elegy tradition, the students are not likely to attack Shelley's motives as insincere. On the basis of our discussion of Milton, I have a student rehearse the way in which Shelley follows the conventions—invocation of the muse, the sympathy of nature, the questioning, the procession of mourners—before the class analyzes particular stages in the process.

We discuss the name, Adonais, by which Shelley conflates Adonis (the subject of Bion's lament and the god associated with fertility and rebirth) and Adonai (the Hebrew name for God). The students usually see parallels with Milton's less complicated act of giving the name Lycidas to Edward King and with Blake's more complex and symbolic naming of his visionary eternals. That discussion leads us to think about Shelley's creation of the name to praise John Keats's godlike imagination and to recognize that more is at stake in the poem than John Keats. ("You mean Adonais is sort of like Los?" one student asked.)

Another revealing name is that of Urania, which most students recognize as Milton's muse. It takes a while to sort out what Shelley is doing with Milton and his muse, who, as my students notice, is both the mother and the lover of Keats. As we work through the passages relating the failure of her mourning, I ask the students why Shelley distances himself from Milton and his muse, hoping that they will see his moving beyond Urania, who is "chained to Time, and cannot thence depart!" (234), and in a different direction from Milton's Christian consolation.

That is usually a good place to have the students think about *Adonais* as not only going through the processes of grief but also testing different philosophical positions and attitudes toward reality. Students who have been studying Shelley for several weeks expect as much. I ask them to think about the major movements of the poem as the speaker's attitude toward time and nature and from the perspective of the three philosophical positions analyzed by Wasserman in *Shelley: A Critical Reading*: stanzas 1–17 (matter is ultimate reality), stanzas 18–37 (mind and matter are distinct), and stanzas 38–55 (mind is eternal). That is also a good place to discuss Shelley's structure of imagery (also thoroughly analyzed by Wasserman) and the way in which patterns of images are transformed and purified (from the elements of earth to fire) in the final movement, as if to confirm the reality of eternal spirit over the changing world of nature.

Twice when discussing those philosophical positions and structures of imagery a student has commented (saving me the task) that Shelley's last movement and the urgent push toward transcendence seem odd or ironic in the light of our reading of Keats and his dis-enchantment with the transcendent realms of the nightingale or the cold world of the Grecian urn. We then talk about Shelley's Keats, for whom transcendence is possible:

> He is made one with Nature: there is heard
> His voice in all her music, from the moan
> Of thunder, to the song of night's sweet bird . . .   (370–72)

We contrast that Keats with the one who loses the "plaintive anthem" of his nightingale as it is "buried deep / In the next valley-glades" ("Ode to a Nightingale" 75–78). Does Shelley, I ask, transform Keats into an ideal Shelleyan poet, a martyr to the cause of transcendent poetry killed by hostile criticism? After students ponder that question, I suggest that what was only a metaphoric identification for earlier poets becomes radical and literal for Shelley: he becomes Keats.

That transformation brings us to the problem of the final movement of *Adonais*, Shelley's apparent death wish: "No more let Life divide what Death can join together" (477) is a different sentiment from on "to fresh Woods, and Pastures new." Although the class is prepared for a different consolation from Milton's Christian affirmation, "Through the dear might of him that walk'd the waves" ("Lycidas" 173), the final stanzas in Shelley's poem pose new problems. The next time I teach *Adonais* I shall introduce Peter Sacks's provocative claim that Shelley brings "his version of the genre to the brink of its own ruin" because he is driven beyond "the detours and saving distances" of life and language (165). Such a suggestion will force the students to return to our original discussion of the social and psychological basis of convention—the pastoral elegy as a work of mourning that through language affirms life and continuity. Reading Shelley with that awareness will also bring the students to "Thyrsis" and *In Memoriam*, later in the semester, full of expectations and ready for the surprises of the genre.

Shelley's Portrayals of Emotion in the Lyrics to Jane Williams

Constance Walker

Students unfamiliar with Romantic poetry often mistakenly assume that it is primarily concerned with portraying unbridled, gushing emotion. While even a brief perusal of what the English Romantics wrote can dispel such a notion, it is useful when teaching Romanticism to examine just how radically Romantic portrayals of emotion differ from the largely inaccurate stereotypes of overwrought passion and from earlier literary treatments of emotion. Shelley's late lyrics to Jane Williams, for instance, are remarkably understated, spare, and oblique; they sound like nothing that had been written in English up to that point. In an undergraduate survey course, one particularly effective way of helping students explore the differences between neoclassical and Romantic expressions of emotion is by contrasting "To Jane. The Invitation" and "To Jane. The Recollection" with Gray's "Ode on a Distant Prospect of Eton College," a poem that highlights Shelley's innovations through its reliance on neoclassical rhetorical conventions.

What all three poems share that makes them useful to be read together is the contrast they draw between the realm of human emotions and the realm of the natural landscape. Shelley's poems and Gray's "Ode" look either back or forward to a natural scene of serenity and calm against which they juxtapose the tumultuous passions of the mind and the heart. Yet the manner in which those emotions are represented differs radically, indicative of a change that took place in the latter half of the eighteenth century in the cultural conception and the articulation of emotion. The "fury Passions" of Gray's poem (line 61) belong to a long tradition of discourse on the passions in the arts and the sciences, which routinely considered them as universal, fixed entities and frequently portrayed them with personification. By contrast, Shelley's depictions of emotion, influenced in part by association psychology, emphasize the fluid, individual nature of feelings and suggest by their obliquity that language may be incommensurate with emotion. Even without an extensive knowledge of eighteenth-century psychology and discourse on emotion and the passions, students can arrive inductively at the two attitudes about language and emotion that inform the poems.

In view of the prominence of the natural landscapes as settings for the emotional dilemmas in the poems, one way to begin a comparison of the texts is by asking students to discuss the characteristics and the functions of the scenes described. In Gray's "Ode," for instance, the green playing fields of Eton become synonymous with the innocence and the youth of the schoolboys who frolic there. The landscape, consistently described as "happy" and "pleasing" (11), acts as a temporary restorative for the narrator, who addresses the fields directly: "I feel the gales, that from you blow / A mo-

mentary bliss bestow" (15–16). However, the landscape is featured prominently only in the first five stanzas of the ode; it disappears from the second
half of the poem, which is devoted to the "fury Passions" that wait to seize
"the little victims" (52). The poem thus creates a sequestered preserve within
itself, a pure haven of five stanzas uncontaminated by the passions and the
cares of the adult emotional life to come depicted in the subsequent stanzas.

The same question about the function of the landscape may also be raised
for Shelley's lyrics. In "The Invitation," natural scenes serve as a haven for
the narrator; the "silent wilderness" (23) to which he invites his companion
represents the antithesis of "men and towns" (21) and an escape from his
"accustomed visitor[s]" of "Sorrow," "Reflexion," and "Despair" (30–35).
Unlike the playing fields of Eton, which are symbolic of the carefree existence
reserved exclusively for its young denizens, the wilderness in Shelley's poem
represents the possibility of mature tranquility, a physical embodiment of
the longing for emotional solace and peace. It is an ideal detailed with
absorbed specificity: the beauty of the clear skies, pines, waves, and reflective pools of winter rains in both poems is described in greater and in more
precise detail than is the vista in Gray's "Ode." There is almost an attempt
to re-create the tangibility of the natural world in its minute particulars, as
if to enter into the primal unity that it seems to promise and to tap its
reserves of calm. In "The Invitation" Shelley describes a landscape and a
seascape "Where the earth and ocean meet, / And all things seem only one /
In the universal Sun" (67–69); even more inclusive is the "magic circle" of
"The Recollection" into which the speaker and his beloved are drawn (41–
52). Here the serene circle itself emanates from human love; the wanderers
are seemingly included in the landscape, rather than excluded, as they are
from Gray's garden of ignorance and bliss.

Yet as students who have noticed Spenser's telling use of the verb *to seem*
in *The Faerie Queene* may observe, Shelley's use of *to seem* has the effect
of qualifying the descriptions of paradise: in "The Invitation," "all things
seem only one" (68); in "The Recollection," "There seemed . . . a magic
circle traced" (41–44), calling the status of that unity into question. And
modifiers in "The Recollection," the darker of the two poems, suggest a
scene less purely innocent and beneficent than the landscape of Gray's ode:
pines are "tortured by storms" (23) and winds are "envious" (81). The speaker
is seemingly allowed to partake of a moment of inviolate stillness and peace,
but he is equally subject to ruptures and disturbances that themselves are
part of nature. In the final stanza of "The Recollection," the image of the
reflective pools disturbed by the wind reminds him of his own turmoil: "Less
oft is peace in S[ ]'s mind / Than calm in water seen" (87–88). The wilderness
serves less as an escape than as a mirror. If Gray has used his landscape as
a symbol of universal innocence, a land of no return, Shelley pursues a more

personal and cautious analogy between natural and emotional potential; peace is momentarily possible, if unlikely.

By contrasting the specific manner in which emotions are presented in each poem, students can best see the formal conventions that Shelley deliberately plays against and ultimately rejects. Stanzas 7 and 8 of Gray's ode consist of a catalog of personified passions, "the vultures of the mind" (62) that prey on every human psyche, including "Disdainful Anger," "pallid Fear," "Shame," "pineing Love," Jealousy, "Envy wan," "faded Care," Despair, and Sorrow. Gray's descriptions of the passions are in keeping with other contemporary portrayals of emotion: the popular drawings by Lavater and Le Brun of the human face distorted by the various passions, the theatrical poses of actors recommended by acting handbooks and illustrated by engravings, and paintings of personified emotions—all testify to a conception of passion as a willful, independent agency. (Blake's illustrations for the "Ode" are particularly apposite; it's helpful to have them available for the class to see.) Gray's passions troop by in the form of a masque, much like the procession of the seven deadly sins in *The Faerie Queene*; one can also point back to the allegorical virtues and vices of medieval morality plays as models. You may ask your students about the effects of such personification here and discuss why a formal, stereotypical depiction of emotion became an artistic norm.

However, Shelley's treatment of emotion in the late lyrics challenges the adequacy of formal conventions and decorum. Nowhere, in fact, does he indicate the difference between his own conception of passion and the conception on which Gray relied more than in "The Invitation." Shelley half-mockingly compiles a catalog of personified passions à la "Ode on a Distant Prospect:" he leaves a notice on his door:

> For each accustomed visitor—
> "I am gone into the fields
> To take what this sweet hour yields.
> Reflexion, you may come tomorrow,
> Sit by the fireside with Sorrow—
> You, with the unpaid bill, Despair,
> You, tiresome verse-reciter Care,
> I will pay you in the grave,
> Death will listen to your stave—
> Expectation too, be off!
> To-day is for itself enough—
> Hope, in pity mock not woe
> With smiles, nor follow where I go;
> Long having lived on thy sweet food,

> At length I find one moment's good
> After long pain—with all your love
> This you never told me of." (30–46)

While precisely the same personified passions as those featured in Gray's ode come to call, Shelley's treatment of emotion differs considerably in allowing for an entire realm of experience not defined by orthodox categories. Even Hope cannot tell him of the "one moment's good" (44) arising from "this sweet hour" (32); Shelley imagines himself escaping from the demands of the traditional passions into an uncharted realm of feeling that he describes only by means of indirection, through imagery that only suggests, rather than explicitly states, the range and the intensity of his emotions. Similarly, "The Recollection" does not explicitly mention the emotions that trouble the speaker's peace: they are simultaneously revealed and hidden—far more amorphous, private, and elusive than their counterparts in eighteenth-century verse. Both poems place a new emphasis on the individuality and the literal unspeakability of passion; again, your students may discuss the assumptions and the values underlying Shelley's innovative literary treatment of emotion.

The late lyrics in general are deliberately oblique about emotion for compelling personal and artistic reasons. You may want to refer your students to the relevant chapters of Richard Holmes's biography of Shelley for an account of the complex emotional circumstances that, in part, engendered the poems; to Judith Chernaik's *Lyrics of Shelley*; and to "Shelley's Last Lyrics" in William Keach's book *Shelley's Style* for an astute analysis of the specific "historical and biographical pressures" (202) that served as context for the poems to Jane Williams. You may also want to link Shelley's presentations of emotions in the late lyrics with his meditations on the difficulties of finding language at all commensurate with emotion in *Epipsychidion* and in his essay "On Love." The lyrics to Jane reveal a writer not only experimenting with lyric style and substance but also searching for a new mode of discourse on emotion.

Transformability in
"The Triumph of Life"

Jean Hall

"The Triumph of Life" is an unfinished poem, one that has provoked sharp disagreement among critics. Was Shelley writing a despairing vision at the time of his death, or is the existing "Triumph" the dark first part of a poem projected to end optimistically? Strong arguments for those positions have been offered by, respectively, Harold Bloom (*Mythmaking* 220–75) and Donald H. Reiman (*Shelley's "The Triumph"* 19–86), and reading them can be a useful prelude for the teacher preparing to lead a discussion of Shelley's last major work. I myself begin by presenting the poem's problem of incompleteness and by inviting students to decide for themselves whether "The Triumph of Life" is likely to have ended in despair or in hope.

We begin by unfolding the poem's pessimistic core: the image developed in lines 110–20 of life as a Roman triumphal procession in which nearly every person is eventually enslaved, as by a conqueror. Here is a vision of life as war and of relationships as inevitably transactions between tyrant and slave, oppressor and oppressed. But the victims in the pageant seem to contribute to their own fate—lovers whirl about each other, kindling and consuming themselves, and "others mournfully within the gloom / Of their own shadow walked, and called it death . . . / And some fled from it as it were a ghost" (lines 58–60). The historical figures in the parade suffer from the same plague of self-oppression; in particular, Shelley's vision of the recent history of Europe—the French Revolution and the Napoleonic wars—makes that clear.

When the students see that the poem projects human self-division as the tragic condition that pollutes history, we turn to the Rousseau of the "Triumph." At that point I mention Shelley's debt to Dante's *Divine Comedy*. Vergil was a reliable guide who correctly interpreted the sights of hell and purgatory for Dante and led him safely to the brink of heaven, but Shelley's equivalent figure, Rousseau, is tormented and unsure of himself. Although he is a profound fatalist, a believer in life's inevitable triumph, Rousseau does not understand the nature of the pageant and even suggests that the poem's narrator interpret the triumph for him: "But follow thou . . . And what thou wouldst be taught I then may learn / From thee" (305–08). He envisions a being he calls the shape all light, who initially seems benificent but then tramples on his mind and delivers him helpless to the triumph of life. Alerted to Rousseau's unreliability, the students begin to realize that we must critically examine his interpretation of the incident.

According to his account, Rousseau queries the shape but does not receive a direct answer. The figure merely extends her cup, inviting Rousseau to "Arise and quench thy thirst" (400). If the students have studied *Prometheus*

Unbound, they can compare that curiously indirect dialog between the shape and Rousseau with Asia's interrogation of Demogorgon in act 2, scene 3 of Shelley's lyrical drama. Asia receives no direct answer to her questions about the cause of the world's evil; Demogorgon will only say that "the deep truth is imageless" (116), and Asia at last realizes that she must envision the truth for herself: "of such truths / Each to itself must be the oracle" (121–23). If each person must be an oracle in *Prometheus Unbound*, possibly Rousseau must also be his own oracle in the "Triumph," and, in fact, perhaps he is performing that function unawares.

Certainly, Rousseau is uneasy in that scene. Although he has awakened into a paradisiacal dawning world, he is troubled because he cannot remember his past life, and he is unable to believe in what he sees. His question to the shape—"Shew whence I came, and where I am, and why— / Pass not away upon the passing stream" (398–99)—betrays a preoccupation with time, with his origins, and with his mysterious present. He thirsts for explanation and control; in reply, he is immediately shown a vision of the triumph of life, in which each person is controlled by his own insatiable desires. The "eddying flood" (458) of the triumph soon replaces the gentle stream paced on by the shape all light.

That transition from stream water to flood water is accompanied by other intensifying successions as the shape all light's world fades at the advance of the triumph. Like the shape, the triumphal charioteer is a woman (148), but whereas the shape is a warm amalgam of dawn light and dew, the charioteer is veiled in black clouds and radiates a harsh, cold glare. Whereas the shape all light walks in rhythm with "the ceaseless song / Of leaves and winds and waves" (375–76), the triumph careers along to the cadences of "savage music, stunning music" (435). The powerful, obtrusive display of the triumph overlays the milder effects surrounding the shape all light; nevertheless, Rousseau knows that the shape remains beside him, although nearly imperceptible: "More dimly than a day appearing dream . . . did that shape its obscure tenour keep / Beside my path, as silent as a ghost" (427–33).

The triumph blots out the shape all light as daylight disperses night's dreams. The narrator of the "Triumph" experiences an equivalent sequence at the poem's beginning; his nocturnal thoughts keep him "as wakeful as the stars that gem / The cone of night" (22–23), but his meditation is interrupted by the coming day, and, like Rousseau, he envisions the triumph of life. It comes as a "waking dream" (42) transparently overlaying the forested Apennine slope where he reclines. Evidently, the narrator and Rousseau both experience the potential presence of two worlds—a harsher one that is in the foreground of another milder, latent presence. In a crucial remark about transitions, Rousseau compares the shape all light to Lucifer, the morning star, which reappears as the first star of evening, and invokes "the presence of that fairest planet," which, "Although unseen is felt by one who hopes / That his day's path may end as he began it / In that star's smile" (416–19).

If the students have discussed *Adonais*, they recognize the potential presence in the "Triumph" of the image complex that governs the major transitions of Shelley's elegy. There, the daylight of mortal existence seems to blot out Adonais, the morning star of poetry, but the poem's transitions bring a night of vision in which the latent starlike presence of poetry is again put in the foreground and affirmed. The teacher should read Earl Wasserman's essay on *Adonais* to fully appreciate the operation of that image complex (*Shelley* 462–502). What can be observed of the existing "Triumph of Life" is that Shelley has laid the groundwork for an *Adonais*-like conclusion to the poem; the shape all light may reappear in a visionary night of poetry that transcends the harsh light of life's triumph.

Shelley may not have intended that solution, but the option needs to be seriously discussed, and the transformability of the poem's images should be noted. The shape all light is a "shape," life's charioteer is also a "Shape" (87), Rousseau himself is a deformed "Feature" (190), and the horribly creative rays of life's chariot "Wrought all the busy phantoms that were there / As the sun shapes the clouds" (534–35). In the world of "The Triumph of Life" everyone and everything is a shape-changer. Rousseau laments change because he sees it as governed by the triumph of life and, therefore, inevitably degenerative and deforming, but the latent presence of visionary elements in the poem opens the possibility of poetry's victory—the triumph of poetic transformation.

Such poetic transformation would probably have temporal, as well as shaping, implications; indeed, in the existing poem, time contributes to the formation of shapes by either speeding or delaying the process. The triumphal charioteer is the "Shape . . . whom years deform" (87–88), and the flood tide speed and savage music of the procession both accelerates the victims' natural aging and produces deformities: "From every firmest limb and fairest face / The strength and freshness fell like dust" (520–21) and "Phantoms diffused around, and some did fling / Shadows of shadows, yet unlike themselves" (487–88). Rousseau says the entire procession takes place between morning and evening (193–95), a remarkable claim—apparently, the triumph reduces all human history to a single day.

Quite on the contrary, time is slowed down by the shape all light. As she treads above the waters "her feet ever to the ceaseless song / Of leaves and winds and waves and birds and bees / And falling drops moved in a measure new" (375–77). The shape all light controls time not through the self-dividing oppressor-oppressed relationship established in the triumph of life but through integrative, poetic processes—song and dance. The shape will not "Pass . . .

away upon the passing stream" (399) as Rousseau fears, because, like the singing and dancing Spirits that initiate act 4 of *Prometheus Unbound*, she can "Weave the dance on the floor of the breeze . . . Enchant the Day that too swiftly flees, / To check its flight" (4.69–72).

The powers of poetry suggested here are discussed at some length in *A Defence of Poetry*, which can be taught profitably in conjunction with "The Triumph of Life." In the *Defence* Shelley begins by claiming that men "dance and sing and imitate natural objects, observing in these actions . . . a certain rhythm or order" and that "there is a certain order or rhythm belonging to each of these classes of mimetic representation" (481). He goes on to assert the transtemporal potential of poetry, which unveils "the permanent analogy of things by images which participate in the life of truth" and is "the echo of the eternal music" (485). The *Defence* also formulates a literary history that affirms the power of poetry to form a "great poem, which all poets, like the co-operating thoughts of one great mind, have built up since the beginning of the world" (493), a vision that reverses the degenerative historical process of "The Triumph of Life." Finally, the *Defence* contains a lengthy and laudatory discussion of Dante as the epic poet who, along with Milton, has "conferred upon modern mythology a systematic form" (499).

Although the transformability of "The Triumph of Life" is demonstrable and although *Prometheus Unbound, Adonais,* and *A Defence of Poetry* do provide strong suggestions of what the finished "Triumph" would have been, I take pains to preserve the incompleteness of the poem, the openness of the options. After all, the Shelley of 1818–21 may have been more optimistic than the Shelley of 1822. In our concluding discussions and in critical papers, the students devise and defend scenarios for the finished "Triumph," and we have the opportunity to consider a range of possibilities.

Teaching "On Life":
An Introduction to Shelley's Skeptical Poetics

Brooke Hopkins

Shelley's poetry presents teachers with a multitude of challenges, not the least of which is that it aims to get its readers to question the assumptions on which their reading first began—for instance, that the world of the opening of *Prometheus Unbound*, the world of Prometheus's opening speech, is the real world. The clearest statement of that skeptical philosophy is to be found in Shelley's fragmentary essay "On Life." Unlike *A Defence of Poetry*, which must be taught on its own terms and in relation to Shelley's argument with Peacock, "On Life" can introduce the complex and largely counterintuitive linguistic world of the middle and late poems. I use it on both the undergraduate and graduate levels to that end.

"On Life" is really about language, about words. (Its title should really be "On 'Life'.") On the surface the essay presents the familiar Wordsworthian argument that, because our earliest experiences are prelinguistic, "words can [not] penetrate the mystery of our being," cannot penetrate what we call, for want of a better word, "life."

> This is, in truth, heroic argument,
> And genuine prowess, which I wished to touch
> With hand however weak; but in the main
> It lies far hidden from the reach of words.
> (*Prelude* 3.182–85)

But Shelley's argument is more philosophical than psychological. "Rightly used" (presumably in either philosophy or poetry), words "may make evident our ignorance to ourselves, and this is much. For what are we? Whence do we come, and whither do we go? Is birth the commencement, is death the conclusion of our being?" (475–76): The promotion of such questions, the acknowledgment of the "ignorance" such questions imply, is one of the aims of the "intellectual system" (476) of skepticism that Shelley celebrates in the essay, the skeptical aporia on which all genuine knowledge must be based.

Words, then, are useful to the extent that they are able to afford us a knowledge of our ignorance. And, the essay's argument continues, the same is true of philosophy.

> Philosophy, impatient as it may be to build, has much work yet remaining as pioneer for the overgrowth of ages. It makes one step towards this object; it destroys error, and the roots of error. It leaves, what is too often the duty of the reformer in political and ethical

> questions to leave, a vacancy. It reduces the mind to that freedom in
> which it would have acted, but for the misuse of words and signs, the
> instruments of its own creation.   (477)

That is, in many ways, a classic account of skepticism. The skeptical project
reverses the normal movement of philosophy, which is to build, to construct
systems. Its aim is to clear away. Its method is reductive, to free the mind
from the codes it has constructed to imprison itself (see Wordsworth's "that
most dreadful enemy to our pleasures, our own pre-established codes of
decision"—Advertisement to *Lyrical Ballads*, 1798). Once again, language
itself is not the problem. The misuse of language, the "misuse of words and
signs," is the problem. The aim of skepticism is to restore the mind to its
potential for action ("that freedom in which it would have acted"), a potential
that can be realized only when it discovers the errors it has made. "Our
whole life is thus an education of error" (477): only with that admission can
the work of reconstruction begin.

The skeptical plot, therefore, involves a reversal of direction, if not a
return. That is what students have such difficulty in seeing, especially in
their initial readings of a poem like *Prometheus Unbound*, where the apparent forward movement of the poem is, in fact, a movement backward,
an undoing, a reduction of "the mind to that freedom in which it would have
acted, but for the misuse of words and signs, the instruments of its own
creation," (477), particularly the curse that has produced the system in which
Prometheus has enslaved himself. That enslavement is primarily linguistic,
as embodied in Prometheus's opening speech, and involves "the misuse of
words and signs," particularly the personal pronouns "Thou" and "I" to refer
to Jupiter and Prometheus himself. Once again, "On Life" is useful in calling
attention to Shelley's concern for the way language can be used to distort
the underlying unity of all things to which we give the name "life":

> the words *I, you, they*, are not signs of any actual difference subsisting
> between the assemblage of thoughts thus indicated, but are merely
> marks employed to denote the different modifications of the one mind
> . . . grammatical devices invented simply for arrangement and totally
> devoid of the intense and exclusive sense usually attached to
> them.   (477–78)

The problem is not with language itself but with the values attached to
certain words—in this case, words that seem to suggest a difference, even
an opposition, when there is none (like the opposition between Prometheus
and Jupiter). The aim of "the intellectual philosophy" (478) Shelley calls
skepticism is to make its practitioners more conscious of "the misuse of

words and signs," to bring them to "that verge where words abandon us
. . . the dark abyss of—how little we know" (478). Even the geography here
resembles that of *Prometheus*, in which the poem's central action, Asia's
encounter with Demogorgon, takes place in the darkness of a cave, a cave
of unknowing.

Approaching a poem like *Prometheus Unbound* from that perspective (and
I usually assign "On Life" before we read the poem) can help students
recognize the rationale on which many of Shelley's rhetorical decisions are
based: the peculiar quality of language in Prometheus's opening speech, the
enormous importance attached to the curse (a paradigm of "the misuse of
words and signs"), the use of parody in the scene in "heaven" at the opening
of act 3, the way the poem dismantles itself before its readers' eyes and in
the act of reading. The poem and others like it ("The Sensitive-Plant" comes
to mind) offers more than skepticism, of course. An understanding of the
intellectual system Shelley celebrates in "On Life" is only a beginning. But
it can be an important beginning in teaching the middle and late poetry.
Students generally assume that poetry, like philosophy, builds worlds. What
does our word *creative* imply, after all? The movement of Shelley's poetry
—like that of many other great poets from Dante on and including Shelley's
contemporaries Blake and Wordsworth—is a radically counterintuitive one.
It works to counter its readers' expectations. Some appreciation of the philosophical basis of that movement is useful.

The Poetics of Re-vision:
Teaching *A Defence of Poetry*

Jerrold E. Hogle

A Defence of Poetry is, to a great extent, a deliberately deceptive statement. In apparently refuting his friend Thomas Love Peacock's "Four Ages of Poetry," Shelley seems to counter an excessively skeptical rationalism with an intensely elevated vocabulary that appears to revive Christian, Neoplatonic, and ancient mystic arguments for the value of inspired poetic vision. This rhapsodic display is offered, however, by an opponent of orthodox Christian absolutes and the social hierarchies they help support, by a writer who feels that Plato's "theories" about "elementary laws" are "not always correct" (Notopoulos 402), and by a poet-philosopher who values skeptical empiricism as much as Peacock does, albeit differently. The *Defence*, it turns out, is following tactics that Shelley attributes to Jesus in the "Essay on Christianity"; in order to be immediately effective, the piece "accommodate[s its] doctrines to the [often religious] opinions of [contemporary] auditors" while undercutting and altering the conceptions usually assumed and constructed by a prophetic language (Clark 198).

Students tend to fall into the prophetic line of interpretation on first reading the *Defence*, even if they are not particularly religious. The poet's rendering of the Imagination as the "spirit" within and behind the "body" of Reason (480) offers the apparent attraction of a deeper level, where a kind of knowledge can be found that is greater and truer than any offered by the modern "rational" systems of science, economics, and law. Teaching what really happens in this essay, in other words, means that we must start with that understandable interpretation and only gradually lead the students to see that the rhetoric that arouses it is iconoclastic, aimed less at rescuing older belief systems and more at releasing the revolutionary potentials in Peacock's own empirical assumptions. I therefore want to propose a sequence of steps through which classes on the *Defence* can proceed toward that realization.

Initially I would ask the students to place the *Defence* in relation to "The Four Ages of Poetry," first in a way that establishes ostensible differences and then in a reexamination of both works that virtually shocks the students into a recognition of their similarities. That look at what prompts the *Defence* should emphasize Peacock's claims, first, that poetry in earlier ages developed the mind's empirical and associative capacities to weave a "comprehensiveness" of interrelated observations and to turn fading memories into living recollections (Adams 491–92); second, that this process at the origins of poetry was used for the virtual deification of tyrant-chieftains in a manner that tried to restrict the expansion of thought relations that poetry had helped set in motion (Adams 491); and third, that the associative drive has finally striven to—and should—break free of poetry's regressive limitations to pursue the "philosophic mental tranquility" that "collects a store of ideas [from perceptions], discriminates their relative value [after assessing their social consequences]," and finally "forms new combinations that impress the stamp of their power and utility on the real business of life" (Adams 496).

Once those assertions are clear to the students, the teacher can ask them to pick out moments in the *Defence* that seem the most forceful denials of those arguments. In my experience the students should point fairly soon at the recasting of Reason's philosophical arrangements by the transformative Imagination (which is now the maker of new associations, 480); at the origins of poetry now seen as re-creative (not restrictive) of basic "impressions" or beliefs (481); at the rising of poetic constructs, in their "vital metaphoricity," to a seemingly transhistorical participation in "the eternal, the infinite, and the one" beyond rational philosophy (482–83); and at the genesis of all those movements in the *un*deliberate, *un*tranquil metamorphosis of a "fading coal" or receding mental state as though there "were the [unwilled] interpenetration of a diviner nature through our own" (504). At that point, the teacher should urge the students to acknowledge how often Shelley starts to answer Peacock with what seems to be the verbiage of absolutist religious beliefs (echoing sources best enumerated by Fanny Delisle)—beliefs that Shelley himself is known for rejecting even in the *Defence* (on 498, for example). The students should now realize that something else is going on within the poet's choice of images, and they should begin to steer away from interpretive conclusions that are too superficial.

The best way to increase and direct that realization is to show how much Peacock's associationist epistemology is also Shelley's (with a few modifications), to such an extent that poetry can be defended in Shelley's eyes because it makes possible, keeps resuscitating, and even carries toward a more generous expansiveness the very activity of the philosophic mind that Peacock has made the goal of human progress. The students should now be directed to Shelley's skeptically empirical assumption—extending Berkeley, Hume, and William Drummond—that "All things exist [only] as they are perceived" (505). That statement should be presented as so true for Shelley that thoughts and objects are not strictly distinguished for him and that thoughts about basic perceptions in his eyes (the interpreters of interpretations in Shelley's essay "On Life") keep the psyche, as Peacock would admit, free from being strictly "subjected to the accident of surrounding impressions" (505). Those beliefs should now be made to color the opening contrast in the *Defence* between Reason and Imagination. The students should soon perceive that the freedom in thoughts about thoughts operates in the passage on two different levels. The first level, the so-called body of thought, is Reason's establishment of the basic, customary relations between different perceptions—or really between memories or signs of perceptions. The second level, a breathing of "spirit" into the "body," is Imagination's recomposition of those signs and relations into "other thoughts" similar to compounds in chemistry (see Hogle, "Poetics" 177–78), producing heretofore "unapprehended combinations of thoughts" (487), "each containing within itself the [interrelational] principle of its own integrity" (480).

The students can now see that for Shelley the "deep knowledge" in poetic creation is not some belated awareness of an existing Light of Truth, despite his use of language with such overtones. It is the generation of a projected heat or brightness (as in chemical reactions) by a revolutionary attraction of thought elements into new analogic relations with each other, an intensification of the same combinatory logic that Peacock regards as supremely philosophical. As Shelley sees it, the original rise of poetry was—and the recurrence of the poetic impulse remains—so much a revision of existing "signs for portions or classes of thoughts" (482) that true poetry never has been and never can be a tyrannizing repression of thought potentials. Instead, it must have always been and must still be an acceleration of what Peacock values most: an enlargement of human awareness by new compoundings of perceptions, so that the psyche becomes the "receptacle of a thousand unapprehended combinations of thought" (487). For Shelley, poetry is more than just the composition of poems; it is a process of Imagination that so "distends, and then bursts the [present] circumference of the [poet's or] hearer's mind" with an increased sense of "the permanent analogy of things" that it overflows all the cultural frames around human possibility that currently limit what analogies can be allowed to form between perceived or perceiving thoughts.

After the class discussion has reached that understanding, the students should be guided toward the next discovery, wherein they may see how this disruptive and uncentered process of Imagination can lead both to a Peacockian "utility" that can improve the future of the human race and to the "participation"—of the poet, the poem, or the reader—in a "universal" or a "oneness" different from any orthodox Christian or Platonic absolute. If the students see imaginative recombination for Shelley as reaching beyond any limited ranges of thought connection, then, if directed to the relevant passages, they can see what the poet means when he envisions such transgressive constructs as inherently looking beyond the individual person to analogies between that person's thoughts and those of others in society. In keeping with the quest for analogies basic to the Imagination, Shelley maintains that "the mind can[not] see itself unless [it is] reflected upon that which it resembles"—most particularly on a person or persons it resembles (491). Moreover, as it pursues that interreflection, the psyche discovers the "great secret of morals" as a "love" going out of the self to "the place of another and of many others" (487–88) and realizes that its inclusion of those "others" in its analogies adds a further "class of emotions" to the ones felt by the outreaching poet (481). The resulting combination of perceptions and desires harkening to one another as they interact produces, we can show the students, a discovery of "those laws according to which things ought to be ordered" so that the fulfillments desired by one person (say, the poet) can be possible for another and many others (483).

The students need to realize that it is the projection of such revolutionary visions in poetic compounds that allows the poet of the *Defence* to be prophetic, in a peculiarly Shelleyan sense of "behold[ing] the future in the present" (483), and that makes the poet's communicated acts of metaphoric reconception seeds or "germs" (483, 485) that cast their projections ahead of the current situation to inseminate eternally potential "motives or actions" throughout "the possible varieties of human nature" (485). Even though— indeed, because—the process keeps looking to future readers and responses, Shelley regards the continual movement of the world-reforming activity in poetry as "the life of truth" and as what conveys "universal" possibilities, the activity of "analogy" being more "permanent" and more beneficial to more people than any time-bound belief system or ideology (485).

Here is perhaps the crux of what the students should be brought to see in Shelley's seemingly absolutist diction: that words once used to suggest fixed essentials or levels now point to iconoclastic *processes* of revisionary reinterpretation in poetic thoughts and metaphors, either within single poetic visions or throughout the history of Western poetry. The reorientations in the *Defence*'s echoes of older phrases perform the very activity that Shelley wants to promote, the one that he works to associate with all the historical stages of true "poetry," whereas Peacock limits the word to the construction of ideological power plays in a few early periods. Eventually, the students should be directed to the passage on "the eternal, the infinite, and the one" and Shelley's placement of it (483) directly after his description of how and why forward-looking "germs" are produced. If the logic just outlined has been clearly talked through, the students should see that the "one" here is the "eternal" process of thought revision, language revision, and reenvisionings of the social order by and in poetic revisions of all codified mental, verbal, and political configurations. A poet participating in that sort of "universal" is, indeed, an "unacknowledged legislator" (508), the facilitator of a loving interplay between different figures that is possible but has yet to exist fully in human thinking, discourse, action, and society.

If class time permits, that last step should not be the final one. The students may still wonder about the "fading coal" passage—the one that they most want to discuss—and they are probably less clear than they should be on what for Shelley is the most basic and transindividual impulse behind the weaving of thought relations by the Imagination and behind the revisionary drive in true poetry that breaks up older schematizations in era after era so as to impel unimagined thought potentials toward articulation. As it happens, the sequence on the coal is the most vivid statement about that impulse in the *Defence*, and a good class discussion can bring the student analysis of the essay to a fitting (though partial) conclusion by probing those paragraphs to see in their metaphors what primally underwrites Shelley's special vision. By that point, the students should realize that Shelley's picture of the "mind in creation" is not a mere repetition of ancient or Christian infusions from on high. In fact, what is occurring for Shelley in the reawakening of a "fading" mental state is a revivifying transfiguration of decaying thought patterns by an "invisible influence" that acts "like the colour of a flower which fades and changes as it is developed" (504). This "power arises from within" thinking, as color does from within the flower's potentials for change, and yet it is outside all present awareness, as though it were the emergence of an oft-repressed and easily forgotten movement deep in thought itself. It resembles Freud's sense of an *Übertragung*, a carrying over or transference, in which, according to *The Interpretation of Dreams*, receding memory traces are transported into another association with more recent memories (fading and changing) to enter a recombination that transforms the desires and the potentials in all the thoughts.

Shelley, the class can conclude, locates the impetus for poetic thought in a transference of mnemonic images from fading associations, which even recall older patterns of discourse, into new and more revolutionary combinations of thoughts and words. Such is the case particularly when he sees the revival of the "coal" as a renewed and revisionist use "of evanescent visitations of thought and feeling sometimes associated with place or person, sometimes regarding our mind alone" (504). If the transformative action that reorders those vestiges recalls forms of divine inspiration, the students can see, it is only as it resembles (or "is as it were," 504) the Hebrew Yahweh's continual self-concealment of power in the effects of it (best described by Herbert Schneidau) and only as the resemblance provides a recognizable metaphor for transpositions between different levels of memory, consciousness, and conscious discourse. Shelley's *Defence* is retroping (or turning) such biblical tropes into symbols for a primordial transference that operates preconsciously to shift thoughts toward one another and into "unapprehended" relationships that lead us to reenvision the world that exists only as we perceive it.

Poets for Shelley are generally more receptive to this subliminal movement in all minds—hence their ability to prompt us back into contact with it—and are more able to release such a tendency in words by exploiting the tendency already in language to define an existing word combination as

"another and many others" that are different. Such a basic or radical transference, once freed (usually by poets) from the binding of it in hegemonic
systems of thought and discourse, can be revealed to students as what empowers imaginative interrelations, transfigurations of discourse patterns, and
revisions of worldviews from era to era in Shelley's eyes, particularly as poets
keep working to continue the developing movement of "that great [but never
finished] poem, which [they, as if they were] the co-operating thoughts of
one great mind, have built up since the beginning of the world" (493).
Certainly that poetic impulse is what makes possible Peacock's sense of
human self-revision, though Peacock does not admit it. Students may not
see what makes Shelley's vision of poetry as brilliant and revolutionary as
it is unless they are drawn by the foregoing stages to that level of insight,
unless they are asked to confront the activity that is "the electric life which
burns" in the words of Shelleyan poets and is "the Power . . . seated on the
throne[s] of their" souls, urging them toward the recombinations of thoughts
that can truly remake the world we perceive (508).

LITERARY AND HISTORICAL CONTEXTS

Shelley in His Times

Donald H. Reiman

How can a teacher best prepare those studying Shelley to learn about the historical period in which he lived and wrote? When I taught freshman rhetoric at the University of Illinois, veteran teachers warned us that old, proven term papers from the fraternity and sorority files might turn up. To forestall that possibility, I required my students to read the pages in the *Encyclopaedia Britannica* article on "English History" devoted to the reigns of George III, George IV, and William IV, and I permitted them to write on any topic that came up in that assignment—any scientific, technological, or agricultural advance of the period, such as the development of Hereford cattle; the music, art, and architecture; the historical events or the economic developments; the intellectual issues or the literary achievements. Students from every specialized curriculum could find something of interest, and most topics were unhackneyed, so far as the freshman theme files were concerned. That experiment convinced me that the historical articles in almost any edition of the *Britannica* provide a quick overview that highlights the central concerns of the Romantic age.

In any course on the Romantics, I include in the syllabus the birth and death dates of all the major writers and ask at the first class period what patterns emerge and what their significance may be. Students quickly learn, through analogies drawn from their own lifetimes, that the age at which the poets encountered a historical event (such as the Reign of Terror, as reported in England) or experienced a social change (such as the hardships brought upon many families by the postwar depression after Waterloo) greatly influenced the attitudes of the various Romantic poets toward the historical events and the changes that often form the subject matter or the basic allusions of their poems, as well as of their voluminous political and social prose and their letters.

To alert students to the importance of such references and allusions, the teacher should give them a list of easily consulted sources, including the appendixes to their desk dictionaries; the *Dictionary of National Biography*; encyclopedias; and a small reserve shelf of relevant books, including studies of Shelley from a social and political point of view (see the "Materials" section of this volume); one or two histories of England during the period 1789–1832; a history of France during the same general period, such as the English version of Georges Lefevbre's two-volume history of *The French Revolution* and two-volume *Napoleon*; and a selection of political and social histories, representing different viewpoints—for example, E. P. Thompson's *The Making of the English Working Class* balanced by such studies as J. E. Cookson's *Lord Liverpool's Administration, 1815–1822* and A. D. Harvey's *Britain in the Early Nineteenth Century*. Include also some books of broader sweep on more specialized topics, such as John Roach's *Social Reform in England, 1780–1880*, G. E. Mingay's *English Landed Society in the Eighteenth Century*, and its companion volume, F. M. L. Thompson's *English Landed Society in the Nineteenth Century*. Since one easy way to learn what issues of the time were implicated in a poem is to read the contemporary reviews, teachers and students alike will also profit from a sampling of the last two volumes of Reiman's *The Romantics Reviewed*, John O. Hayden's *Romantic Bards and British Reviewers*, or (for reviews of Shelley only) Newman Ivey White's *The Unextinguished Hearth*.

Romantic literature can become more vital and relevant to students when they become familiar with the sociopolitical issues contemporary with its origins. The point can be made by handing out texts of two unannotated poems—one on a modern event familiar to the students and the other on an early nineteenth-century event, such as Shelley's poem on the bombardment of Copenhagen from the Esdaile Notebook—and asking them to explicate the poems in class. They will soon recognize that they must do some research to cross the gap between Shelley's historical milieu and their own.

Students at any level learn more about the historical and social background (or anything else) if they actively participate as coteachers, responsible for part of the preparation for each class. Both to get acquainted with the individuals in a new class and to involve them in the course, I ask two students at each of the first few sessions to prepare a two- to four-minute presentation (one or two double-spaced typescript pages—no more), to be read at one meeting and handed in at the next, as revised in the light of questions and discussions; these papers provide the class with introductions to a variety of people, places, events, and issues important to the poems under discussion. For example, at the class preceding the discussion of "The Mask of Anarchy," I may ask one student to introduce John Scott, Earl of Eldon, and Shelley's relations with him and ask another to outline the events of Peterloo. I hold all the students responsible for the material in these reports (and any additions and corrections brought up in class) by including some of the topics in the short-answer objective questions on the midterm or the final exam. The teacher need not count the oral reports in the final grade, but I mark up the short papers with detailed comments to establish the standards of research, logic, and writing to which students will be held in their longer papers.

Different poems by Shelley present particular problems of distance to overcome. With *Queen Mab*, for example, the literary background is more important than the historical. That is, although Shelley's poem (like a number of his later poems, such as *Prometheus Unbound*) depicts the evils of past historical periods, the conflicts of the present, and the hopes of an idealized future, its presentation of history derives from a literary convention. If the teacher has access to a translation of Volney's *Les ruines*, or to Peacock's *Palmyra*, reading or handing out duplicated passages from those works, together with reference to the earlier Utopian tradition—Thomas More's *Utopia* and Swift's *Gulliver's Travels*, for example—will help the student place *Queen Mab* in its genre while clarifying some of the objects of Shelley's attack. With "The Mask of Anarchy," *Swellfoot the Tyrant* (on Queen Caroline's trial), "Ode to Naples," *Hellas*, or "Written on Hearing the News of the Death of Napoleon," on the other hand, students should be encouraged to supplement the notes in their texts with brief historical accounts—a few pages reproduced from an encyclopedia or general history—that contain the relevant factual background, with some indication of what Shelley himself would have been likely to know about the event when he wrote the poem.

Shelley's prose, though not yet available in a truly reliable edition, is useful as a way of convincing students of the social and philosophical dimensions of his thought that his poetry tends to abstract or mythologize. Shelley consistently believed that he was more intelligent than most of his readers and that, by shaping his language and argument to his sense of their motivations, he could persuade them to adopt his viewpoint. By trying to identify Shelley's intended audience and his rhetorical purpose for each prose work—for example, his Irish tracts—students can avoid the mistake of taking every word literally. But even as poetic and rhetorical an essay as *A Defence of Poetry* (in part, Shelley's defense of his own career as a poet against the ironic attack of his friend Thomas Love Peacock, who had recently given up attempts to write poetry for a career at the East India Company) conveys so much information about Shelley's intellectual background and displays his deepest feelings so clearly that it is invaluable to understanding his characteristic modes of thought and expression.

If possible, some work of Shelley's prose should be set as a reading assignment along with each poem or group of poems. Common pairings include "On Life" with "Mont Blanc" and "Hymn to Intellectual Beauty"; "On Love" with *Alastor* and the lyrics published with it; *A Defence of Poetry* with *Adonais* or *Epipsychidion*; and, for a two- or three-day assignment, *A Philosophical View of Reform* between *Prometheus Unbound* and "The Mask of Anarchy." Note that, in most of those specific cases, the poems were written before the accompanying prose; and the ideas developed first in Shelley's mythic and imaginistic imagination before he reduced them to a prose discourse. (This pattern thus supports his contention in *A Defence of Poetry* that poetic creativity is both the root and the flower of the mind's operations.)

Additional assignments, involving the works of other Romantic writers, may also utilize Shelley's prose works. His fragmentary essay "On the Punishment of Death" can be treated in conjunction with his more rhetorical *Address to the People on the Death of the Princess Charlotte* to approach his thinking on capital punishment, while the latter, taken with his brief *Declaration of Rights*, presents his attitudes on social inequality and the responsibilities of the upper classes toward the poor. Shelley's views on the death penalty can be profitably compared with those expressed in Wordsworth's fourteen "Sonnets on the Punishment of Death" (a good exercise for students who claim that they've already studied thoroughly all the Romantics). Shelley's views on social responsibility—seen directly in his Irish and "Hermit of Marlow" pamphlets—appear from another perspective in Peacock's portraits of him as Forester in *Melincourt* and as Falconer in *Gryll Grange*; a term paper on the topic, delightful for both student and teacher, can be spiced by engaging Marilyn Butler's contention in *Peacock Displayed* that Shelley is *not* portrayed in these characters.

Hellas provides a clear case of how Shelley's artistry merges literary tradition with contemporary events and issues. A full study of the drama would begin with a look at Aeschylus's *The Persians* and a brief discussion of how it differs from the other surviving Athenian tragedies. (The matter is treated in the section of Woodring's *Politics in English Romantic Poetry* reprinted in Reiman and Powers, and the notes to that book provide additional details.) Then the contemporary political situation can be surveyed—Metternich's repressive Holy Alliance, which in 1821 dashed Shelley's and Byron's hopes by crushing the 1820 constitutional revolution in Naples (which paralleled a similar movement in Spain); the struggle for the Balkans between Turkey and Russia (presented graphically in cantos 7 and 8 of Byron's *Don Juan*); the history of Ali Pasha (Byron's host in 1809) and his war against the Turkish sultan; the Shelleys' friendship with Prince Mavrocordato and other Phanariot Greek exiles at Pisa; and the revolution in Greece itself and the echoes of this conflict in western Europe, which can be sketched by someone assigned to read the early chapters of William St. Clair's *That Greece Might Still Be Free*.

To move from the practical to the theoretical level, I adumbrate my unconventional view of the social and political issues of the period and their effects on Shelley's writings—a view that other teacher-scholars can test for themselves against the facts of his life and the tenor of his writings. (This view is argued more fully in my "Shelley as Agrarian Reactionary.") The chief economic and sociopolitical development of the period was the industrial, technical, and scientific revolution that, as capital accumulated, was transforming agriculture, manufacturing, and transportation more rapidly with each passing decade. This increase in production and accumulation of new wealth reduced the relative wealth (and power) of traditional landed proprietors, such as Shelley's family and friends. (Byron's family and the patrons of Wordsworth's and Coleridge's families derived their *original* power from agriculture, but there were also coal mines on Byron's Rochdale estate, while both mines and a shipping port had brought new wealth to the Lowther earls of Lonsdale, the Wordsworths' patrons.) Those brought up on American Western movies may view the conflict through an analogy with the conflict between the old wealth of cattle barons and the new wealth of those who struck oil on their lands.

The French Revolution signaled the spread of the capitalist revolution to the Continent and the transfer of power from the landed aristocracy to the middle classes there. This burgeoning of industry originally threatened competition with British manufacturing and trade, causing those interests and balance-of-power tacticians in the government, as well as more traditional adherents of Church and Crown, to support a war to stop the spread of bourgeois revolutionary fervor on the Continent. At first, such agricultural magnates as the Russell dukes of Bedford and the Howard dukes of Norfolk (the latter were patrons of the Shelleys) did not foresee the threat to their own interests and joined with antiroyalists among the middle-class dissenters and the idealistic liberals in support of the French Revolution.

Percy Bysshe Shelley—like Wordsworth, William Cobbett, and other thinkers of the period—was deeply committed to the values of the old preindustrial way of life. But as he saw the misery of the growing urban working class, he called for changes in the political structure that would enable it to respond in a humanitarian way to the new social and economic conditions. The tension between Shelley's reactionary social ideals and his humanitarian and republican political goals led him to treat social and political issues in imprecise, symbolic terms, thereby freeing his poetry from merely local or transitory issues. His prose, especially *A Philosophical View of Reform*, demonstrates his clear understanding of the history of Europe since the seventeenth century and proposes a useful course of social action that provides generally conservative, gradualist solutions to the problems. When Shelley embodies his comprehension in idealized poems, such as *Prometheus Unbound*, that transcend the particular and the local, he presents a far more radical picture of social transformation. But even in his call for direct action in "The Mask of Anarchy," the injustices he attacks and the solutions he proposes derive from a conservative or even reactionary viewpoint, resisting at every point the development of the commercial-industrial society that Marxists deem a necessary way station on the road to the workers' paradise.

Even "revolutionary" steps in "The Mask of Anarchy" are not designed to enhance the "progressive" forces of commerce and industry, the triumph of which later in the century ushered in the various stages of reform legislation, leading to universal suffrage and, ultimately, to the victory of the Labour Party. Rather, Shelley advocates that society return to an idealized version of preindustrial England, when the poor would have enough food, clothing, and shelter—"a neat and happy home"—and when peace would allow the common people to enjoy the blessings of their domestic virtues. Yet the tone of "The Mask of Anarchy" and Shelley's other "exoteric" or popular songs, such as "Men of England," is so militant that they became rallying cries and hymns for the British Chartists and Marxists of several generations. In an age of heightened political consciousness and fervor, even an expression of support for the "Good Old Days" grew into a radical expression of revulsion against the status quo.

The writings of Shelley and other Romantics remain valid, when so much political poetry of earlier and later periods has become passé, because their poetry and prose hold in tension both the old humane, classical-Christian values of the politically active Western literary tradition (epitomized in the writings of Dante and Milton) and the new hopes for representative government and material redistribution that the explosion of new wealth resulting from the capitalist revolution at last seemed to make possible for the entire British society. As subsequent history has shown, it is difficult, in practical terms, both to adhere to the ideals of individual freedom and to implement egalitarian redistribution of material wealth and political power, because the coercion required to enforce the latter goals tends to inhibit individual liberties, while to permit individuals to live by their personal agendas tends to militate against social and economic equality. The Romantics remain pertinent to us today precisely because they sensed and articulated in timeless words and symbols the ambivalence about these questions that most of us continue to feel.

Wordsworth and the Shelleyan Self

Leon Waldoff

We need a term under which we can assimilate the different representations of *I* in Shelley's poetry and bring into focus a psychological profile of the self that is dramatized. Taken in that way, the term *self* can be thought of as representing the critical counterpart of a biographical portrait, referring primarily to the self dramatized in a poem but also to the self revealed in biography. That Shelleyan self includes the speakers in first-person lyrics and many of the central characters in dramatic and narrative poems, who are versions of the poet's self.

My approach relies on a psychoanalytically informed understanding of the makeup of the self, the recurrence and structure of crucial moments in the life of the self, and what a poet's characteristic way of representing those moments can reveal about the self. But I do not try to develop psychoanalytic readings in the classroom. Rather, I use insights taken from psychoanalysis in formulating questions about the way the self is imagined in a poem, the relationship the self has with the object or the character encountered or addressed, and the patterns of experience most frequently repeated in the poetry.

In undergraduate courses, particularly in advanced surveys of Romantic literature and in honors seminars, I rely mainly on "To Wordsworth," "Mont Blanc," and *Prometheus Unbound* to develop the idea of the Shelleyan self, though I also refer to other poems that we read, such as "Hymn to Intellectual Beauty," "Ode to the West Wind," *Julian and Maddalo*, and *Adonais*. I begin with the 1816 sonnet in which Shelley expresses an ambivalent attitude toward Wordsworth, praising the early poet, whose voice "did weave / Songs consecrate to truth and liberty," but deploring the loss of that voice in the later poet. Most students recognize Shelley's ironic use of the theme of loss—what G. Kim Blank calls Shelley's "Wordsworthian loss of Words-worth" (48)—and identify "Intimations of Immortality" as the poem most central to the irony. Many recall Wordsworth's sympathies with the poor and his depiction of human suffering, and they point to "The Old Cumberland Beggar," "Michael," and "Resolution and Independence" as possible sources of Shelley's admiration. In support of those observations I mention Shelley's attraction to the radical ideas of William Godwin, his political activities in Dublin in support of Catholic emancipation, and the theme of moral, social, and political reform in his poetry. Two aspects of Shelley's representation of himself in the sonnet, however, usually go unnoticed but deserve to be emphasized: the implicit challenge of a figure of authority in the act of addressing him and the tone of moral superiority that, in effect, usurps the authority attributed to Wordsworth.

The Shelleyan self in "Mont Blanc" now becomes the main subject of discussion, and I ask my students to compare it with the Wordsworthian self in "Tintern Abbey," referring them to a set of study questions handed out at the end of the previous session. Critics have frequently read "Mont Blanc" as an antithetical version of "Tintern Abbey." My questions call attention to four aspects of the two poems that reveal the different selves in them: the dramatic situations, the descriptions of nature, the conceptions of the presences found in nature, and the relationships the speakers imagine themselves having with those presences.

In answering the first question—"What similarities and differences do you find in the settings of 'Tintern Abbey' and 'Mont Blanc' "?—students immediately distinguish the rolling hills of the Wye valley from the stark countenance of Mont Blanc. Many recognize the stationing of a meditative speaker in a natural setting as a typical dramatic situation in Romantic poetry, and some recall our discussion earlier in the semester of the structure of the greater Romantic lyric (as defined by M. H. Abrams) and mention examples we have read, such as "Nutting," "The Eolian Harp," and "Hymn before Sun-Rise, in the Vale of Chamouni." As the discussion proceeds, however, I shift the focus from the formalist similarity of the dramatic situations to the psychological significance of the Romantic poet's stationing of a self before a personified presence in Nature to dramatize the speaker's reflections. Such a presence or Other is a recurrent feature of the greater Romantic lyric, and how it is imagined in "Mont Blanc" reveals much about the character of the Shelleyan self in the poem.

To show how the Other is imagined, I begin by examining the radical differences between the scene of the Wye valley and that of Mont Blanc and the Ravine of Arve. I ask my students to compare lines 60–83 of "Mont Blanc" (in which Shelley describes the mountains as "unearthly forms" and the vales between as "frozen floods, unfathomable deeps," and the whole scene as a "desart" with shapes "rude, bare, and high, / Ghastly, and scarred, and riven") with lines 1–22 of "Tintern Abbey" (in which Wordsworth observes "steep and lofty cliffs," "orchard-tufts," "hedge-rows," "little lines / Of sportive wood run wild," and "pastoral farms, / Green to the very door"). Other passages in the two poems can be contrasted with equal effect, pointing up the difference between Wordsworth's "meadows . . . woods . . . mountains" and "this green pastoral landscape" (103–04, 158) and Shelley's "primaeval mountains," first called "A city of death," then "a flood of ruin" (99, 105, 107). The legacy of the New Criticism is nowhere more evident than in the practice of close reading in the classroom, and I use it to highlight the differences in the two poets' representations of nature.

More difficult to grasp and define are the divergent conceptions of the presence that the poets assume resides in or behind nature. To illustrate how the conceptions diverge, I ask my students to list four or five attributes of the presence in "Tintern Abbey" and then contrast them with those of the presence in "Mont Blanc." The attributes of the presence in "Tintern Abbey" most frequently listed are those of being infinite, beneficent, maternal, nurturing, constant, and consoling. "Nature never did betray / The heart that loved her" (122–23) is on the lips of the best students. The presence in "Tintern Abbey" is felt by the speaker, and "something far more deeply interfused" is said to have its "dwelling" both in external nature and "in the mind of man" (96–99). The attributes of the presence in Shelley's poem, by contrast, are almost exactly opposite: though infinite and eternal, the presence is mysterious, inconstant, amoral, and unconsoling. Shelley does not feel or experience a presence so much as an absence: "Power dwells apart in its tranquillity / Remote, serene, and inaccessible" (96–97).

Beyond those differences there is the issue of the gender of each presence, which students as well as critics often overlook. And that issue leads to another: does it matter that Wordsworth uses the word "presence" ("And I have felt / A presence," 93–94), whereas Shelley uses "Power" ("Where Power in likeness of the Arve comes down," 16)? The question of gender has already been implicitly answered with regard to Wordsworth's poem (though it assumes a new significance now) but not to Shelley's, and students are genuinely puzzled by it. Throughout most of the poem Shelley uses the pronoun "it" in references to the mountain and the "Power," and to a reader the effort to identify Shelley's pronoun antecedents may well seem to reenact the speaker's attempt to identify the Power and to end in similar uncertainty. Lines 16–17, however, contain an important clue: "Power in likeness of the Arve comes down / From the ice gulphs that gird *his* secret throne" (italics mine). Despite some ambiguity in the use of the pronoun (it could refer to the Power or to the Arve), Shelley gives the Power a masculine identity (or gives it the appearance of one: "in likeness of"), as he did the mountain in a long letter to Peacock written at roughly the same time (22 July to 2 August 1816) as the poem: "One would think that Mont Blanc was a living being & that the frozen blood forever circulated slowly thro' his stony veins." In the same letter Shelley wonders if the ruler of the mountain is Ahriman and describes him "throned among these desolating snows" in language remarkably similar to that of the poem—"among these palaces of death & frost, sculptured in this their terrible magnificence . . . these deadly glaciers [are] at once the proofs & symbols of his reign" (F. L. Jones 1: 500, 499). Shelley's conception of the Power in "Mont Blanc" has more in common with Coleridge's "kingly Spirit" and "Great hierarch" in "Hymn before Sun-Rise" (81–83) than with Wordsworth's "presence."

Establishing the different gender identifications of Wordsworth's "presence" and Shelley's "Power" provides a psychological key to the different relationships that the Wordsworthian and Shelleyan selves have with their respective Others. The fact that the speaker in "Tintern Abbey" sees Nature as maternal and beneficent reveals more about him than about Nature. On that point I frequently mention Richard Onorato's psychoanalytic study of the character of the poet in *The Prelude* to help explain the dimension of the Wordsworthian self that relies on a fantasy of Nature as maternal and seeks and finds modes of consolation in its relationship with the "presence."

How different is the presence wondered at in "Mont Blanc" and how different the speaker's relationship with it! The fact that the presence is masculine, is thought of as a Power and monarch ruling over "subject mountains" (62), and is perceived to be secretive, solemn, and inaccessible suggests the stationing of a self before an unapproachable patriarchal figure. In "Tintern Abbey" the beauteous forms of Nature, even when visible only in memory and imagination, enable the Wordsworthian self to "see into the life of things" (49); in "Mont Blanc," by contrast, "the naked countenance of earth . . . [and] these primaeval mountains / Teach the adverting mind" (98–100) a different lesson. Standing before Mont Blanc and in the shadow, as it were, of its resident Power, the Shelleyan self can only wonder at "The secret strength of things" (139). In "Tintern Abbey" the presence is a nurse, a guide, a guardian; in "Mont Blanc" the Power remains an "unknown omnipotence" (53). The differences reach into the very modes of thought dominating the two poems. Wordsworth's reliance on memory emphasizes his continuing relationship with Nature and supports the mood of consolation with which "Tintern Abbey" ends. Shelley's reliance on speculation in "Mont Blanc" underscores the absence of communication with the Power and foreshadows the mood of uncertainty and doubt with which "Mont Blanc" concludes. For Wordsworth, as Robert Langbaum has observed, memory ensures the continuity of self; for Shelley, speculation reveals the uncertainty of selfhood.

To bring the Shelleyan self of "Mont Blanc" into sharper focus and give it greater psychological credibility, I relate it to Shelley's life and to other images of the self in his poetry. I remind my students of Shelley's authorship of *The Necessity of Atheism*, his refusal to recant, his consequent expulsion from Oxford, and his unresolved conflict with and ultimate estrangement from his father. That pattern in Shelley's experience and thought suggests a lifelong and deeply troubled relationship with authority as it appeared to him in the forms of earthly and divine father figures (see Waldoff). I then mention the plots of *The Revolt of Islam*, *Prometheus Unbound*, and *The Cenci* and the ways in which a Shelleyan self (Laon, Cythna, Prometheus, and Beatrice Cenci) confronts a tyrannical and patriarchal figure (Othman, Jupiter, Count Cenci).

The searching and reflective Shelleyan self in "Mont Blanc" cannot be thought of as interchangeable with the haunted figure of the young poet in

Alastor, the speaker of the companion poem "Hymn to Intellectual Beauty," or the long-suffering and defiant figure of Prometheus. On the contrary, the variation in its representation in Shelley's poetry is one of the intriguing problems a reader must deal with in attempting to define the Shelleyan self. But certain essential features of the self are dramatized in the poetry and constitute a core of the Shelleyan self. The self is repeatedly represented as stationed in relation or opposition to figures, principles, or traditions of inconstant, mysterious, tyrannical, or inaccessible authority or power, and it is dramatized to work out or maintain its own separate identity through opposition, skepticism, doubt, defiance, moral superiority, or continued quest.

In the famous imagination passage in book 6 of *The Prelude* Wordsworth says, "Our destiny, our being's heart and home, / Is with infinitude, and only there; / With hope it is, hope that can never die . . . And something evermore about to be" (604–08). Wordsworth makes hope and unending expectation central to his definition of human nature. Shelley also defines human nature in terms of hope in his essay "On Life," yet he does so in a way that converts similarity into difference: "man is a being of high aspirations . . . whose 'thoughts that wander through eternity' [*Paradise Lost* 2.148] disclaim alliance with transience and decay" (476). In his echo of Belial he aligns himself with beings who maintain hope only in the context of struggle and defiance. The mind has no home in infinitude, but must wander through eternity. Shelley does not claim immortality, only disclaims transcience and decay. "Whatever may be his [man's, human nature's] true and final destination," Shelley goes on to say, "there is a spirit within him at enmity with nothingness and dissolution. . . . This is the character of all life and being" (476). And this is the character of the Shelleyan self: it defines itself in terms of opposition, and it asserts hope, not in a sense of harmony with an "invisible world" (*Prelude* 6.602), but in defiance of a threatening uncertainty.

The Younger Romantics:
Teaching Shelley with Byron and Keats

John A. Hodgson

Shelley, Byron, and Keats—the younger Romantics—constitute a natural subgroup in English Romantic poetry. They are, first of all, a new and distinct generation of poets, first heirs of a Romantic tradition that their immediate forebears, Wordsworth and Coleridge, had already established and of a world not verging obliviously on revolution but all too experienced in it. In their "revived and conscious classicism" after 1817, when they drew more on the Mediterranean south than (as their predecessors had) on the Germanic north; in their "formal sense and their inclination to objectivity"; and in their "use [of] traditional genres," they head a new and "clearly defined literary group" (Butler, *Romantics* 123–24). In the resonances between their lives and their writings, too—particularly the parallelings in life and art of their intertwined emphases on love, suffering, and death—the three poets merge into a pastiche to which our students all too often owe their notion of the Romantic poet and the poetic life.

There is one brief moment, at once highly charged and anticlimatic, when Byron, Shelley, and Keats come together in their poetry. In *Adonais*, stanzas 30–34, Byron, "The Pilgrim of Eternity," and Shelley, "a Power / Girt round with weakness," come into the presence of the dead Keats, Adonais, as the greatest and the least of his fellow poet mourners. The scene encapsulates a number of issues and motifs in late Romantic poetry. Here I focus on two: the poets' self-presentations and role playings and the swerves of their poetic careers, indicated by each one's alienation from a former muse.

It is almost impossible to teach the poetry of Shelley, Byron, or Keats effectively today without addressing the matter of the poet's self-presentation and self-dramatization in his work. The problem that Shelley's self-portrait in *Adonais* poses for students is obvious: they tend to find it vexing, baffling, and embarrassing, a caricature inviting condescension if not scorn. Here, as elsewhere in Shelley's poetry, their lack of sympathy with what may seem a neurotic or precious oversensitivity—"I shrieked, and clasped my hands in extacy!" ("Hymn to Intellectual Beauty" 60)—can bar their openness to the poem. But the issue of the poet's self-dramatization is even more prominent in Byron; and in Keats, too, particularly in the great odes and *The Fall of Hyperion*, it affects our appreciation of the poetry.

An attentiveness to the dramatic distancing of the author from his characters can alter a student's attitude to the poetry. This is especially true of *Alastor*, not merely in Shelley's distance from the wandering Poet, but also in his separateness (as his preface suggests) from his narrator, and of Byron's

"Prometheus," a solemn ode that becomes pretentious if read as a self-portrait (the supposedly isolated sufferer gathers an audience, his readers, to whom he proclaims his determination to speak only when he is sure he won't be overheard; see 10–14). Distancing is also important in *Epipsychidion*, which in its advertisement at least proffers the fiction of being a fiction, and in *Childe Harold's Pilgrimage*, canto 3, in which Byron at once retains and blurs the distinction between himself and Harold.

But typically, even in these last two examples, the poet's intermingling of his life and his poetry is vital to the poem. Here we need to help our students consider to what degree those self-dramatizations are performances and to what ends. We need to guide them to some awareness of the literary traditions, as well as the personal histories, lying behind those appearances (see Matthews, "Shelley's Lyrics"; Chernaik 8–31; Webb, *Voice* 1–73). To be a shepherd-mourner in a pastoral elegy (*Adonais*) or a poet-dreamer in a dream vision (*The Fall of Hyperion*) is to play in or with a venerable and complex tradition. The student who does not know or remember that tradition inevitably has difficulties reading the poetry.

Shelley's self-portrait in *Adonais* is particularly careful and allusive. The figure's self-expression, as opposed to the narrator's speculations about him, is entirely emblematic. He carries a light thyrsus-spear (significantly, it is neither a mere thyrsus nor a shepherd's crook), associating him as over-matched poet-hunter with Adonais. He wears pansies and violets not as affectations or merely pastoral touches but because they are emblematically appropriate to himself and to the occasion: they signify thoughts (usually heavy) and faithfulness, respectively. He identifies himself by his brow marked "like Cain's or Christ's" (306) as indifferently the murderer and the crucified; and that indifference, crucial to the poem but alien to Urania's understanding, further emphasizes his present foreignness to her. If the figure is not an anonymous, generic poet, neither is it simply Shelley: it is Shelley playing a particular traditional role in a particular individual way.

The same is true of the vatic Shelley of "Hymn to Intellectual Beauty" and "Ode to the West Wind." It is true of Byron when he patterns his protagonists after himself (or himself after his protagonists) and when he casts himself as the "broken Dandy" (410) of "Beppo" or the ironic, shifty, conversational narrator of *Don Juan*. And it is true of the Keats who describes his soul as "a lawn besprinkled o'er / With flowers, and stirring shades, and baffled beams," who "burned / And ached for wings" when he recognizes the three Shadows passing before him ("Ode on Indolence" 43–44, 23–24), or who, "half in love with easeful Death," listens "Darkling" to the nightingale's song ("Ode to a Nightingale" 51–52). Only by sensitizing our students to the contexts of those performances can we relieve them from sharing

Urania's bafflement by the strange poet's "accents of an unknown land" (301) and enable them to understand and interpret the voices of the younger Romantics.

Early in 1821, when Shelley was writing A *Defence of Poetry* in response to Thomas Love Peacock's witty attack, he told Peacock (in a letter also praising Keats's recently published *Hyperion* as "very fine") that he rose to the defense "in honour of my mistress Urania" (F. L. Jones 2: 261). Urania had been Milton's muse in *Paradise Lost* and implicitly Keats's in *Hyperion*; and so, Shelley represents her in *Adonais*. Least and last among Adonais's mourners, Shelley comes before her, and,

> As in the accents of an unknown land,
> He sung new sorrow; sad Urania scanned
> The Stranger's mien, and murmured: "Who art thou?"
> (301–03)

It is a stunning, unexampled moment of pathos in English poetry: Shelley comes into the presence of his muse—and she does not recognize him, cannot even understand his song. He, too, is her child, yet she does not know him.

Why doesn't Urania recognize Shelley? We must take his strangeness to her and the foreignness of his tongue to indicate that he now has become, instead, the poet of an inspiration that is strange and foreign to her. Specifically, he has become the author of *Adonais*, which among other things constitutes an exposé of her inadequacy, as Shelley sees it, and a rejection of her beliefs (see Cronin 178–90; Hodgson 94–96): her hopes for Adonais were deluded, for "the contagion of the world's slow stain" (356) is inevitable.

That shock of nonrecognition is peculiarly Shelleyan and also allusively Miltonic (see Satan's nonrecognition of his son, Death, in *Paradise Lost* 2.681, and Ithuriel's and Zephon's nonrecognition of Satan, 4.823–40). We encounter it again and again in almost the same words in scenes where a central character meets but fails to recognize a familiar but now alienated other—when Shelley's Prometheus hears the voice of his mother, the Earth (1.151), when he beholds the Furies of his own mutinous thoughts (1.446), when Jupiter beholds his dreadful child Demogorgon (3.1.51), when the narrator of "The Triumph of Life" meets the shade of Rousseau (199). But such a scene also marks the turns from an earlier muse, an earlier poetic voice, in both Byron's and Keats's careers.

For Byron, the change from his earlier voice comes late in the composition of *Manfred* or just after. As he wrote then about *Manfred* to his publisher, "It is too much in my old style—. . . I certainly am a devil of a mannerist

—& must leave off—" (*Letters* 5: 185); six months later, just after starting "Beppo," he added that he and most contemporary poets "are upon a wrong revolutionary system" and that "if I had to begin again—I would model myself accordingly" after classical examples (5: 265). In "Beppo," Byron does just that, taking up with a new muse; and here again, as in *Adonais*, the transformed poet introduces himself into his own poem as an apparent alien unrecognized by his mistress and his native audience. Manfred, unable to forget, finally contents himself to die, but Beppo feels "a desire to see his home again" (754). Just as Beppo abandons his exotic life as a pirate and a Turk to rejoin his society, so the Byronic persona comes back from his own Eastern tales into his native, classic tradition of letters. He comes back, whatever his private cynicism, as an entertaining if outlandish storyteller, enlivening a staid but comfortable society—an avatar of the narrator of *Don Juan*.

Though Keats in *Endymion* hesitantly hails his muse as the "Muse of my native land!" (4.1), he presently finds that he has mistaken her. *Endymion* proceeds from Keats's poetic faith that, as he soon put it in his famous letter likening the imagination to Adam's dream, "What the imagination seizes as Beauty must be truth" (*Letters* 1: 184). But soon he abandons that conviction, troubled by the doubts he voices in the "Epistle to John Hamilton Reynolds," and moves beyond *Endymion*, still seeking his proper, native muse, "looking into new countries with 'O for a Muse of fire to ascend!' " (*Letters* 1: 239). The Hyperion poems further represent that progress. The Titans, in their "blind . . . supremacy" (*Hyperion* 2.185) types of the dreamer-poet of pure imagination that Keats had formerly believed himself to be, are undeceived "by course of Nature's law" (2.181) and die out of their poetic bliss into blind suffering. In contrast, the new and truer poet figure, Apollo, "Die[s] into life" (3.130), his mind schooled by his heart (see *Letters* 2: 101–04) by virtue of his newly mature appreciation of how beauty takes its bloom from suffering—from experience, pain, mortality. Mnemosyne, the new muse figure, forsakes the old thrones for the promise of her new devotee.

But when Keats recasts and internalizes the myth of his poetic development in *The Fall of Hyperion*, focusing not on Apollo but on his own persona Poet, he displaces Mnemosyne with Moneta, a muse figure who, when we first encounter her, is still Saturn's priestess (though she evolves in the poem), still true to the old, discredited order. Moneta still preaches the tenets that Keats now rejects—that joy can be separated from pain (1.172–74; see "Lamia" 1.191–96) and that "The poet and the dreamer are distinct, / Diverse, sheer opposite, antipodes" (1.199–200). She is thus recognizable as something like his earlier muse, the muse of *Endymion*; in turn, she mistakes him as what he no longer is, her own poet, mischaracterizing him in phrases ("a dreaming thing, / A fever of thyself . . . venom[ing] all [thy] days" [1.168–75]) that describe her own present self. Urania, beholding Shelley, sees his foreignness but fails to recognize him as her former worshiper; Moneta, beholding Keats, recognizes him as her former worshiper but fails to see his present foreignness.

Shelley and Modern Poetry

George Bornstein

"Shelley . . . shaped my life," wrote W. B. Yeats in a retrospective essay of 1932 (*Essays* 424). Indeed, Shelley helped shape the life and the art of a surprising number of modern poets, inspiring either imitation or reaction. Yeats remains the one whom Shelley influenced most directly and most pervasively (see Bloom, *Yeats*; Bornstein, *Yeats, Transformations*), and his career displays a paradigmatic pattern of imitation, reaction, and final reconciliation. Beyond Yeats, Shelley's impact was greatest on the modern poets, like Wallace Stevens, who saw themselves as continuing, if modifying, Romantic tradition, but Shelley also affected avowedly anti-Romantic poets, like T. S. Eliot, who saw themselves as rejecting the English poetry of the previous century. Whether seeing Shelley as model or as menace, modern poets seem not to have grasped the full subtlety of Shelley's skeptical dialectic; instead, their Shelley is usually a variant of the idealistic poet who in his own life sometimes fell short of the ideals upheld in his work.

Yeats's early devotion to Shelley centered on their shared pursuit of Intellectual Beauty. That similarity shows up most clearly in the section of Yeats's *Poems* called *The Rose*, a major grouping of his work from the early 1890s. I have found it helpful to begin with one of Yeats's numerous prose comments about the relation of those poems to Shelley—for example his 1925 remark that

> I notice upon reading these poems for the first time for several years that the quality symbolized as The Rose differs from the Intellectual Beauty of Shelley and of Spenser in that I have imagined it as suffering with man and not as something pursued and seen from afar.   (*Poems* 589)

Perhaps more important than the sole difference Yeats detects is one that he omits: Shelley finds Intellectual Beauty more elusive and in his poems continually strives to capture a trace of it, whereas Yeats shows more confidence in his ability to invoke Intellectual Beauty and continually guards against his complete absorption into it. A good pairing of poems to demonstrate both the affinity and the difference is Shelley's "Hymn to Intellectual Beauty" and Yeats's "To the Rose upon the Rood of Time." Shelley begins his poem by putting Intellectual Beauty at a triple remove ("The awful shadow of some unseen Power / Floats though unseen amongst us"), goes on to ask "where art thou gone" (line 15), and urges it to "Depart not" (46). In contrast, Yeats merges his invocation of the same power with a warning for it to keep its distance: "Come near, come near, come near—Ah, leave me still / A little space for the rose-breath to fill!" (13–14).

Shelley affected Yeats's early narrative poems as well. Yeats particularly admired Shelley's *Alastor*, whose hero he ranked among the "great symbols of passion and of mood" in Romantic poetry (*Prose* 1: 271). For Yeats, Shelley's youth exemplified the solitary, sensitive poet vainly seeking to realize an ideal dream vision on earth. Yeats's own "Song of Wandering Aengus" constitutes an Irish *Alastor* in miniature, with Aengus at the end vainly wandering in search of the visionary woman he had once glimpsed. The same theme recurs in "He Hears the Cry of the Sedge," which also has links to Keats's "La Belle Dame Sans Merci."

Shelley affected Yeats not only through specific poems but also through poetic technique, particularly the tendency Shelley shared with Blake to deploy systematically organized imagery. As Yeats remarked:

> Shelley seemed to Matthew Arnold to beat his ineffectual wings in the void, and I only made my pleasure in him contented pleasure by massing in my imagination his recurring images of towers and rivers, and caves with fountains in them, and that one Star of his, till his world had grown solid underfoot, and consistent enough for the soul's habitation.   (*Essays* 294)

Yeats clearly applied that technique to his own verse as well, massing his own recurrent symbols, such as Rose, bird, mask, tree, and tower.

Besides the Rose, Yeats's tower symbol offers the best image for revealing his relation to Shelley, partly because he explicitly linked it to his precursor in the poems themselves. That particularly happens after Yeats's purchase of the Norman tower Thoor, Ballylee, for use as a summer home. For example, in "The Phases of the Moon" Robartes invokes *Prince Athanase* in speculating that the Yeatslike protagonist has

> chosen this place to live in
> Because, it may be, of the candle-light
> From the far tower where Milton's Platonist
> Sat late, or Shelley's visionary prince.   (13–16)

Similarly, Yeats himself invokes *Prometheus Unbound* among the symbolic associations of the tower in "Blood and the Moon": "And Shelley had his towers, thought's crowned powers he called them once" (15). The specific echoes make it easier for students to see not only that Shelley's uses of towers lie behind Yeats's own but also that the general manipulation of a repeated symbol was something Yeats learned partly from Shelley.

I have found that the best texts to juxtapose to show the mature Yeats's difference from Shelley are a stanza from Shelley's "The World's Great Age

Begins Anew" chorus from *Hellas* and one from Yeats's "Two Songs from a Play." Because both poems ultimately derive from a famous passage about the return of the Golden Age in Vergil's eclogue 4, an even more complicated instance of intertextuality can be explored. Here is Shelley's redaction:

> A loftier Argo cleaves the main,
> Fraught with a later prize;
> Another Orpheus sings again,
> And loves, and weeps, and dies;
> A new Ulysses leaves once more
> Calypso for his native shore.   (1072–77)

And here is Yeats's:

> Another Troy must rise and set,
> Another lineage feed the crow,
> Another Argo's painted prow
> Drive to a flashier bauble yet.   (1.9–12)

That pairing works particularly well for class discussion; students are quick to contrast Shelley's elevating language—"loftier," "fraught"—with Yeats's more deflating "feed the crow" and "flashier bauble." They can usually go on from there to contrast Shelley's apparent optimism about cyclical return with Yeats's disillusioned harshness at a seemingly meaningless repetition. The best students notice that Shelley introduces a note of skepticism, too, in the last stanza, which the instructor can supplement by pointing out the overall plot of *Hellas*.

If more than one class session can be devoted to Shelley and Yeats, it is helpful to have the students read some of Yeats's copious prose about Shelley. The three most important pieces are the early essay "The Philosophy of Shelley's Poetry," the later one on *Prometheus Unbound*, and the description of "Phase Seventeen" in *A Vision*. The first essay shows a sympathetic understanding of Shelley's philosophy and symbolism remarkable for the time at which it was written. The second is a much less perceptive condemnation of Shelley as a naively optimistic poet. The condemnation carries over into *A Vision*, where Yeats assigned Shelley to the same phase as Dante (and, privately, himself) and arraigned Shelley for lacking Unity of Being.

I ask the students whether Yeats's late criticisms of Shelley fit better Shelley himself or Yeats's own early work; that question usually leads to a lively discussion both of Shelley's effect on Yeats's development and of the role of displacement in poetic influence. A second strand that emerges from the prose is Yeats's persistent claim to have "corrected" Shelleyan Romanticism by fastening that vision to a national landscape, rather than to Shelley's more international or cosmopolitan ones: Yeats usually grounds his work in specifically Irish settings.

The drive to revise Romanticism by rooting it in a different locale was shared by Wallace Stevens, particularly during the 1930s, when he resumed publication under the banner of his "new romantic" theories (see Litz). The concept of a new Romanticism particularly informs the poem "Sailing after Lunch" and the essay on Marianne Moore entitled "A Poet That Matters." Shelley played a key role in Stevens's defense of poetry against simplistic calls for political engagement, as the cento of passages from Shelley's *Defence* in Stevens's "Figure of the Youth as Virile Poet" makes clear.

The discussion of those two essays and of "Sailing after Lunch" prepares the students for a discussion of particular Stevens poems with a clear and explicit relation to Shelley, chief among them "Mr. Burnshaw and the Statue," "Mozart, 1935," and two sections from part 2 of *Notes toward a Supreme Fiction*. In the second section of "Mr. Burnshaw" Stevens makes clear that "Astral and Shelleyan" lights can alter our sense of the world but not the actual structure of Nature; and in part 4, when maintaining that even the creation of an "Italy of the mind" would not suffice the perpetually restless imagination, he punningly suggests that "Shelley lies / Less in the stars than in their earthy wake" (1–2). "Mozart, 1935" presents the diminished claims of the modern poet against the foil of Shelley's invocation in "Ode to the West Wind":

> Be thou the voice,
> Not you. Be thou, be thou
> . . . Be thou that wintry sound
> As of the great wind howling.   (16–17, 20–21)

Stevens's crucial "as" replaces Shelley's cry for the wind to inspirit him with Stevens's more modest one to make a cry "as" of the wind. The same Shelleyan poem stands behind the sixth lyric in part 2 ("It Must Change") of *Notes toward a Supreme Fiction*. There Stevens counterposes the "Bethou, bethou, bethou me" of the sparrow to the "Ké-ké" of the wren in a musical standoff in which neither predominates. Stevens's tendency to provisionalize the imagination and its claims culminates two poems later, when Nanzia Nunzio confronts Ozymandias. Asking students to read Stevens's poem against Shelley's sonnet can engender lively discussion. The students usually see first that Stevens reverses his Shelleyan source by replacing the longevity of art with its perpetual change: "A fictive covering / Weaves always glistening from the heart and mind" (20–21). Some notice that the fictive filaments and coverings of the poem revise Shelley's characteristic image of the veil. And a few always point out that the poem acts out its own doctrines by providing the Shelleyan figure of Ozymandias himself with modern poetic dress. In that way it also enacts the central principle of modern theories of post-Romantic poetic influence, which Stevens rendered in "Sailing after Lunch":

> The romantic should be here.
> The romantic should be there.
> It ought to be everywhere.
> But the romantic must never remain. . . .   (11–14)

Additional pairings of poems for papers or class discussion include (1) "To a Sky-Lark" and Thomas Hardy's "Darkling Thrush," Robert Frost's "Oven Bird" or "Kitty Hawk," or Paul Laurence Dunbar's "Prometheus"; (2) "The Triumph of Life" and section 2 of T. S. Eliot's "Little Gidding" in the light of Eliot's contention in his essay "What Dante Means to Me" that the passage describing Rousseau in Shelley's poem "is better than I could do" (*To Criticize the Critic*); and (3) "Ode to the West Wind" and D. H. Lawrence's "Song of a Man Who Has Come Through" or Marianne Moore's "Half Deity."

CRITICAL PERSPECTIVES

Shelley and Current Critical Debates

Paul Magnuson

Recently, I have recast my two-semester graduate survey in the English Romantic poets to include one representative essay of contemporary criticism in each class. In selecting the essays for each week, I have followed several principles: First, the essays were only recommended reading; they were not required of all students. Second, the selections were brief, either a relatively self-contained essay or a short selection from a full book of criticism. Third, the essays were directly on the texts that were to be discussed in class; they contained a good amount of practical criticism. Fourth, the essays were written, if possible, by major representatives of the various critical schools as both an introduction and an illustration of those approaches. The implicit argument (and at times it was a real argument) was that an understanding of Romanticism is essential to an understanding of contemporary criticism.

I introduced the course by saying that the recommended reading in contemporary criticism would constitute a relatively small portion of our time and that the course could be completed with distinction by traditional work on the primary texts of poetry. While I was quick to stick critical labels on the essays that were recommended reading, I was much more evasive about what constituted traditional criticism or primary reading. In fact, traditional critics kept having labels stuck on them and being categorized as belonging to schools of twentieth-century criticism, which expedient seemed the easiest way to end classes after the bell. Traditionalists in this decade usually turned out to include M. H. Abrams, Earl Wasserman, Kenneth Neill Cameron, C. E. Pulos, and Donald Reiman.

The survey of the second-generation Romantics began with Byron and covered Shelley and Keats. My general thesis throughout the course was that the literature of the second generation constituted several dialogues. There was the dialogue between idealism and skepticism within each poet's work and a dialogue between the second generation and the earlier Romantics and among the poets of the second generation. I began the semester with a discussion of Romanticism and its definitions contained in Abrams's *Natural Supernaturalism* and the qualifications of Abrams's definitions in Anne Mellor's *English Romantic Irony*, Tilottama Rajan's *Dark Interpreter*, and Jerome McGann's *Romantic Ideology*. The latest edition of Frank Jordan's *English Romantic Poets: A Review of Research and Criticism* is helpful in mapping the fields of recent criticism of Romanticism.

Shelley illustrated my central thesis well. The emphasis fell on the irony in the play between idealism, the hope for a transcendent reality and the faith in the mind's ability to know it, and skepticism, the realization that the mind is severely limited to the chaos of sensation in its quest for knowledge. In some works, the idealistic impulse leads Shelley to escape the world of phenomena and to disregard the chaos of sensation; in others, idealism leads him to imagine the reordering of the world, particularly its political and sexual orders.

For each of the four sessions on Shelley, I assigned a large number of poems but planned to concentrate on one or two poems for class discussion. Originally, I planned to keep the discussion of the poetry separate from that of the criticism in order to define the critics' premises, to identify the criticism with which they argued (implicitly or explicitly), and to point out their weaknesses or blind spots. It often proved difficult, however, to keep the two discussions separate. For the first session on Shelley, I concentrated on *Alastor* with essays from the Reiman and Powers edition, particularly those by Wasserman and Pulos, to encourage the students to see the conflict between the idealistic quest and its failure in the skeptical conclusion that the well, which is the source of the river, is "inaccessibly profound." I also used Harold Bloom's account of *Alastor* in the opening chapter of *Yeats* for the dialog between Shelley and Wordsworth on the issue of the value and the function of Nature and the natural world.

For the second session, I assigned both *The Defence of Poetry* and *Prometheus Unbound*, knowing full well that I have never been able to complete both in one class. For the recommended critical reading I included both Frye's "Prometheus: The Romantic Revolutionary" from *A Study of English Romanticism* and Harold Bloom's "Internalization of Quest Romance" from *Romanticism and Consciousness*. In the discussion of the *Defence*, I pointed out the various idealistic and skeptical statements and tried to reconcile them by referring to Shelley's definition of metaphorical language: it "marks the before unapprehended relations of things" (482). The poet's job is to continually create new orders.

Then, for the traditional students, I illustrated Shelley's creation of the Prometheus figure from diverse myths. In demonstrating the composite figure of Shelley's Prometheus, I drew on Frye's and Bloom's essays. At the same time, I was able to illustrate the differences between Frye's archetypal criticism and Bloom's phenomenological approach. Frye locates the hero's journey through worlds of Nature, and he illustrates those worlds by referring to Shakespeare's romances. The struggle of the hero that Bloom traces leads his Prometheus into the realms of consciousness in which Nature has no part.

The third week was devoted to cleaning up after the second week and then creating more chaos with *The Cenci* and *A Vindication of the Rights of Women* by Mary Wollstonecraft. My argument was twofold. First, I wanted to demonstrate the similarities between the two works on the issues of kings and fathers. In both Shelley and Wollstonecraft the tyranny of kings and fathers was a result of their weaknesses, not their strengths. My second purpose was more controversial. Obviously, *The Cenci* parallels the tyrannical father with the tyrannical priest, Pope, and God. The domestic tragedy is only thinly veiled political commentary. I then (too boldly, as I was to discover) argued that many domestic tales in the period, written by both men and women, were also political commentaries, including those by Wollstonecraft and Helen Maria Williams. Thus, I argued, domestic narrative was not the exclusive domain of women writers but was a matter of politics shared by men and women authors alike. In fact, I suggested, most domestic narratives of the day could be and indeed probably were read as political commentaries. Another mess to clean up.

Finally, the last week was given to an analysis of *Adonais*, read in the light of Wasserman's essay on it in *Shelley: A Critical Reading*, a fine example of Wasserman's fevered New Criticism. I ended with a most inconclusive discussion of "The Triumph of Life" and the essays by Paul de Man and Hillis Miller in *Deconstruction and Criticism*, edited by Harold Bloom and others. The de Man essay proved a good choice, for the first part of the essay pursues its deconstructive purpose by referring to explicit thematic statements in Shelley's poem, particularly those of effacement and erasure. Only when those thematics are clearly established does the essay turn to the more subtle and more controversial deconstructive strategies of reading. The second half of the essay and Miller's somewhat similar procedure of reversing categories provided the students with some examples of deconstructive analysis.

Would that procedure work for an undergraduate survey of the Romantics that included Shelley? Yes, with some modification. I would not hesitate to use some of the essays, those in Reiman and Powers or those by Frye and Wollstonecraft, in a general survey course. They are clear enough so that they contribute to a general discussion of the poetry, and, with a little explication by an instructor, their critical procedures are clear. In a more advanced course, one that focuses on the second generation or on Byron and Shelley, some of the other essays work if there is enough class time for the instructor to explain their methods. The instructor is then relieved from the task of rehearsing the same old plots-and-themes routine. The final purpose is for the student to see clearly that the Romantic poets were struggling with the same critical issues as contemporary critics.

Shelley's Endings:
Formalist and Postformalist Perspectives

Susan J. Wolfson

Shelley's poems are remarkable for the frequency with which their endings involve terms and syntaxes that complicate or even subvert satisfactory closure. Sometimes it is an effect of conclusions that come to rest in states of vacancy and absence: "Those who remain behind" to mourn the poet in *Alastor*, for instance, do not have even

> The passionate tumult of a clinging hope;
> But pale despair and cold tranquillity,
> Nature's vast frame, the web of human things,
> Birth and the grave, that are not as they were. (716–20)

At other times, Shelley's terms of closure entail uncertain surmise—*if, as if*—or are perplexed by tones of hesitation—*may, might*—or the language of tentative suggestion—*whether . . . or*. The clearly labeled "Conclusion" of "The Sensitive-Plant," for example, sets into play two *"whether . . . or"* possibilities, to which the poet can respond only with "I cannot say . . . I dare not guess" (4, 9) before advancing "a modest creed" (14) whose own language is as slippery as it is suggestive.

That Shelley's imaginative impulses seem more powerfully engaged with problems than with solutions affects the endings of his poems, which typically complicate their motions of closure. A study of the complications offers a productive focus for classroom attention. For undergraduates the approach is a stimulating way of bringing close reading to bear on the relation between Shelley's formalist practices and his philosophical values; for more advanced students, Shelley's poems, long and short, offer fruitful cases in point for exploring the different theoretical emphases displayed by New Critical-formalist readings and deconstructive-postformalist ones. Such a focus on problems of closure, moreover, can provoke a lively writing assignment in which the students are asked to consider the problem, conceived in both conceptual and formalist terms, in a poem or set of poems not already treated in class.

One may begin the approach by presenting for discussion a few differing assessments of Romantic poetics: a general one by M. H. Abrams, one focused more specifically on Shelley by Earl Wasserman, and a theoretical statement by Paul de Man. In 1965 Abrams published an influential analysis of the formal and, by implication, psychological procedures of "the Greater Romantic Lyric":

> In the course of [his] meditation the lyric speaker achieves an insight, faces up to a tragic loss, comes to a moral decision, or resolves an

emotional problem. Often the poem rounds upon itself to end where it began, at the outer scene, but with an altered mood and deepened understanding which is the result of the intervening meditation.   (201)

Although Abrams's analyses usually concern literary history and the history of ideas, his sentences in that essay offer a summary of New Critical unity. With that extract in hand, I ask students which of Shelley's poems seem to accord with Abrams's model and why. Then, as a way of anticipating de Man's radical deconstruction of Abrams's paradigm, I turn to an intermediate statement, Wasserman's comment in 1971 about "the half-skeptical note on which [Shelley] ends so many of his poems" (*Shelley* 251). Wasserman has "Ode to the West Wind," "The Sensitive-Plant," and "Mont Blanc" in mind, but, rather than tip his hand, I ask the students to propose and explain their own cases; even if they cannot yet talk about the specific terms of Shelley's skepticism, with some prodding they should be able to hear tones and recognize syntaxes—uncertain resolutions, ambiguous decisions, incomplete understandings, troubled insights—that suggest both the value and the limitation of Abrams's categories.

Undergraduates may have enough of a challenge interpreting Shelley's poetry in relation to those two statements. For more advanced students de Man offers a paradigm that is about as opposite to Abrams's as one can imagine. Anticipating and in many ways inaugurating the deconstructive practices of the 1970s, de Man squares off against Abrams to argue that Romantic rhetoric is implicated in ironies that reveal "the existence of a temporality that is definitely not organic, in that it relates to its source only in terms of distance and difference and allows for no end, for no totality" ("Rhetoric" 203). At that point I ask the students whether they think it is possible to extend Wasserman's sense of Shelley's "half-skeptical" notes of closure that far and, if so, which poems seem most to resist a totality of understanding or a closure to the intellectual crisis represented.

It helps to recount the situation of Shelley's poetry in both assessments of Romanticism. Abrams mentions "Stanzas Written in Dejection" and "Ode to the West Wind" in passing as examples of meditation dominating the description of external landscape, but the most productive examples for his paradigm do not include Shelley. In general, New Critical formalism tends to be dissatisfied with the "looseness" of Shelleyan poetics. W. K. Wimsatt, for instance, does not seem to be able to accommodate much of Shelley's poetry beyond citing "Ode to the West Wind" as an instance of how some kinds of Romantic poetry "achieve iconicity by a more direct sensory imitation of something headlong and impassioned, less ordered, nearer perhaps to the subrational" than what obtains in Neoclassical forms (115). Interesting shifts of emphasis appear as early as the 1960s in the work of Wasserman and David Perkins, and deconstructive approaches to Romanticism were strongly energized, if not in some ways enabled, by Shelley's practices—in particular, his tendency to push language to the limits of its expressive power and his corresponding willingness to bend the poetics of closure to indeterminacy and deferral. In fact, *Deconstruction and Criticism*, edited by Harold Bloom and others (1979), was planned as a collection of interpretive essays on Shelley's last and, provocatively for this approach, unfinished poem, "The Triumph of Life"; although the volume has a wider focus, Shelley is still the central figure.

With the theoretical terrain of closure mapped out, one may turn to two especially engaging practical applications, the closing lines of "Mont Blanc" and the last stanzas of "Ode to the West Wind." Both voice questions addressed to the world of Nature, and the tone of both questions—"rhetorical" or "genuine"?—is deeply ambiguous. Although "Mont Blanc" is the earlier poem, its thematic issues are so complexly elusive and the internal elements of its questioning are so slippery that I have found it best to work first with the apparently more straightforward conclusion of "Ode to the West Wind"; the fact that the ode is shorter also facilitates a consideration of its ending in relation to the text as a whole. All the stanzas of the poem are organized as terza rima sonnets, a scheme that (like the Shakespearean form) presses toward epigrammatic summary in a concluding couplet. In the final stanza of Shelley's ode, this couplet yields a climactic question, one so familiar that it has become a cliché, a significant point in itself:

> Drive my dead thoughts over the universe
> Like withered leaves to quicken a new birth!
> And, by the incantation of this verse,
>
> Scatter, as from an unextinguished hearth
> Ashes and sparks, my words among mankind!
> Be through my lips to unawakened Earth
>
> The trumpet of a prophecy! O Wind,
> If Winter comes, can Spring be far behind?   (63–70)

Students are usually able to note how the image of "leaves dead . . . driven" (2–3) before the West Wind in stanza 1 is here recovered as the vehicle of a simile through which the speaker calls on the Wind to inspire a rebirth of poetic voice. That the voice is projected as "The trumpet of a prophecy" (69) casts both the act of calling and the desired rebirth in the highest register of imagination. The transformation of wind into a trumpet is both a summons to and, by virtue of its inspiration, an enactment of that reawakening. Those tropes of rebirth tempt students to read Shelley's summary question as the equivalent of a statement whose terms escalate the vocabulary of natural rebirth to an implied universal rebirth for "mankind." The interrogative syntax, they often suggest, solicits our assent and quickens thereby our participation in the new birth for which the poet petitions. There is good support for that interpretation: the *Princeton Encyclopedia of Poetry and Poetics* cites this apostrophe as probably the most famous English example of the "rhetorical question," which is defined as one "asked for effect rather than information, one to which the speaker knows the answer in advance" (705). The wide acceptance of that view is underscored by one of the most sensitive readers of Shelley's poetry, David Perkins, who quotes the couplet without the question mark, as if that terminal punctuation had no effect on the "symbolic ground for optimism" so claimed (*Quest* 165).

Such views notwithstanding, Shelley's verse exposes some interesting ruptures. The full logic of the simile that compares "dead thoughts" to "withered leaves" may be more forceful than its rhetorical intent can manage, for dead leaves are not "winged seeds" (7) and only indirectly quicken "new birth." What is the implication of "dead thoughts"? That issue is aggravated by the verse form of the next tercet, which troubles its simile with another subversive equation. Shelley's syntax aligns the potential for spiritual awakening with an "unextinguished hearth" and the poet's words with the "Ashes and sparks" that will rekindle consciousness. But his verbal sequence, abetted by the stanza form, brackets the tenor and the vehicle in line 67 in a way that suggests an equation: the poet's words are only "Ashes and sparks," half-opaque debris, half-incendiary. What events are borne in the prophecy? And how are we to coordinate those two similes with the symbolically potent language of the final question?

Furthermore, how far can one apply the seasonal succession to the dynamics of spiritual awakening "among mankind"? Is human nature wholly explicable as physical nature? Or is Shelley showing how, even at such heightened moments of apparent self-confidence, the poet's words may inscribe "mankind's" difference from the the natural forces he petitions? My patent pedagogy in the interrogative mode is designed to help students challenge the view that the poem's concluding question is equivalent to a statement; Shelley himself sensed some difference, for he decided not to close with the assertion, "When Winter comes Spring lags not far behind" (Wasserman, *Shelley* 251), but to rephrase the issue of succession in a way that turns rhetoricial questioning into genuine inquiry and plays that inquiry into the rhetoric of temporality.

As a way of offsetting the vexed terms of that conclusion, I turn to the end of another poem in the *Prometheus Unbound* volume of 1820, "The Cloud." From the playfully experimental perspective of a speaker who is the cloud itself, rather than a poet petitioning Nature for inspiration and energy, the dynamics of change are unequivocally harmonious, and the voice contains no pressure of dire necessity or entreaty. The last lines, instead, seem gleefully matter-of-fact:

> I change, but I cannot die—
> For after the rain, when with never a stain
>   The pavilion of Heaven is bare,
> And the winds and sunbeams, with their convex gleams,
>   Build up the blue dome of Air—
> I silently laugh at my own cenotaph,
>   And out of the caverns of rain,
> Like a child from the womb, like a ghost from the tomb,
>   I arise, and unbuild it again.—   (76–84)

Unlike "Ode to the West Wind," "The Cloud" presents no death that needs to be trumpeted awake. Imagining change from the perspective of perpetual transformation, Shelley indulges a tone and an imagery that are everywhere playful, not at all fraught with the urgency of death and prophecy that drives the ode. Even the cenotaph, a sign of mortal ending, becomes for the cloud a word to be rhymed with *laugh* and a metaphor to be subverted in a witty play of simultaneities: whereas the "Ode" bases its optimism, qualified as it is, on sequence, the two penultimate similes in "The Cloud" are concurrent, equivalent, and share the same energy; the resurrection of the "I" is achieved by an act of unbuilding, and the whole process is governed by the never-ending cycle of repetition implied by the last word of the poem, *again*. Indeed, the terminal punctuation, a dash (which appears in some manuscripts and is authorized by the Reiman and Powers edition), has the effect of inscribing an expansive ending, a sign of closure that writes a line of connection to the resurrected cloud that speaks the first lines of the poem.

If little is ambiguous or troubling about the vision of happy change chanted by the cloud, that voice of Nature sharply contrasts with what obtains in Shelley's "Ode to the West Wind," where the wind does not reply to the poet's exhortation, and with what obtains in "Mont Blanc," where the mountain does not speak and where the poet cannot escape the grip of that silence. Indeed, the ambiguous poetics of interrogative closure in the "Ode" are forecast by the conclusion of "Mont Blanc":

> 　　　　　　　　The secret strength of things
> Which governs thought, and to the infinite dome
> Of heaven is as a law, inhabits thee!
> And what were thou, and earth, and stars, and sea,
> If to the human mind's imaginings
> Silence and solitude were vacancy? (139–44)

Students need to weigh both parts of the conclusion, the exclamation and the question, and the relation between them; students also need to articulate a provisional distinction between what Shelley may be suggesting by "Silence and solitude" on the one hand and "vacancy" on the other. A consideration of the rhetoric of direct address may help, for the interpretation of "Silence and solitude" seems to imply a resistant presence and a latent potential for responsiveness (here held in abeyance), whereas the alternative, "vacancy," seems to relinquish the mountain to remoteness and nonreferential otherness.

One can challenge that distinction, but it helps first to consider the relation between the exclamation and the question. If the exclamation advances the argument that mind and Nature alike are governed by "the power" named at the beginning of this stanza—"Mont Blanc yet gleams on high:—the power is there, / The still and solemn power of many sights" (127–28)—the question suggests that it is only by virtue of the "the human mind's imaginings" (143) that blankness, silence, and solitude may be repealed from the condition of mere vacancy, for such imaginings are themselves a power that reads and interprets signs of "secret strength" (139). We can ask students to consider whether the two halves of the conclusion are, therefore, cooperating statements or competing claims. The *And* (142), which seamlessly joins the exclamation to the question, and the couplet rhyme of *thee* with *sea* (141–42), which imposes a formal binding on the two sentences, suggest the logic of the former; but the imperfect rhyming of *vacancy* with the preceding *thee* . . . *sea* couplet disrupts continuity (see Keach 200), and the situations conveyed—"inhabits thee" (141), "were vacancy" (144)—are sufficiently opposed to form a crux of competing priorities: would power exist without a mind to think it does and to say so? If one wants to shift the emphasis slightly, one can press at the word *imaginings* (143), which suggests something less emphatic than, say, *imagination* or *understanding*.

More advanced students can assess the competing and emphatically different arguments of Bloom (*Mythmaking* 34–35), Wasserman (*Shelley* 238), and Ferguson (203, 211–12) on what exactly is being proposed in the poem's summary question and what sort of conclusion is being drawn. Students can also be challenged to apply de Man's rhetoric of temporality: Does the blank mountain tease the mind with significance only to reveal the irony of such projects? Or do the 144 lines it takes to get to the question suggest an unwillingness to relinquish material nature to mere blankness and opacity? Here one may query the issue of vacancy itself: Is the notion strictly opposed to what is implied by the attributes of "Silence and solitude" (144)? Or is it an ironic restatement, inscribing a subtext of potential inhabitation? Students who wrestle with those questions without achieving interpretive closure discover just how potently Shelley's poetry transmits his speaker's struggle with a sensation of power that remains teasingly unlocatable.

Teaching and Un-teaching Shelley's Texts: Textual Criticism in the Classroom

Neil Fraistat

In a way that scarcely would have surprised the author of *A Defence of Poetry*, Shelley has come to exist in, through, and even as his texts. Yet, as Stuart Curran has commented, "The embarrassing state of the Shelley texts, after so many years and so many editors, is legion" ("Review" 214). However embarrassing, the vexed state of the texts themselves and the nearly bewildering array of questionable practices and cultural pressures that have affected their transmission are seldom commented on in the classroom by those of us who teach Shelley's poetry, and they are even more rarely developed as subjects capable of rewarding sustained attention. By and large then, we remain silent about the extent to which the Shelley that students encounter is a function of the textual representation of his work.

Most of us, as Jerome J. McGann has observed, tend to view textual criticism as a precondition to, rather than as a necessary part of, the critical act ("Monks" 182). Nor is it likely that the roles of textual and literary critics will become productively integrated until textual criticism ceases to be understood solely as the construction of scholarly editions and is seen, instead, in the more expansive terms argued for by McGann and others, as a "special method that students of literature must and should use when they examine, interpret, and reproduce the works we inherit from the past" ("Monks" 187). Certainly, in presenting the palimpsestlike development of some of Wordsworth's most crucial works, the Cornell Wordsworth series has done an admirable job of suggesting the importance of textual criticism for hermeneutics and has provided, in the process, a valuable tool for teaching students the interrelations of those functions.

With the recent initiation of the Bodleian Shelley Manuscripts series, edited to date by Dawson, Massey, Murray, Reiman, and Tokoo; the ongoing publication of the other Shelley manuscripts in *Shelley and His Circle*, edited by Cameron and Reiman; and the publication of the Manuscripts of the Younger Romantics series, edited by Reiman, teachers of Shelley's works have been gaining the means to increase their students' engagement in what textual criticism has to offer to the interpretation of Shelley's poetry. (In addition to those resources, students of Shelley's manuscripts can turn with caution to Forman, *Note Books*, and to Woodberry, *Notebook*.) In view of the instability that characterizes Shelley's texts, some engagement at the level of a text's formation and an awareness of how history has handed it down to us is valuable, perhaps crucial, to an informed critical reading and to the teaching of Shelley's works. In what follows, I suggest several forms that the engagement may take in the classroom.

In my experience, not only are students easily engaged in learning about the various social pressures and market relations that conditioned the composition and the production of Shelley's texts, but they can also become surprisingly interested in matters concerning the reproduction of the texts. (For a cogent overview, see the relevant essays in Reiman, *Romantic Texts*.) My students, for example, are usually shocked to learn that there is as yet no reliable collected edition of Shelley's poetry or prose and that the twenty-two Shelley notebooks in the Bodleian Library, the largest repository of Shelley holdings in the world, have never been systematically indexed or studied bibliographically, so that after more than 150 years and several major editions, even the size and the shape of Shelley's canon has yet to be firmly established. Those facts, in turn, lead us to discuss the implications of reading the poetry in a selected edition that has no textual apparatus and to consider in what ways critical arguments based solely on a close reading of such a text may be open to question.

Asking students to perform a few sample collations further drives the point home and can usefully raise some other points. Although any number of Shelley's works may serve a similar purpose, I usually ask students to collate the fourteen lines concluding act 3 of *Prometheus Unbound* as presented in the fair copy manuscript, the first edition, and the Hutchinson, Ingpen and Peck, and Reiman and Powers editions. (Readings from the fair copy and the first edition of *Prometheus Unbound* can be reconstructed from Zillman, *Variorum*.) The exercise not only engages us in a careful reading of a difficult and important passage but also provides me with an opportunity to demonstrate the crucial significance of Shelley's punctuation to the meaning of his poetry and the problematic way that his punctuation has been transmitted and represented by editors.

In discussing those issues, I also describe the dispute between editors such as William Michael Rossetti, Thomas Hutchinson, and Neville Rogers who, as self-proclaimed "polishers" of Shelley's texts, altered Shelley's grammar, punctuation, syntax, and even diction when they seemed deficient and editors such as Harry Buxton Forman and Donald Reiman who believe that Shelley punctuated along rhetorical, rather than grammatical, lines and that he took great pains to prepare his poems so that they could be copied to the letter by the press. (See Rogers, "Spelling," "Punctuation," and "Texts"; Reiman, *Romantic Texts*; and McGann, *Critique* 107–09.)

The collation of "To Constantia" as printed in the Hutchinson, Ingpen and Peck, and Chernaik editions can be a stunning lesson in textual differences. Beyond local variants among the editions, Chernaik's recuperation of Shelley's intended ordering of the poem's stanzas dramatically alters the poem's effects and meaning, as students invariably point out—often with indignation at the earlier editors. Classroom discussion of student collations and the relative instability of Shelley's texts, moreover, provides an opportunity to address such important theoretical issues as the authority of an author, the role that an author's intentions could and should play in the establishment of a text, and—as Stanley Fish might phrase it—just where the text is located.

Students are quick to understand the difficulties of providing reliable texts for many of the poems—particularly those posthumously published and those, such as *Prometheus Unbound*, with whose printing Shelley was dissatisfied—after some acquaintance with Shelley's manuscripts in all their notorious inscrutability. The often indecipherable handwriting scrawled in two or three sometimes crisscrossing directions on the same page, the scattering of drafts for the same poem throughout the pages of a notebook and among notebooks, the difficulty in discriminating between the hands of Percy and Mary Shelley—all those problems are evident in the photographic reproductions presented and discussed in the volumes of the Bodleian Shelley Manuscripts and the Manuscripts of the Younger Romantics series. But the volumes in those series can also be put to other, more significant pedagogical uses.

In Shelley's notebooks, drafts and fair copies of various works intersect with each other and with other matters from the daily lives of Percy and Mary Shelley to form a rich and largely still untapped record of his mind's encounter with the material conditions of its existence, thus anchoring the life and the work firmly in the ground of history. (With the exception of Cameron and Reiman's valuable *Shelley and His Circle*, the most comprehensive critical study of Shelley's manuscripts remains Rogers's *Shelley at Work*.) Moreover, the notebooks highlight connections among Shelley's works that may otherwise go unnoticed by readers looking at the texts only as poems published in a scholarly edition, and hence the notebooks suggest new ways to structure students' reading. An entire course on Shelley can be constructed, for example, on the intertextual network of poetry and prose involving *Prometheus Unbound* as those relations are disclosed by the notebooks. For those wishing to trace the interrelations, the most reliable guide to the contents of Shelley's notebooks at the Bodleian is Tokoo's "Index," which can be supplemented for the poetry by Locock's *Examination* and for the prose by Koszul's book *Shelley's Prose*.

Classroom attention to the genesis and the evolution of a particular work from early draft to fair copy to press copy (in the few press copies extant) can also be directed to Shelley's initial personal and ideological investments as they interact, first with the pressures of poetic form and rhetorical strategy and then with the exigencies of the publishing process. For example, Donald Reiman's edition of the intermediate fair-copy holograph of "The Mask of Anarchy," Mary Shelley's transcription for the press, and the proofs of Leigh Hunt's first edition can be used in the classroom in a discussion of the stages through which Shelley's manuscripts passed as they were prepared for the press, the collaborative role Mary Shelley played in the process, and the various ways in which Shelley was powerless to have his poems printed when and how he wished them to appear. Certainly, an important point to make in the classroom is the way in which "The Mask" is an occasional poem that is sundered from its own immediate occasion and published only in the changed political climate of 1832 after substantive alterations by both Mary Shelley and Leigh Hunt.

Furthermore, Shelley's notebooks make it clear that his poems often evolve through a complex series of displacements. As Timothy Webb has observed in "The Avalanche of Ages," Shelley's public poems frequently have their genesis in private experiences or desires that are subsequently effaced from the surface of the text through revision. A study of the genesis and the development of such poems as "Ode to the West Wind," *Julian and Maddalo*, *Prometheus Unbound*, *Adonais*, and *Epipsychidion* may raise questions from students about whether the ideological content and the social concerns of Shelley's poems are primarily a reflex of his own unfulfilled, even escapist, private desires; evidence of false consciousness, bad faith, or even personal reticence (of which Shelley had plenty); or the result of rhetorical purposiveness and poetic form.

Whatever answers we come to, it can be demonstrated from a study of the notebooks that for Shelley the personal and social realms are so deeply inscribed within each other that there is no neat way to keep them separate, even when editors of his work have, in effect, attempted to do so. "Invocation to Misery," for example, a seemingly private lyric written sometime between fall 1818 and fall 1819, while tensions were high in the Shelley household, appears in one of the Bodleian fair-copy books for *Prometheus Unbound*. The draft of the "Invocation," which Shelley never completed, begins with Shelley's personal unhappiness but, as Joseph Raben has pointed out ("Invocation"), moves on to explore the repressive political conditions of England in a section that has never been transmitted by editors of the text.

The depoliticized, ethereal Shelley is thus, as I take some pains to point out in the classroom, partly a creation of Shelley's editors, who were responding to a complex set of social relations, foremost among which ranks, first, a middle-class readership to whom they wanted to present an acceptable Shelley; second, the reputation and the livelihood of the surviving members of the Shelley circle, who required protection; and, third, the continued threat of prosecution for publication of some of Shelley's most radical statements. Indeed, a study of the textual fates of such works as *Queen Mab*, *Laon and Cythna*, "The Mask of Anarchy," *Peter Bell the Third*, and the notorious lyric frequently mistitled "The Indian Serenade" proves rewarding not only because many of Shelley's poems (some of which were published posthumously) were subject to various forms of censorship, suppression, and dismemberment by Mary Shelley and others, including biographers Medwin and Hogg, but also because the act of selecting and arranging the Shelley canon helped to produce and was itself a product of contemporary conceptions of Shelley (a statement no less true of our own contemporary editions).

Regardless of whether it is taught as a course in itself or as a component of a course and whether it is taught to introductory or advanced students, the teaching of Shelley at the level of textual formation has much to offer. At the least, in asking our students to consider such issues as the production, the reproduction, and the transmission of Shelley's texts, we help free them from what Michael J. Warren has characterized as the daunting "degree of finality if not definitiveness" that scholarly editions "arrogate to themselves by their mere being" (27). The cost of such freedom may be the loss of textual innocence. But the fall into textual criticism is fortunate for those literary critics and their students who consequently seek to wrest from history an expansive understanding of what they are reading when they read Shelley.

A Feminist Approach to
Teaching Shelley

Barbara Charlesworth Gelpi

In 1792, the year that Percy Bysshe Shelley was born, a surprising fashion caused much comment in the press: the sixth-month pad, a garment designed to make its wearer, whatever her age or marital status, appear to be pregnant (Werkmeister 328–30). More common knowledge but something often surprising to students is fashion's emphasis throughout the Romantic period on women's breasts, their visibility and accessibility. While historians differ on how much the conduct books' strong encouragement of maternal breast-feeding affected women's practice, there seems to be no question that women's clothing reflected an almost obsessional interest within the culture about the significance of maternal care. I suggest in advanced classes that students read eighteenth-century and early-nineteenth-century conduct books (such as those by Cadogan, Nelson, Pennington, and Wollstonecraft), noting the sexualization of maternity on the one hand and, on the other, the suggestion that a mother's care for her children is providential in its consistency, power, beneficence, and scope (see M. C. Massey).

Biographers differ strongly on the nature of Shelley's relationship with his mother (N. I. White, *Shelley* 1: 14; Cameron, *Young Shelley* 4–5; Holmes, *Pursuit* 11), and, without more definitive knowledge, a strictly biographical approach to that question is not possible. My point is that the cultural significance of mothering has an effect on Shelley's work, whether his own experience of being mothered was positive or negative.

Over the past several years a number of feminist critics working in Romanticism have found psychoanalytic theory about the mother-infant bond to be useful for analyzing the work of both generations of Romantics (Durham; Homans; Mellor, *Romanticism*; Schapiro), but Wordsworth, Coleridge, and Mary Shelley are the writers who have received the most attention in that regard. Indeed, little feminist work has been done on Percy Bysshe Shelley. The work of a poet who complicated, endangered, and—to a real if immeasurable degree—destroyed the lives of many women can reasonably seem a disheartening topic, too obvious an example of the nature of sexism to engage extensive feminist thinking. So that students can understand the nature of the problem, they need to be given the biographical background, with information coming from biographers of Harriet and Mary Shelley, as well as of Percy (Boas; Mellor, *Mary*; Holmes, *Pursuit*).

Some form of mother identification may lie behind Shelley's disastrous relationships with women; his repeated urge is to adopt young women who seem emotionally needy, but, having done so, he becomes the one demanding total understanding and care. He switches, in other words, between mother and infant, still caught up in that dyadic relationship. Relevant here is Holmes's statement that the feelings between Shelley and his mother were "exceptionally close and warm" until Shelley went to school but that after that he felt rejected by her (11). In that connection students will find it useful to analyze the language of Shelley's prose fragment "On Love" (473–74).

A link between Shelley's relations with women and his theoretical position is the fact that Shelley considered himself a feminist. While I (pace Brown) decidedly do not consider Shelley a feminist, I agree that Shelley's own understanding of a feminist position—especially that of Mary Wollstonecraft, whose work he passionately admired—casts light on a connection between free love and women's liberation that is still unresolved in today's feminist movement. Advanced students may be interested in looking at James Lawrence's *Empire of the Nairs* and Shelley's reaction to that book (F. L. Jones 1: 322–25), along with Godwin's strictures against institutional marriage (2: 848–52), as a way of understanding Shelley's reading of Wollstonecraft and as an exemplum of what a sexual revolution actually accomplishes when a system of male dominance remains in place.

The prose fragment "On Life" is even more important than "On Love" for the insight it gives into central aspects of Shelley's thinking. A consensus within Shelley scholarship holds that Pulos was right in the emphasis he gave to Shelley's endorsement of the intellectual system, with particular mention of its exposition in William Drummond's *Academical Questions* (Pulos 24–41). Pulos concentrates on the eclecticism made possible by Shelley's skeptical thinking; while in agreement with Pulos, I nonetheless give more attention than he does to Shelley's thoughts about the inadequacy of the intellectual system and to his strategy for overcoming that failing.

That philosophy, encapsulated in the phrase "Nothing exists but as it is perceived," destroys error, but "it leaves, what it is often the duty of the reformer in political and ethical questions to leave, a vacancy" (477). Shelley may arguably be admitting that one must simply live with that vacancy, but his next paragraph pushes into new territory by speculating on the nature of perception itself. Significantly, the mode of perception that most catches his interest is the oceanic one that Freud in *Civilization and Its Discontents* (12–16) links to the infant's identification with the mother. Recalling "our sensations as children," Shelley adds, "We less habitually distinguished all that we saw and felt from ourselves. They seemed as it were to constitute one mass" (477). Yet while the faculty for identification serves, like Keats's "negative capability," as an answer to the solipsism threatened by the Humean intellectual philosophy, it opens up a terrifying split within subjectivity itself: "The words *I*, and *you* and *they* are grammatical devices invented simply for arrangement and totally devoid of the intense and exclusive sense usually attached to them" (478).

Shelley at that point draws back from "the dark abyss—of how little we know" (478) and does not verbalize a connection between the abyss and "our sensations as children" (477). Still, the mythic preoccupations reflected in the imagery and the incidents of many of his poems—among them *Alastor*, *Prometheus Unbound*, *Julian and Maddalo*, *Epipsychidion*, *Adonais*, and "The Triumph of Life"—suggest that for Shelley the pivotal mystery in the nature of subjectivity resides in the bond between mother and infant. Since Shelley subscribes without question to his culture's equation of the human norm with the male subject, his intellectual focus and his emotional identification are with the son-lovers of the Great Mother—figures such as Attis, Osiris, and Adonis.

Shelley's wide and diverse reading makes it a daunting task to trace his sources in Western, Middle Eastern, and Eastern mythological texts and in their scholarly exegeses. Stuart Curran's achievement in *Shelley's Annus Mirabilis* in bringing an extraordinary number of those sources together while considering the works that Shelley wrote in 1819 helps considerably, since the materials Curran brings forward, including illustrations, are also relevant to Shelley's earlier and later works.

Shelley's poetry manifests great ambivalence toward the idea of maternal power, often leaning to the negative side of that double-mindedness. It thereby offers another example in support of Dorothy Dinnerstein's analysis of the fear of the feminine—fear of it as an abyss threatening one's subjectivity—that assails both women and men when women serve as all infants' primary caretakers. But if some of Shelley's works express a culturally shared terror of the maternal feminine, they do so with an unusual urgency and violence and from a specifically masculine point of view.

The first woman critic to notice Shelley's peculiarly obsessive desire to get at and possess the secret of an abhorrent yet fascinating feminine power was, of course, Mary Godwin Shelley, who alluded to it in her characterization of Frankenstein (Woodman, "Urania" 64–5; Mellor, *Mary*). Passages in *Frankenstein* virtually dovetail with lines in "Hymn to Intellectual Beauty" and *Alastor* and in Shelley's early Gothic fictions, such as *St. Irvyne* and *The Wandering Jew*. The violence in those two works gives emphasis to feminism's argument that men's fear of women stems from irrational sources (see Lederer) and from guilt about a dominance they refuse nonetheless to relinquish. For its vivid exemplifications of such attitudes, I think Shelley's writings illuminating. However, he is one among so many others that I would not give his work particular significance from a feminist perspective for that reason alone. Much more important and interesting is the way in which Shelley's theories about language and its uses turn on his fascination with the mother imago.

A consideration of the mother's relation to the acquisition of subjectivity and language should, in advanced classes, take into account Julia Kristeva's revision of Lacanian theory. Kristeva's prose makes difficult reading, but scholarly discussions and explications of it (for example, Homans 6–10; K. Silverman 132–93) are making it more accessible, and Kristeva's own recent work helps clarify her central ideas (*Tales of Love* 33–34). Kristeva, adopting a developmental hypothesis common to psychoanalysis and object relations theory, posits a period that she calls "the semiotic," in which the infant has no sense of differentiation from the mother and, as a result, no language but is infused with the rhythms and the sounds of language, which are intimately associated with body rhythms and sensations. Entrance into the symbolic ordering of language requires separation from the mother and acquiescence in the judgment that she belongs to the father.

Because Kristeva, like Lacan, believes that language and consciousness are produced by the intervention of a masculine "third term," she places it in the male camp. Still, she believes that the infiltrating presence of the maternal semiotic is necessary to the existence of a Poetic language. According to Kristevan theory, the mother-infant relationship is the breath or the impulse behind the poet's words, and the writing of poetry involves a reexperiencing of it (which Kristeva describes in terms of incest, *Desire* 136) but only as a past dead relationship that cannot in actuality be reexperienced without regression into the abyss of nonsubjectivity. How pertinent that theory is to Shelley poems in which the speaker waits on an inspirational breath from a feminine presence is obvious. Equally central in Shelley's thought is the desolating recognition that the poet's attempt, with the aid of the breath, to re-create imaginatively a once-experienced unity is impossible: "The mind in creation is as a fading coal . . ." (503–04). (See also Hughes, "Potentiality" 107–08.)

Shelley's cultural preconceptions about the nature of the feminine and his acculturated experiences of the feminine were similar to Freud's. In consequence, like Freud and Freudian theorists, Shelley often seems to place women outside a language that celebrates them only as absent—celebrates their absence, indeed, since their presence would threaten engulfment (Homans 10). But one must always remember (I speak here, first of all, to myself) that Shelley never read Freud. Were Shelley alive now, he might find Daniel Stern's developmental theory about the infant's acquisition of language within a relationship to a primary caretaker at least equally compelling. Certainly, that theory has striking relevance to Shelley's poetic practice, particularly his extraordinarily frequent use of synesthesia. (See Stern 288, O'Malley 3–34, Marks 236–42.)

From the observed behavior of infants and mothers, Stern concludes that a crucial stage in language development occurs because the mother through "attunement" recasts the infant's responses into another sensory modality (161). In the process the infant learns about both the substitutive nature of symbols, such as words, and the concept of symbols shared through the common meaning assigned to them. Stern's work may offer a more positive concept of the mother's relation to language than Freudian theory does. Stern describes the infant's acquisition of language without ever using the terms *penis* or *phallus*. In his analysis the mother-infant relationship inheres in words as the mother's or primary caretaker's gift. To my mind that more positive sense of the mother's relation to language can also be found in Shelley's work, perhaps most strikingly in *Prometheus Unbound*.

To give one brief example: How, as a feminist critic, would I discuss *Adonais* with a class? I would begin by noting the centrality and the omnipresence of the Venus and Adonis myth within the poem (see Hungerford 216–39; C. Baker, *Major Poetry* 239–54; O'Malley 113; Woodman, "Urania" 61; Knerr 129–30) and point out the emphasis Shelley gives to Urania's maternal and sexual relationship with Adonais (Woodman 63). Next must be laid out the tripartite function in the poem of this Urania/Venus (1) as a creative and unifying spirit of love manifesting itself throughout the universe, (2) as Nature, and (3) as planet. O'Malley sketches in some of those interrelations under the rubric of "the Venus complex" (27–33). Within the body of the poem I would note the ancient Middle Eastern connection between the Venus-Adonis theme and the central themes of the pastoral (*Mythology of All Races* 5: 24; Halperin 112) and discuss the function and the effect of Shelley's use of synesthesia. Finally, I would note the way in which the poem's ending recapitulates that moment in culture (deduced, rather than documented, to be sure) in which a male pantheon of gods wrest power from the mother goddess.

In Woodman's interpretation, Urania, whom he defines as purely an earth goddess (63), has disappeared altogether from the end of the poem. I agree about her disappearance but on totally different terms. In stanzas 42 and 43 Adonais has been "made one with Nature" (line 370) and with "the loveliness / Which once he made more lovely" (379–80), but in stanza 46 he is invited to ascend to the kingship of Venus, which, as a planet, is described as a "blind" and "silent" "kingless sphere" (411–13); the son-lover is now also the master of the goddess.

Shelley's perspective is not feminist. He envisions a world in which male poet-legislators overturn the existing tyranny of the father, replacing it with the (presumably beneficent) rule of the son (Nye 685). Women's situation does not change. Still, implicit in his poetic practice can be found revelatory ideas about a feminine presence in the mother tongue that is transmitted as a part of the process of infant care.

CONTRIBUTORS TO THE VOLUME AND SURVEY PARTICIPANTS

The following scholars and teachers contributed essays or participated in the survey of approaches to teaching Shelley's poetry that preceded preparation of this book or both. Their assistance made the volume possible.

Jonathan Arac, Duke University; Stephen C. Behrendt, University of Nebraska, Lincoln; Betty T. Bennett, American University; Kim Blank, University of Victoria; George Bornstein, University of Michigan, Ann Arbor; Claude Brew, Gustavus Adolphus College; Nathaniel Brown, Mary Washington College; William Crisman, Pennsylvania State University, Altoona; Stuart Curran, University of Pennsylvania; Dennis Dean, University of Wisconsin, Parkside; Roland Duerkson, Miami University, Ohio; Helen Ellis, University of Waterloo; David Erdman, State University of New York, Stony Brook; William Evans, Kean College; Neil Fraistat, University of Maryland, College Park; Adam J. Frisch, Briar Cliff College; Thomas R. Frosch, Queens College; Barbara Charlesworth Gelpi, Stanford University; Nancy Moore Goslee, University of Tennessee, Knoxville; Mildred Greene, Arizona State University; John Greenfield, McKendree College; J. H. Haeger, San Jose State University; Jean Hall, California State University, Fullerton; Spencer Hall, Rhode Island College; John A. Hodgson, University of Georgia; Diane Long Hoeveler, Marquette University; Jerrold E. Hogle, University of Arizona; Brooke Hopkins, University of Utah; Eileen Johnston, US Naval Academy; Kenneth Johnston, Indiana University, Bloomington; William Keach, Brown University; Theresa Kelley, University of Texas, San Antonio; J. Douglas Kneale, University of Western Ontario; Beth Lau, Ripon College; David Leigh, Seattle University; Seraphia D. Leyda, University of New Orleans; Fleming McClelland, Northeast Louisiana University; Jerome McGann, University of Virginia; Paul Magnuson, New York University; John L. Mahoney, Boston College; Ralph Manogue, Middlesex County College; Gyde Christine Martin, Texas Christian University; Irving Massey, State University of New York, Buffalo; Anne Mellor, University of California, Los Angeles; Judith W. Page, Millsaps College; David Perkins, Harvard University; Stuart Peterfreund, Northeastern University; Vincent F. Petronella, University of Massachusetts, Boston; Mary A. Quinn, University of San Diego; Tilottama Rajan, University of Wisconsin, Madison; Donald H. Reiman, Carl H. Pforzheimer Library; Jeffrey C. Robinson, University of Colorado, Boulder; Charles Rzepka, Boston University; Morris Schappes, New York, New York; Beverly Schneller, Marist College; Bryan Shelley, Oxford University; Frederick Shilstone, Clemson University; Stuart Sperry, Indiana University, Bloomington; Eugene Stelzig, State University of New York, Geneseo; Patrick Story, George Mason University;

Lou Thompson, New Mexico Tech; Leonard Trawick, Cleveland State University; George Van Devender, Hardin-Simmons University; K. D. Verma, University of Pittsburgh, Johnstown; Leon Waldoff, University of Illinois, Urbana; Constance Walker, Carleton College; Aileen Ward, New York University; Susan J. Wolfson, Rutgers University, New Brunswick; Ross Woodman, University of Western Ontario; Art Young, Clemson University.

WORKS CITED

Books and Articles

Abbey, Lloyd. *Destroyer and Preserver: Shelley's Poetic Skepticism*. Lincoln: U of Nebraska P, 1979.

Abrams, M. H. *The Correspondent Breeze: Essays on English Romanticism*. New York: Norton, 1984.

———, ed. *English Romantic Poets: Modern Essays in Criticism*. 2nd ed. New York: Oxford UP, 1975.

———. *The Mirror and the Lamp: Romantic Theory and the Critical Tradition*. 1953. New York: Norton, 1958.

———. *Natural Supernaturalism: Tradition and Revolution in Romantic Literature*. New York: Norton, 1971.

———, gen. ed. *The Norton Anthology of English Literature*. 5th ed. 2 vols. New York: Norton, 1986.

———. "Structure and Style in the Greater Romantic Lyric." 1965. Bloom, *Romanticism* 201–29.

Adams, Hazard, ed. *Critical Theory since Plato*. New York: Harcourt, 1971.

Aers, David, Jonathan Cook, and David Punter. *Romanticism and Ideology: Studies in English Writing 1765–1830*. London: Routledge, 1981.

Albright, Daniel. *Lyricality in English Literature*. Lincoln: U of Nebraska P, 1985.

Allott, Miriam, ed. *Essays on Shelley*. Totowa: Barnes, 1982.

Allsup, James. *The Magic Circle: A Study of Shelley's Concept of Love*. Port Washington: Kennikat, 1976.

Anderson, Erland. *Harmonious Madness: A Study of Musical Metaphors in the Poetry of Coleridge, Shelley, and Keats*. Wolfeboro: Longwood, 1975.

Applewhite, James. *Seas and Inland Journeys: Landscape and Consciousness from Wordsworth to Roethke*. Athens: U of Georgia P, 1986.

Baker, Carlos. *The Echoing Green: Romanticism, Modernism, and the Phenomena of Transference in Poetry*. Princeton: Princeton UP, 1984.

———, ed. *The Selected Poetry and Prose of Percy Bysshe Shelley*. New York: Random, 1951.

———. *Shelley's Major Poetry: The Fabric of a Vision*. Princeton: Princeton UP, 1948.

Baker, Joseph E. *Shelley's Platonic Answer to a Platonic Attack on Poetry*. Iowa City: U of Iowa P, 1965.

Ball, Patricia. *The Central Self: A Study in Romantic and Victorian Imagination*. London: Athlone, 1968.

Barcus, James E., ed. *Shelley: The Critical Heritage*. London: Routledge, 1975.

Barnard, Ellsworth. *Shelley's Religion*. Minneapolis: U of Minnesota P, 1937.

Barrell, Joseph. *Shelley and the Thought of His Time: A Study in the History of Ideas*. 1947. Hamden: Archon, 1967.

Bate, Jonathan. *Shakespeare and the English Romantic Imagination*. Oxford: Clarendon, 1986.

Bate, Walter Jackson. *The Burden of the Past and the English Poet*. Cambridge: Harvard UP, 1970.

Beaty, Frederick. *Light from Heaven: Love in British Romantic Literature*. DeKalb: Northern Illinois UP, 1971.

Behrendt, Stephen, ed. *Percy Bysshe Shelley:* Zastrozzi *and* St. Irvyne. London: Oxford UP, 1986.

Bennett, Betty T., ed. *The Letters of Mary Wollstonecraft Shelley*. 3 vols. Baltimore: Johns Hopkins UP, 1980–88.

Benziger, James. *Images of Eternity: Studies in the Poetry of Religious Vision from Wordsworth to T. S. Eliot*. Carbondale: Southern Illinois UP, 1962.

Blake, William. *The Complete Poetry and Prose of William Blake*. Ed. David Erdman. Commentary by Harold Bloom. Rev. ed. Garden City: Doubleday, 1982.

Blank, G. Kim. *Wordsworth's Influence on Shelley: A Study of Poetic Authority*. New York: St. Martin's, 1988.

Bloom, Harold. *The Anxiety of Influence: A Theory of Poetry*. New York: Oxford UP, 1973.

———, ed. *English Romantic Poets*. New York: Chelsea, 1986.

———. *A Map of Misreading*. New York: Oxford UP, 1975.

———, ed. *Percy Bysshe Shelley*. New York: Chelsea, 1985.

———. *Poetry and Repression: Revisionism from Blake to Stevens*. New Haven: Yale UP, 1976.

———. *The Ringers in the Tower: Studies in Romantic Tradition*. Chicago: U of Chicago P, 1971.

———, ed. *Romanticism and Consciousness: Essays in Criticism*. New York: Norton, 1970.

———, ed. *The Selected Poetry and Prose of Shelley*. 1966. New York: Meridian-NAL, 1978.

———. *Shelley's Mythmaking*. New Haven: Yale UP, 1959.

———. *The Visionary Company: A Reading of English Romantic Poetry*. Rev. ed. Ithaca: Cornell UP, 1971.

———. *Yeats*. New York: Oxford UP, 1970.

Bloom, Harold, and Lionel Trilling, eds. *Romantic Poetry and Prose*. Vol. 4 of *The Oxford Anthology of English Literature*. 6 vols. London: Oxford UP, 1973.

Bloom, Harold, et al., eds. *Deconstruction and Criticism*. New York: Seabury, 1979.

Boas, Louise (Schutz). *Harriet Shelley: Five Long Years*. London: Oxford UP, 1962.

Bornstein, George, ed. *Romantic and Modern: Revaluations of Literary Tradition.* Pittsburgh: U of Pittsburgh P, 1977.

———. *Transformations of Romanticism in Yeats, Eliot, and Stevens.* Chicago: U of Chicago P, 1976.

———. *Yeats and Shelley.* Chicago: U of Chicago P, 1970.

Bowra, C. M. *The Romantic Imagination.* 1949. New York: Oxford UP, 1961.

Brand, C. P. *Italy and the English Romantics: The Italianate Fashion in Early Nineteenth-Century England.* Cambridge: Cambridge UP, 1957.

Briggs, Asa. *The Age of Improvement, 1783–1867.* London: Longmans, 1959.

Brisman, Leslie. *Milton's Poetry of Choice and Its Romantic Heirs.* Ithaca: Cornell UP, 1973.

———. *Romantic Origins.* Ithaca: Cornell UP, 1978.

Brown, Nathaniel. *Sexuality and Feminism in Shelley.* Cambridge: Cambridge UP, 1979.

Bush, Douglas. *Mythology and the Romantic Tradition in English Poetry.* 1937. New York: Norton, 1969.

Butler, Marilyn. *Peacock Displayed: A Satirist in His Context.* Boston: Routledge, 1979.

———. *Romantics, Rebels and Reactionaries: English Literature and Its Background 1760–1830.* Oxford: Oxford UP, 1981.

Butter, Peter. *Shelley's Idols of the Cave.* 1954. New York: Haskell, 1969.

Buxton, John. *Byron and Shelley: The History of a Friendship.* New York: Harcourt, 1968.

———. *The Grecian Taste: Literature in the Age of Neo-Classicism, 1740–1820.* New York: Barnes, 1978.

Byron, George Gordon, Lord. *Byron's Letters and Journals.* Ed. Leslie A. Marchand. 12 vols. Cambridge: Harvard UP, 1973–82.

———. *Poetical Works.* Ed. Frederick Page. Corr. John Jump. New York: Oxford UP, 1970.

[Cadogan, William]. *An Essay upon Nursing and the Management of Children from Their Birth to Three Years of Age.* 3rd ed. London: J. Roberts, 1749.

Cameron, Kenneth Neill, ed. *The Esdaile Notebook.* London: Faber, 1964.

———, ed. *Percy Bysshe Shelley: Selected Poetry and Prose.* New York: Holt, 1951.

———. *Shelley: The Golden Years.* Cambridge: Harvard UP, 1974.

———. *The Young Shelley: Genesis of a Radical.* New York: Macmillan, 1950.

Cameron, Kenneth Neill, and Donald H. Reiman, eds. *Shelley and His Circle, 1773–1822.* 8 vols. to date. Cambridge: Harvard UP, 1961–.

Cantor, Paul. *Creature and Creator: Myth-Making and English Romanticism.* New York: Cambridge UP, 1984.

Chase, Cynthia. *Decomposing Figures: Rhetorical Readings in the Romantic Tradition.* Baltimore: Johns Hopkins UP, 1986.

Chernaik, Judith. *The Lyrics of Shelley.* Cleveland: Case Western Reserve UP, 1972.

Churchill, Kenneth. *Italy and English Literature, 1764–1930.* Totowa: Barnes, 1980.

Clark, David Lee, ed. *Shelley's Prose: Or, The Trumpet of a Prophecy.* Corr. ed. Albuquerque: U of New Mexico P, 1966.

Clubbe, John, and Ernest J. Lovell, Jr. *English Romanticism: The Grounds of Belief.* De Kalb: Northern Illinois UP, 1983.

Cooke, Michael. *Acts of Inclusion: Studies Bearing on an Elementary Theory of Romanticism.* New Haven: Yale UP, 1979.

———. *The Romantic Will.* New Haven: Yale UP, 1976.

Cookson, J. E. *Lord Liverpool's Administration, 1815–1822.* Hamden: Shoe String, 1975.

Crawley, C. W., ed. *War and Peace in an Age of Upheaval, 1793–1830.* New Cambridge Modern History 9. Cambridge: Cambridge UP, 1965.

Cronin, Richard. *Shelley's Poetic Thoughts.* New York: St. Martin's, 1981.

Crook, Nora, and Derek Guiton. *Shelley's Venomed Melody.* New York: Cambridge UP, 1986.

Culler, Jonathan. "Apostrophe." *Diacritics* 7 (1977): 59–69.

Curran, Stuart. "Percy Bysshe Shelley." F. Jordan. 593–663.

———. *Poetic Form and British Romanticism.* New York: Oxford UP, 1986.

———. Rev. of *The Manuscripts of the Younger Romantics. Shelley. Vols. 1–3. Keats-Shelley Journal* 36 (1987): 213–16.

———. *Shelley's Annus Mirabilis: The Maturing of an Epic Vision.* San Marino: Huntington, 1975.

———. *Shelley's* Cenci: *Scorpions Ringed with Fire.* Princeton: Princeton UP, 1970.

Davie, Donald. "Shelley's Urbanity." *Purity of Diction in English Verse.* London: Chatto, 1952. 133–59.

Davies, R. T., and B. G. Beatty, eds. *Literature of the Romantic Period, 1750–1850.* New York: Barnes, 1976.

Dawson, P. M. S., ed. *Bodleian MS Shelley e.4 (Including Drafts of "Ozymandias," "Prince Athanase," "Essay on Christianity," and Other Poetry, Prose, and Translations.)* New York: Garland, 1988.

———. *The Unacknowledged Legislator: Shelley and Politics.* Oxford: Clarendon, 1980.

de Man, Paul. *The Rhetoric of Romanticism.* New York: Columbia UP, 1984.

———. "The Rhetoric of Temporality." *Interpretation: Theory and Practice.* Ed. Charles S. Singleton. Baltimore: Johns Hopkins UP, 1969. 173–209.

Delisle, Fanny. *A Study of Shelley's* A Defence of Poetry: *A Textual and Critical Evaluation.* 2 vols. Salzburg: Universität Salzburg, 1974.

Dictionary of National Biography. Ed. Leslie Stephen and Sidney Lee. 63 vols. + supplements. 1885–1901. London: Oxford UP, 1937–39.

Dinnerstein, Dorothy. *The Mermaid and the Minotaur: Sexual Arrangements and Human Malaise.* New York: Harper, 1976.

Donohue, Joseph. *Dramatic Character in the English Romantic Age*. Princeton: Princeton UP, 1970.

Duerksen, Roland A. *Shelley: Political Writings*. New York: Appleton, 1970.

———. *Shelleyan Ideas in Victorian Literature*. The Hague: Mouton, 1966.

Duffy, Edward. *Rousseau in England: The Context for Shelley's Critique of the Enlightenment*. Berkeley: U of California P, 1979.

Dunbar, Clement, ed. *A Bibliography of Shelley Studies: 1823–1950*. New York: Garland, 1976.

———, ed. *Shelley Studies, 1950–1984: An Annotated Bibliography*. New York: Garland, 1986.

Durham, Margery. "The Mother Tongue: 'Christabel' and the Language of Love." *The (M)other Tongue: Essays in Feminist Psychoanalytic Interpretation*. Ed. Shirley Nelson Garner, Claire Kahane, and Madelon Sprengnether. Ithaca: Cornell UP, 1985. 169–93.

Eaves, Morris, and Michael Fischer, eds. *Romanticism and Contemporary Criticism*. Ithaca: Cornell UP, 1986.

Edwards, Thomas R. *Imagination and Power: A Study of Poetry on Public Themes*. New York: Oxford UP, 1971.

Eliot, T. S. *For Lancelot Andrewes: Essays on Style and Order*. Garden City: Doubleday, 1929.

———. *To Criticize the Critic: Eight Essays on Literature and Education*. New York: Farrar, 1965.

Ellis, F. S. *Lexical Concordance to the Poetical Works of Percy Bysshe Shelley*. 1892. New York: Franklin, 1968.

Ellis, Steve. *Dante and English Poetry: Shelley to T. S. Eliot*. Cambridge: Cambridge UP, 1983.

Encyclopaedia Britannica. 23 vols. + index. Chicago: Encyclopaedia Britannica, 1973.

Engell, James. *The Creative Imagination: Enlightenment to Romanticism*. Cambridge: Harvard UP, 1981.

Enscoe, Gerald. *Eros and the Romantics: Sexual Love as a Theme in Coleridge, Shelley, and Keats*. The Hague: Mouton, 1967.

Erdman, David, et al., eds. *The Romantic Movement: A Selective and Critical Bibliography*. New York: Garland, 1979–.

Evans, Bertand. *Gothic Drama from Walpole to Shelley*. Berkeley: U of California P, 1947.

Evans, G. Blakemore, et al., eds. *The Riverside Shakespeare*. Boston: Houghton, 1974.

Everest, Kelvin, ed. *Shelley Revalued: Essays from the Gregynog Conference*. Totowa: Barnes, 1983.

Ferguson, Frances. "Shelley's 'Mont Blanc': What the Mountain Said." Reed 202–14.

Fletcher, Richard M. *English Romantic Drama, 1795–1843: A Critical History.* New York: Exposition, 1966.

Foakes, R. A. *The Romantic Assertion: A Study in the Language of Nineteenth Century Poetry.* 1958. New York: Barnes, 1971.

Fogle, R. H. *The Imagery of Keats and Shelley: A Comparative Study.* Chapel Hill: U of North Carolina P, 1949.

———. *The Permanent Pleasure: Essays on Classics of Romanticism.* Athens: U of Georgia P, 1974.

Foot, Paul. *Red Shelley.* London: Sidgwick, 1980.

Ford, Boris. *From Blake to Byron.* 1957. Harmondsworth: Penguin, 1982.

Ford, Newell, ed. *The Poetical Works of Shelley.* 1901. Boston: Houghton, 1975.

Forman, Harry Buxton, ed. *Note Books of Percy Bysshe Shelley: From the Originals in the Library of W. K. Bixby.* 3 vols. Boston: Bibliophile, 1911.

———, ed. *The Poetical Works of Percy Bysshe Shelley.* 4 vols. London: Reeves, 1876.

———, ed. *The Poetical Works of Percy Bysshe Shelley.* Aldine Edition. 5 vols. London: George Bell, 1892.

Fraistat, Neill. *The Poem and the Book: Interpreting Collections of Romantic Poetry.* Chapel Hill: U of North Carolina P, 1985.

Franklin, Phyllis. "From the Editor." *MLA Newsletter* 19.3 (1987): 4–5.

Frazer, James George. *The New Golden Bough: A New Abridgement of the Classic Work.* Ed. Theodore H. Gaster. New York: Criterion, 1959.

Freud, Sigmund. *Civilization and Its Discontents.* Trans. James Strachey. New York: Norton, 1962.

———. *The Interpretation of Dreams.* Trans. James Strachey. New York: Avon, 1965.

Fry, Paul. *The Poet's Calling in the English Ode.* New Haven: Yale UP, 1980.

Frye, Northrop. *Anatomy of Criticism: Four Essays.* Princeton: Princeton UP, 1957.

———, ed. *Romanticism Reconsidered: Selected Papers from the English Institute.* New York: Columbia UP, 1963.

———. *A Study of English Romanticism.* New York: Random, 1968.

Furst, Lilian R. *Romanticism in Perspective: A Comparative Study of Aspects of the Romantic Movements in England, France, and Germany.* New York: St. Martin's, 1969.

Gaull, Marilyn. *English Romanticism: The Human Context.* New York: Norton, 1988.

Gerard, Albert. *English Romantic Poetry: Ethos, Structure, and Symbol in Coleridge, Wordsworth, Shelley, and Keats.* Berkeley: U of California P, 1968.

Gleckner, Robert, and Gerald Enscoe, eds. *Romanticism: Points of View.* 2nd ed. Detroit: Wayne State UP, 1970.

Godwin, William. *An Enquiry concerning Political Justice.* 2 vols. London: [1793].

Goslee, Nancy Moore. *"Uriel's Eye": Miltonic Stationing and Statuary in Blake, Keats, and Shelley.* Tuscaloosa: U of Alabama P, 1985.

Gottlieb, Erika. *Lost Angels of a Ruined Paradise: Themes of Cosmic Strife in Romantic Tragedy.* Victoria, BC: Sono, 1981.

Grabo, Carl. *The Magic Plant: The Growth of Shelley's Thought.* Chapel Hill: U of North Carolina P, 1936.

——. *The Meaning of "The Witch of Atlas."* Chapel Hill: U of North Carolina P, 1935.

——. *A Newton among Poets: Shelley's Use of Science in* Prometheus Unbound. Chapel Hill: U of North Carolina P, 1930.

——. Prometheus Unbound: *An Interpretation.* Chapel Hill: U of North Carolina P, 1935.

Gray, Thomas. *The Complete Poems of Thomas Gray.* Ed. H. W. Starr and J. R. Hendrickson. Oxford: Clarendon P, 1966.

Green, David Bonnell, and Edwin Graves Wilson, eds. *Keats, Shelley, Byron, Hunt, and Their Circles: A Bibliography: July 1, 1950–June 30, 1962.* Lincoln: U of Nebraska P, 1964.

Hall, Jean. *The Transforming Image: A Study of Shelley's Major Poetry.* Urbana: U of Illinois P, 1980.

Hall, Spencer. "Power and the Poet: Religious Mythmaking in Shelley's 'Hymn to Intellectual Beauty.'" *Keats-Shelley Journal* 32 (1983): 123–49.

Halperin, David. *Before Pastoral: Theocritus and the Ancient Tradition of Bucolic Poetry.* New Haven: Yale UP, 1983.

Halsted, John B., ed. *Romanticism: Definition, Explanation, and Evaluation.* Boston: Heath, 1965.

Harris, R. W. *Romanticism and the Social Order, 1780–1830.* London: Blandford, 1969.

Hartley, Robert A., ed. *Keats, Shelley, Bryon, Hunt, and Their Circles: A Bibliography: July 1, 1962–December 31, 1974.* Lincoln: U of Nebraska P, 1978.

Harvey, A. D. *Britain in the Early Nineteenth Century.* New York: St. Martin's, 1978.

——. *English Poetry in a Changing Society, 1780–1825.* New York: St. Martin's, 1980.

Hayden, John O., ed. *Romantic Bards and British Reviewers: A Selected Edition of the Contemporary Reviews of the Works of Wordsworth, Coleridge, Byron, Keats, and Shelley.* Lincoln: U of Nebraska P, 1971.

Heath, William, ed. *Major British Poets of the Romantic Period.* New York: Macmillan, 1973.

Hildebrand, William. *Shelley's Polar Paradise: A Reading of* Prometheus Unbound. Salzburg: Universität Salzburg, 1974.

——. *A Study of* Alastor. Kent: Kent State UP, 1954.

Hilles, Frederick, and Harold Bloom, eds. *From Sensibility to Romanticism.* New York: Oxford UP, 1965.

Hillman, James. *Archetypal Psychology.* Dallas: Spring, 1983.

——. *Suicide and the Soul.* New York: Harper, 1964.

Hoagwood, Terence. *Prophecy and the Philosophy of Mind: Traditions of Blake and Shelley.* Tuscaloosa: U of Alabama P, 1985.

———. *Skepticism and Ideology: Shelley's Political Prose and Its Philosophical Context from Bacon to Marx.* Iowa City: U of Iowa P, 1988.

Hobsbawm, E. J. *The Age of Revolution 1789–1848.* New York: NAL, 1964.

Hodgart, Patricia. *A Preface to Shelley.* London: Longman, 1985.

Hodgson, John A. *Coleridge, Shelley, and Transcendental Inquiry: Rhetoric, Argument, Metapsychology.* Lincoln: U of Nebraska P, 1989.

Hoffman, Harold. *An Odyssey of the Soul: Shelley's* Alastor. New York: Columbia UP, 1933.

Hogle, Jerrold E. "Shelley's Poetics: The Power as Metaphor." *Keats-Shelley Journal* 31 (1982): 159–97.

———. *Shelley's Process: Radical Transference and the Development of His Major Works.* New York: Oxford UP, 1988.

Holmes, Richard. *Footsteps: Adventures of a Romantic Biographer.* New York: Viking, 1985.

———. *Shelley: The Pursuit.* London: Weidenfeld, 1974.

Homans, Margaret. *Bearing the Word: Language and the Female Experience in Nineteenth-Century Women's Writing.* Chicago: Chicago UP, 1986.

Hughes, Daniel J. "Coherence and Collapse in Shelley, with Particular Reference to *Epipsychidion.*" *ELH* 28 (1961): 260–83.

———. "Kindling and Dwindling: The Poetic Process in Shelley." *Keats-Shelley Journal* 13 (1964): 13–28.

———. "Potentiality in *Prometheus Unbound.*" *Studies in Romanticism* 2 (1963): 107–26.

Hungerford, Edward B. *Shores of Darkness.* New York: Columbia UP, 1941.

Hutchinson, Thomas, ed. *The Complete Poetical Works of Percy Bysshe Shelley.* 1904. Reset as Oxford Standard Authors edition, 1905 and 1934. Corr. by G. M. Matthews. London: Oxford UP, 1970.

Ingpen, Roger, and Walter E. Peck, eds. *The Complete Works of Percy Bysshe Shelley.* 10 vols. 1926–30. Julian Edition. New York: Gordian, 1965.

Jack, Ian. *English Literature, 1815–1832.* Oxford History of English Literature. Oxford: Clarendon, 1963.

———. *The Poet and His Audience.* Cambridge: Cambridge UP, 1985.

Jackson, James Robert de J. *Poetry of the Romantic Period.* London: Routledge, 1980.

Jeffrey, Lloyd. *Shelley's Knowledge and Use of Natural History.* Salzburg Studies in English Literature. Salzburg: Universität Salzburg, 1976.

Johnson, Samuel. "The Life of Milton." *Lives of the English Poets.* Ed. G. Birkbeck Hill. 3 vols. New York: Octagon, 1967.

Jones, Frederick L., ed. *The Letters of Mary W. Shelley.* 2 vols. Norman: U of Oklahoma P, 1944.

————, ed. *The Letters of Percy Bysshe Shelley*. 2 vols. Oxford: Clarendon, 1964.

Jones, Howard Mumford. *Revolution and Romanticism*. Cambridge: Harvard UP, 1974.

Jordan, Frank, ed. *The English Romantic Poets: A Review of Research and Criticism*. 4th ed. New York: MLA, 1985.

Jordan, John E., ed. A Defence of Poetry *(Shelley)*, *"The Four Ages of Poetry" (Peacock)*. Indianapolis: Bobbs, 1965.

Keach, William. *Shelley's Style*. New York: Methuen, 1984.

Keats, John. *The Letters of John Keats*. 2 vols. Ed. Hyder E. Rollins. Cambridge: Harvard UP, 1958.

Keats, John, and Percy Bysshe Shelley. *The Complete Poems of Keats and Shelley*. New York: Random, 1931.

King-Hele, Desmond. *Shelley: His Thought and Work*. 3rd ed. Rutherford: Fairleigh-Dickinson UP, 1984.

Klapper, Roxana. *The German Literary Influence on Shelley*. Wolfeboro: Longwood, 1975.

Knerr, Anthony, ed. *Shelley's* Adonais: *A Critical Edition*. New York: Columbia UP, 1984.

Knight, G. Wilson. *The Starlit Dome: Studies in the Poetry of Vision*. 1941. London: Oxford UP, 1971.

Korshin, Paul. *Typologies in England, 1650–1820*. Princeton: Princeton UP, 1982.

Koszul, A. H., ed. *Shelley's Prose in the Bodleian Manuscripts*. London: Frowde, 1910.

Kramer, Lawrence. *Music and Poetry: The Nineteenth Century and After*. Berkeley: U of California P, 1985.

Kristeva, Julia. *Desire in Language: A Semiotic Approach to Literature and Art*. Ed. Leon S. Roudiez. New York: Columbia UP, 1980.

————. *Tales of Love*. New York: Columbia UP, 1987.

Kroeber, Karl, and William Walling, eds. *Images of Romanticism: Verbal and Visual Affinities*. New Haven: Yale UP, 1978.

Kubler-Ross, Elisabeth. *On Death and Dying*. New York: Macmillan, 1969.

Kumar, Shiv K., ed. *British Romantic Poets: Recent Revaluations*. New York: New York UP, 1966.

Langbaum, Robert. "Wordsworth: The Self as Process." *The Mysteries of Identity*. New York: Oxford UP, 1977.

Larrabee, Stephen. *English Bards and Grecian Marbles: The Relationship between Sculpture and Poetry, Especially in the Romantic Period*. New York: Columbia UP, 1943.

Lawrence, James Henry. *The Empire of the Nairs: Or, The Rights of Woman*. 2nd ed. London: 1811.

Lea, Frank A. *Shelley and the Romantic Revolution*. 1945. New York: Haskell, 1971.

Leavis, F. R. *Revaluation: Tradition and Development in English Poetry*. 1936. London: Chatto, 1962.

Lederer, Wolfgang. *The Fear of Women*. New York: Harcourt, 1968.

Lefevbre, Georges. *The French Revolution*. Trans. E. M. Evanson, J. H. Stewart, and J. Friguglietti. 2 vols. New York: Columbia UP, 1964.

———. *Napoleon*. Trans. H. F. Stockhold and J. E. Anderson. 2 vols. New York: Columbia UP, 1969.

Leighton, Angela. *Shelley and the Sublime: An Interpretation of the Major Poems*. New York: Cambridge UP, 1984.

Levinson, Marjorie. *The Romantic Fragment Poem: A Critique of a Form*. Chapel Hill: U of North Carolina P, 1986.

Litz, A. Walton. "Wallace Stevens' Defense of Poetry: *La poesie pure*, the New Romantic, and the Pressure of Reality." Bornstein, *Romantic and Modern* 111–32.

Locock, C. D., ed. *An Examination of the Shelley Manuscripts in the Bodleian Library*. Oxford: Clarendon, 1903.

McElderry, Bruce R., Jr., ed. *Shelley's Critical Prose*. Lincoln: U of Nebraska P, 1967.

McGann, Jerome J. *A Critique of Modern Textual Criticism*. Chicago: U of Chicago P, 1983.

———. "The Monks and the Giants: Textual and Bibliographical Studies and the Interpretation of Literary Works." McGann, *Textual Criticism* 180–99.

———. *The Romantic Ideology: A Critical Investigation*. Chicago: U of Chicago P, 1983.

———. ed. *Textual Criticism and Literary Interpretation*. Chicago: U of Chicago P. 1985.

Mack, Maynard, gen. ed. *The Norton Anthology of World Masterpieces*. 4th ed. 2 vols. New York: Norton, 1979.

McNiece, Gerald. *Shelley and the Revolutionary Idea*. Cambridge: Harvard UP, 1969.

Mahoney, John L., ed. *The English Romantics: Major Poetry and Critical Theory*. Lexington: Heath, 1978.

Marks, Lawrence E. *The Unity of the Senses: Interrelations among the Modalities*. New York: Academic, 1978.

Massey, Irving, ed. *Bodleian MS Shelley Adds. d.7. (Containing 131 Transcripts by Mary Shelley of Poems and Fragments by Percy Bysshe Shelley.)* New York: Garland, 1988.

Massey, Marilyn Chapin. *Feminine Soul: The Fate of an Ideal*. Boston: Beacon, 1985.

Matthews, G. M. "Shelley's Lyrics." Reiman and Powers 681–94.

———. "A Volcano's Voice in Shelley." *ELH* 24 (1957): 191–228.

Matthews, G. M., and Kelvin Everest, eds. *The Poems of Shelley*. 1 of 3 vols. to date. London: Longman, 1989–.

Mellor, Anne K. *English Romantic Irony*. Cambridge: Harvard UP, 1980.

————. *Mary Shelley: Her Life, Her Fiction, Her Monsters*. New York: Methuen, 1988.

————, ed. *Romanticism and Feminism*. Bloomington: Indiana UP, 1988.

Metzger, Lore. *One Foot in Eden: Modes of Pastoral in Romantic Poetry*. Chapel Hill: U of North Carolina P, 1986.

Miller, J. Hillis. *The Linguistic Moment: From Wordsworth to Stevens*. Princeton: Princeton UP, 1985.

Milton, John. *Complete Poems and Major Prose*. Ed. Meritt Y. Hughes. New York: Odyssey, 1957.

Mingay, G. E. *English Landed Society in the Eighteenth Century*. London: Routledge, 1963.

Murphy, John. *The Dark Angel: Gothic Elements in Shelley's Works*. Cranbury: Bucknell UP, 1975.

Murray, E. B., ed. *Bodleian MS Shelley d.l. (Including Drafts of* A Defence of Poetry, Epipsychidion, *and "Speculations on Morals and Metaphysics," Fair Copies of "Ode to Naples," and "The Witch of Atlas," and Other Poetry, Prose, and Translations, with Mary W. Shelley's Draft of "Matilda.")* New York: Garland, 1988.

Mythology of All Races: Semitic. Ed. Stephen Herbert. Boston: Marshall Jones, 1931.

Nelson, James. *An Essay upon the Government of Children*. 1756. New York: Garland, 1985.

Notopoulos, James. *The Platonism of Shelley: A Study of Platonism and the Poetic Mind*. Durham: Duke UP, 1949.

Noyes, Russell, ed. *English Romantic Poetry and Prose*. New York: Oxford UP, 1956.

Nye, Andrea. "Woman Clothed with the Sun: Julia Kristeva and the Escape from/ to Language." *Signs: Journal of Women in Culture and Society* 12 (1987): 664–86.

O'Malley, Glenn. *Shelley and Synaesthesia*. Evanston: Northwestern UP, 1964.

Onorato, Richard J. *The Character of the Poet: Wordsworth in* The Prelude. Princeton: Princeton UP, 1971.

Otten, Terry. *The Deserted Stage: The Search for Dramatic Form in Nineteenth-Century England*. Athens: Ohio UP, 1972.

Parker, Reeve. *Coleridge's Meditative Art*. Ithaca: Cornell UP, 1975.

Peacock, Thomas Love. *The Novels of Thomas Love Peacock*. Ed. David Garnett. 1948. Corr. ed. London: Hart-Davis, 1963.

————. *The Works of Thomas Love Peacock*. Ed. H. F. B. Brett-Smith and C. E. Jones. 10 vols. Halliford Edition. New York: Wells, 1924–34.

Pennington, Sarah. *A Mother's Advice. . . .* 1817. New York: Garland, 1986.

Perkins, David, ed. *English Romantic Writers*. New York: Harcourt, 1967.

————. *The Quest for Permanence: The Symbolism of Wordsworth, Shelley, and Keats*. Cambridge: Harvard UP, 1959.

Peterfreund, Stuart. "Wordsworth, Milton, and the End of Adam's Dream." *Milton and the Romantics* 3 (1977): 14–21.

Pottle, Frederick A. "The Role of Asia in the Dramatic Action of Shelley's *Prometheus Unbound*." Ridenour 133–43.

Prickett, Stephen, ed. *The Romantics*. New York: Holmes, 1981.

Princeton Encyclopedia of Poetry and Poetics. Ed. Alex Preminger, et al. Princeton: Princeton UP, 1974.

Pulos, C. E. *The Deep Truth: A Study of Shelley's Scepticism*. Lincoln: U of Nebraska P, 1954.

Purkis, John. *The World of the English Romantic Poets*. London: Heinemann, 1982.

Quennell, Peter. *Romantic England: Writing and Painting, 1717–1851*. New York: Macmillan, 1970.

Quigly, Isabel, ed. *Shelley: Poems*. 1956. Harmondsworth: Penguin, 1985.

Raben, Joseph. "Shelley's 'Invocation to Misery': An Expanded Text." *Journal of English and Germanic Philology* 65 (1966): 65–74.

————. "Shelley the Dionysian." Everest 21–36.

Raine, Kathleen. *Defending Ancient Springs*. London: Oxford UP, 1967.

Rajan, Balachandra. *The Form of the Unfinished: English Poetics from Spencer to Pound*. Princeton: Princeton UP, 1985.

Rajan, Tilottama. *Dark Interpreter: The Discourse of Romanticism*. Ithaca: Cornell UP, 1980.

Redpath, Theodore, ed. *The Young Romantics and Critical Opinion 1807–1824: Poetry of Byron, Shelley, and Keats as Seen by Their Contemporary Critics*. London: Harrap, 1973.

Reed, Arden, ed. *Romanticism and Language*. Ithaca: Cornell UP, 1984.

Reiman, Donald H., ed. *English Romantic Poetry, 1800–1835: A Guide to Information Sources*. Detroit: Gale, 1979.

————, ed. *The Esdaile Notebook: A Facsimile of the Holograph Copybook*. New York: Garland, 1985.

————, ed. *Hellas: A Lyrical Drama: A Facsimile of the Press-Copy Transcript*. New York: Garland, 1985.

————. *Intervals of Inspiration: The Skeptical Tradition and the Psychology of Romanticism*. Greenwood: Penkeville, 1988.

————, ed. *"The Mask of Anarchy": Facsimiles of the Intermediate Fair-Copy Holograph Manuscript and Mary Shelley's Press-Copy Transcript*. New York: Garland, 1985.

————. *Percy Bysshe Shelley*. 1969. 2nd ed. Boston: Twayne-Hall, 1988.

————, ed. Peter Bell the Third: *A Facsimile of the Press-Copy Transcript and "The Triumph of Life": A Facsimile of Shelley's Holograph Draft*. Garland: New York, 1986.

————, ed. *The Romantics Reviewed: Contemporary Reviews of British Romantic Writers, 1793–1830.* 9 vols. New York: Garland, 1972.

————. *Romantic Texts and Contexts.* Columbia: U of Missouri P, 1987.

————. "Shelley as Agrarian Reactionary." *Keats-Shelley Memorial Bulletin* 30 (1979): 5–15. Rpt. in Reiman, *Romantic Texts* 260–74.

————. *Shelley's "The Triumph of Life": A Critical Study, Based on a Text Newly Edited from the Bodleian Manuscript.* Urbana: U of Illinois P, 1965.

Reiman, Donald H., Michael C. Jaye, and Betty T. Bennett, eds. *The Evidence of the Imagination: Studies of Interactions between Life and Art in English Romantic Literature.* New York: New York UP, 1978.

Reiman, Donald H., and Sharon B. Powers, eds. *Shelley's Poetry and Prose.* 1977. 3rd printing corr. New York: Norton, 1981.

"The Relation of the Death of the Family of the Cenci." Woodberry, *Works* 2: 447–63. (Forthcoming: Shelley, Mary Wollstonecraft, trans. "The Relation of the Death of the Family of the Cenci." *Bodleian MS Shelley Adds. d.2 and Adds. e.13.* Ed. Betty T. Bennett and Charles E. Robinson. Gen. ed. Donald H. Reiman. New York: Garland: 1988–.)

Ridenour, George, ed. *Shelley: A Collection of Critical Essays.* Twentieth Century Views. Englewood Cliffs: Prentice, 1965.

Rieger, James. *The Mutiny Within: The Heresies of Percy Bysshe Shelley.* New York: Braziller, 1967.

Roach, John. *Social Reform in England 1780–1880.* New York: St. Martin's, 1978.

Robinson, Charles E. *Shelley and Byron: The Snake and Eagle Wreathed in Fight.* Baltimore: Johns Hopkins UP, 1976.

Rodway, Allan. *English Comedy: Its Role and Nature from Chaucer to the Present Day.* Berkeley: U of California P, 1975.

————. *The Romantic Conflict.* London: Chatto, 1963.

Rogers, Neville, ed. *The Complete Poetical Works of Percy Bysshe Shelley.* 2 vols. of 4 to date. Oxford: Clarendon, 1972–.

————, ed. *The Esdaile Poems.* Oxford: Clarendon, 1966.

————. "The Punctuation of Shelley's Syntax." *Keats-Shelley Memorial Bulletin* 17 (1966): 20–30.

————, ed. *Shelley: Selected Poetry.* London: Oxford UP, 1969.

————. "Shelley: Texts and Pretexts, The Case of First Editions." *Keats-Shelley Memorial Bulletin* 19 (1968): 41–46.

————. *Shelley at Work: A Critical Inquiry.* 2nd ed. Oxford: Clarendon, 1967.

————. "Shelley's Spelling: Theory and Practice." *Keats-Shelley Memorial Bulletin* 16 (1965): 21–28.

Rosenbaum, Jean Watson. "Shelley's Witch: The Naked Conception." *Concerning Poetry* 10 (1977): 33–43.

Rossetti, William Michael, ed. *The Poetical Works of Percy Bysshe Shelley.* 1870. Rev. in 3 vols. London: Moxon, 1878.

Rubin, David. "A Study of Antinomies in Shelley's 'The Witch of Atlas.' " *Studies in Romanticism* 8 (1959): 216–28.

Sacks, Peter. *The English Elegy: Studies in the Genre from Spenser to Yeats.* Baltimore: Johns Hopkins UP, 1985.

St. Clair, William. *That Greece Might Still Be Free: The Philhellenes in the War of Independence.* London: Oxford UP, 1972.

Sales, Roger. *English Literature in History, 1780–1830: Pastoral and Politics.* London: Hutchinson, 1983.

———. *Literary Inheritance.* Amherst: U of Massachusetts P, 1984.

Schapiro, Barbara. *The Romantic Mother: Narcissistic Patterns in Romantic Poetry.* Baltimore: Johns Hopkins UP, 1983.

Schneidau, Herbert. *Sacred Discontent: The Bible and Western Tradition.* Berkeley: U of California P, 1977.

Schulze, Earl J. *Shelley's Theory of Poetry: A Reappraisal.* The Hague: Mouton, 1966.

Scrivener, Michael Henry. *Radical Shelley: The Philosophical Anarchism and Utopian Thought of Percy Bysshe Shelley.* Princeton: Princeton UP, 1982.

Shawcross, John, ed. *Shelley's Literary and Philosophical Criticism.* 1909. Folcroft: Folcroft, 1973.

Shealy, Ann. *The Ravaged Garden: A Critical Study of Shelley's* Epipsychidion. Pompano Beach: Exposition, 1985.

Shelley. Spec. issue of *Studies in Romanticism* 23 (1984): 295–423.

Silverman, Edwin. *Poetic Synthesis in Shelley's* Adonais. The Hague: Mouton, 1972.

Silverman, Kaja. *The Subject of Semiotics.* New York: Oxford UP, 1983.

Simpson, David. *Irony and Authority in Romantic Poetry.* Totowa: Rowman, 1979.

Singer, Irving. *The Nature of Love, 2. Courtly and Romantic.* Chicago: U of Chicago P, 1984.

Smith, Eric. *By Mourning Tongues: Studies in English Elegy.* Totowa: Rowman, 1977.

Spender, Stephen, ed. *A Choice of Shelley's Verse.* London: Faber, 1971.

Sperry, Stuart. *Shelley's Major Verse: The Narrative and Dramatic Poetry.* Cambridge: Harvard UP, 1988.

Stern, Daniel N. *The Interpersonal World of the Infant: A View from Psychoanalysis and Developmental Psychology.* New York: Basic, 1985.

Tetreault, Ronald. *The Poetry of Life: Shelley and Literary Form.* Toronto: U of Toronto P, 1987.

Thompson, E. P. *The Making of the English Working Class.* 1963. New York: Random, 1968.

Thompson, F. M. L. *English Landed Society in the Nineteenth Century.* London: Routledge, 1963.

Thorpe, Clarence D., Carlos Baker, and Bennett Weaver, eds. *The Major English*

Romantic Poets: A Symposium in Reappraisal. Carbondale: Southern Illinois UP, 1957.

Thorslev, Peter, Jr. *Romantic Contraries: Freedom versus Destiny.* New Haven: Yale UP, 1984.

Tokoo, Tatsuo, ed. *Bodleian MS Shelley d.3 (Fair Copy and Press Copy for* The Revolt of Islam [Laon and Cythna]. New York: Garland, 1988.

———. "Index to the Contents of Shelley's Notebooks and Other Literary MSS., Mainly in the Bodleian Library." (Japanese periodical, title of which translates into English as: *Humanities: Bulletin of the Faculty of Letters, Kyoto Prefectural University*) 34 (1982): 1–28.

Trevelyan, G. M. *British History of the Nineteenth Century and After.* 2nd ed. New York: Longman, 1938.

Twitchell, James. *Dreadful Pleasures: An Anatomy of Modern Horror.* New York: Oxford UP, 1985.

———. *Romantic Horizons: Aspects of the Sublime in English Poetry and Painting, 1770–1850.* Columbia: U of Missouri P, 1983.

Veeder, William. *Mary Shelley and* Frankenstein: *The Fate of Androgyny.* Chicago: U of Chicago P, 1986.

Volney, Constantin-François Chasseboeuf. *A New Translation of Volney's Ruins: Or, Meditations on the Revolutions of Empires.* 2 vols. 1802. Rpt. with an introd. by Robert D. Richardson, Jr. New York: Garland, 1979.

Waldoff, Leon. "The Father-Son Conflict in *Prometheus Unbound*: The Psychology of a Vision." *Psychoanalytic Review* 62 (1975): 79–96.

Warren, Michael J. "Textual Problems, Editorial Assertions in Editions of Shakespeare." McGann, *Textual Criticism* 23–37.

Wasserman, Earl. *Shelley: A Critical Reading.* Baltimore: Johns Hopkins UP, 1971.

———. *Shelley's* Prometheus Unbound. Baltimore: John Hopkins UP, 1965.

———. *The Subtler Language: Critical Readings of Neo-Classic and Romantic Poems.* Baltimore: Johns Hopkins UP, 1959.

Watson, George, ed. *The New Cambridge Bibliography of English Literature.* Vol 3. Cambridge: Cambridge UP, 1969.

Watson, J. R. *English Poetry of the Romantic Period, 1789–1830.* New York: Longman, 1985.

———, ed. *An Infinite Complexity: Essays in Romanticism.* Edinburgh: Edinburgh UP, 1983.

Weaver, Bennett. *Prometheus Unbound.* Ann Arbor: U of Michigan P, 1957.

Webb, Timothy. " 'The Avalanche of Ages': Shelley's Defence of Atheism and *Prometheus Unbound.*" *Keats-Shelley Memorial Bulletin* 35 (1984): 1–39.

———. *Shelley: A Voice Not Understood.* Atlantic Highlands: Humanities, 1977.

———, ed. *Shelley: Selected Poems.* London: Dent, 1977.

———. *The Violet in the Crucible: Shelley and Translation.* Oxford: Clarendon, 1976.

Weiskel, Thomas. *The Romantic Sublime: Studies in the Structure and Psychology of Transcendence.* Baltimore: Johns Hopkins UP, 1976.

Welburn, Andrew. *Power and Self-Consciousness in the Poetry of Shelley.* New York: St. Martin's, 1986.

Werkmeister, Lucy. *A Newspaper History of England, 1792–1793.* Lincoln: Nebraska UP, 1967.

Weston, Jessie L. *From Ritual to Romance.* 1920. New York: Doubleday, 1959.

White, Newman Ivey. *Portrait of Shelley.* New York: Knopf, 1945.

———. *Shelley.* 2 vols. New York: Knopf, 1940.

———, ed. *The Unextinguished Hearth: Shelley and His Contemporary Critics.* 1938. New York: Octagon, 1966.

White, R. J. *From Waterloo to Peterloo.* London: Heinemann, 1957.

———. *Life in Regency England.* New York: Putnam's, 1963.

Whitman, Robert F. "Beatrice's 'Pernicious Mistake' in *The Cenci.*" *PMLA* 74 (1959): 249–53.

Wilkie, Brian. *Romantic Poets and Epic Tradition.* Madison: U of Wisconsin P, 1965.

Williams, Raymond. *The Country and the City.* New York: Oxford UP, 1973.

———. *Culture and Society: 1780–1950.* 1958. New York: Columbia UP, 1966.

Wilson, Milton. *Shelley's Later Poetry: A Study of His Prophetic Imagination.* New York: Columbia UP, 1959.

Wimsatt, W. K., Jr. *The Verbal Icon: Studies in the Meaning of Poetry.* 1954. New York: Farrar, 1966.

Winegarten, Renée. *Writers and Revolution: The Fatal Lure of Action.* New York: New Viewpoints, 1974.

Wittreich, Joseph, Jr., ed. *Milton and the Line of Vision.* Madison: U of Wisconsin P, 1975.

Wollstonecraft, Mary, ed. *The Female Reader.* 1789. Delmar: Scholar's Facsimiles, 1980.

Woodberry, George Edward, ed. *The Complete Poetical Works of Percy Bysshe Shelley.* 4 vols. Boston: Heath, 1892. Cambridge: Cambridge UP, 1901.

———, ed. *The Shelley Notebook in the Harvard College Library.* Cambridge: Barnard, 1929.

Woodings, R. B., ed. *Shelley.* London: Macmillan, 1968.

Woodman, Ross. *The Apocalyptic Vision in the Poetry of Shelley.* Toronto: U of Toronto P, 1964.

———. "Shelley's Urania." *Studies in Romanticism* 17 (1978): 61–75.

Woodring, Carl. *Politics in English Romantic Poetry.* Cambridge: Harvard UP, 1970.

———, ed. *Prose of the Romantic Period.* Boston: Riverside-Houghton, 1961.

Wordsworth, Jonathan, Michael C. Jaye, and Robert Woof, eds. *William Wordsworth and the Age of English Romanticism.* New Brunswick: Rutgers UP, 1987.

Wordsworth, William. *The Prelude, 1799, 1805, 1850.* Ed. Jonathan Wordsworth, M. H. Abrams, and Stephen Gill. New York: Norton, 1979.

Wright, John. *Shelley's Myth of Metaphor*. Athens: U of Georgia P, 1970.

Yeats, W. B. *Essays and Introductions*. New York: Macmillan, 1961.

———. *Poems: A New Edition*. Ed. Richard Finneran. New York: Macmillan, 1983.

———. *Uncollected Prose*. Ed. John P. Frayne. 2 vols. New York: Columbia UP, 1970–76.

Young, Art. *Shelley and Nonviolence*. The Hague: Mouton, 1975.

Zillman, Lawrence J., ed. *Shelley's* Prometheus Unbound: *A Variorum Edition*. Seattle: U of Washington P, 1959.

———, ed. *Shelley's* Prometheus Unbound: *The Texts and Drafts*. New Haven: Yale UP, 1968.

Audiovisual Aids

Films, Sound Filmstrips, and Videocassettes

English Literature: The Romantic Period. 16-mm film. Coronet Instructional Films, 1957.

The Glorious Romantics, Pt. 3: Percy Bysshe Shelley. Videocassette. Great Plains Instructional TV Library.

The Rise of Romanticism. Sound filmstrip. United Learning, 1974.

The Romantic Age. Sound filmstrip. Thomas S. Klise, 1976.

The Romantic Era. Sound filmstrip. Educational Audio-Visual, 1970.

Romanticism: The Revolt of the Spirit. 16-mm film. Learning Corporation of America, 1971. (Available in videocassette.)

Romantic Poetry. Sound filmstrip. Films for the Humanities, 1982.

The Romantic Protest. Sound filmstrip. Multi-Media Productions.

The Spirit of Romanticism. Videocassette. Encyclopedia Brittannica Educational Corporation.

The Younger Romantics. Videocassette. Films for the Humanities.

Readings

Bloom, Claire, et al. *English Romantic Poetry*. Caedmon.

Edwards, Hilton. *Golden Treasury of Milton, Keats, and Shelley*. Spoken Arts.

Fletcher, Bramwell. *English Romantic Poets*. Listening Library.

Price, Vincent. *Poetry of Percy Bysshe Shelley*. Caedmon. (Available as *Poetry of Shelley* from Learning Arts.)

Speaight, Robert, and Robert Eddison. *Treasury of Percy Bysshe Shelley*. Spoken Arts.

Recorded Criticism

English Romantics and the French Revolution. Audiocassette. CBC Learning Systems.

Holloway, John. *Shelley, Percy Bysshe.* Audiocassette. Gould Media.

"Ozymandias" by Percy Bysshe Shelley. Audiocassette. National Tape Repository.

Percy Bysshe Shelley. Audiocassette. Classroom Film Distributors.

Poetry of Percy Shelley, Pts. 1 and 2. Audiocassette. National Tape Repository.

Salvensen, Christopher, and William Walsh. *The Romantics.* Audiocassette. BFA Educational Media.

INDEX OF WORKS BY SHELLEY

Address to the People on the Death of the Princess Charlotte, An, 123

Adonais, 8, 11, 21, 23, 35, 41, 42, 45, 63, 67, 100–02, 109, 110, 123, 127, 132, 133, 134, 135, 144, 155, 159, 161

Alastor, 21, 32–33, 41, 43, 45, 51, 54–58, 75, 76–78, 83, 94, 123, 131, 132, 138, 143, 146, 159

Cenci, The, 3, 15, 21, 28–30, 75, 86–89, 90, 130, 144

"Cloud, The," 149, 150

Declaration of Rights, 123

Defence of Poetry, A, 3, 5, 6, 8, 13, 31, 32, 33, 34, 41, 42, 57, 66, 69, 79, 83–85, 110, 111, 114–19, 122, 123, 134, 140, 143, 144, 152

Epipsychidion, 21, 45, 94, 96–99, 106, 123, 133, 155, 159

Esdaile Notebook, 3, 7, 121

"Essay on Christianity, An," 63, 114

Hellas, 3, 81, 122, 123, 139

"Hermit of Marlow" pamphlets, 123

"Hymn to Intellectual Beauty," 29, 32, 33, 41, 42, 50, 62–64, 67, 123, 127, 131, 132, 133, 137, 159

"Indian Serenade, The" ("The Indian Girl's Song"), 155

"Invocation to Misery," 155

Irish pamphlets, 123

Julian and Maddalo, 15, 67–69, 127, 155, 159

Laon and Cythna (The Revolt of Islam), 155

"Lines Written among the Euganean Hills," 64, 79

"Mask of Anarchy, The," 51, 70, 90–92, 122, 123, 125, 154, 155

"Mont Blanc," 11, 29–30, 41, 42, 43, 45, 49, 57, 59–61, 64, 67, 123, 127–30, 147, 148, 150–51

Necessity of Atheism, The, 130

"Ode to Naples," 122

"Ode to the West Wind," 36–40, 41, 42, 49, 50, 64, 67, 79–82, 127, 133, 140, 141, 147, 148–50, 155

"On Life," 3, 111–13, 115, 123, 131, 158

"On Love," 3, 106, 123, 158

"On the Punishment of Death," 123

"Ozymandias," 23, 65–66, 140–41

Peter Bell the Third, 45, 155

Philosophical View of Reform, A, 7, 123, 125

"Posthumous Fragments of Margaret Nicholson," 15

Prince Athanase, 138

Prometheus Unbound, 3, 5, 7, 11, 12, 15, 18, 20, 21, 23, 30–31, 33–34, 36, 41, 42–43, 63, 67, 68, 70–75, 76–78, 107, 108, 110, 111, 112, 113, 122, 123, 125, 127, 130, 134, 138, 139, 143, 144, 149, 153, 154, 155, 159, 161

Queen Mab, 3, 11, 41, 72, 122, 155

Refutation of Deism, A, 56

Revolt of Islam, The, 130

St. Irvyne, 5, 159

"Sensitive-Plant, The," 11, 36–40, 57, 113, 146, 147

"Song to the Men of England," 41, 42, 125
"Sonnet: England in 1819," 41, 42
"Stanzas Written in Dejection," 147
Swellfoot the Tyrant, 122

"To a Sky-Lark," 41, 43, 64, 83–85, 141
"To Constantia," 153
"To Jane. The Invitation," 103–06
"To Jane. The Recollection," 103–06
"To Wordsworth," 127

"Triumph of Life, The," 7, 13, 15, 21, 31, 32–33, 35, 41, 42, 43, 45, 83, 107–10, 134, 141, 144, 148, 159

Wandering Jew, The, 159
"Witch of Atlas, The," 21, 93–95
"Written on Hearing the News of the Death of Napoleon," 122

Zastrozzi, 5

INDEX OF NAMES

Abbey, Lloyd, 19, 54, 56
Abrams, M. H., 6, 12, 15, 17, 36, 128,
    142, 143, 146–47
Adams, Hazard, 6, 114, 115
Aers, David, 14
Aeschylus, 42, 43, 72, 78, 123
Albright, Daniel, 15
Ali Pasha, 124
Allott, Miriam, 21
Allsup, James, 18
Anderson, Erland, 16
Applewhite, James, 16
Arnold, Matthew, 43, 138

Baker, Carlos, 4, 12, 14, 17, 20, 93, 161
Baker, Joseph E., 83
Barcus, James E., 10
Barnard, Ellsworth, 18
Barrell, Joseph, 18
Bate, Jonathan, 14
Bate, Walter Jackson, 14
Beatty, B. G., 17
Beaty, Frederick, 16
Bedford, Russell dukes of, 124
Behrendt, Stephen, 5
Bennett, Betty T., 17
Benziger, James, 16
Berkeley, George, 29, 115
Bion, 100, 101
Blake, William, 18, 32, 34, 42, 44, 90,
    101, 105, 113, 138
Blank, G. Kim, 20, 127
Bloom, Claire, 23
Bloom, Harold, 4, 6, 11, 12, 13, 14, 15,
    16, 17, 19, 21, 61, 93, 107, 137, 143,
    144, 148, 151
Boas, Louise (Schutz), 157
Bornstein, George, 14, 17, 20, 137
Bowra, C. M., 16
Brand, C. P., 16–17
Brawne, Fanny, 97
Briggs, Asa, 13
Brisman, Leslie, 14, 15
Brown, Nathaniel, 20, 93, 158
Browning, Robert, 18
Brun, Frederike, 60
Bush, Douglas, 15
Butler, Marilyn, 13, 96, 123, 132
Butter, Peter, 19, 20

Buxton, John, 16, 20
Byron, George Gordon, Lord, 20, 44, 51,
    67–69, 90, 97, 123, 124, 132–36, 143,
    145

Cadogan, William, 157
Cameron, Kenneth Neill, 4, 7, 8, 11, 142,
    152, 154, 157
Cantor, Paul, 15
Caroline, Queen, 122
Castlereagh, Robert Stewart, 91
Cenci, Beatrice, 86
Cenci, Francesco, 86
Chase, Cynthia, 13
Chaucer, Geoffrey, 42
Chernaik, Judith, 7, 12, 20, 41, 79, 84,
    106, 133, 153
Chopin, Frederic, 16
Churchill, Kenneth, 16
Clark, David Lee, 5, 114
Clubbe, John, 13
Cobbett, William, 124
Coleridge, Hartley, 96
Coleridge, Samuel Taylor, 44, 57, 59–61,
    69, 96, 124, 129, 132, 157
Constable, John, 16
Constant, Benjamin, 97
Cook, Jonathan, 14
Cooke, Michael, 13, 16
Cookson, J. E., 121
Crawley, C. W., 14
Cronin, Richard, 20, 134
Crook, Nora, 20
Culler, Jonathan, 36
Curran, Stuart, 3, 9, 10, 12, 15, 19, 21,
    87, 91, 152, 159

Dante Alighieri, 17, 31, 42, 98, 107, 110,
    113, 125, 139
Darwin, Charles, 43
Davie, Donald, 39, 40
Davies, R. T., 17
Dawson, P. M. S., 19, 152
de Beauvoir, Simone, 98
Delisle, Fanny, 8, 115
de Man, Paul, 13, 144, 146, 147, 151
Dinnerstein, Dorothy, 159
Donohue, Joseph, 15

Drummond, William, 115, 158
Duerksen, Roland A., 5, 20
Duffy, Edward, 18
Dunbar, Clement, 9
Dunbar, Paul Laurence, 141
Durham, Margery, 157

Eaves, Morris, 13, 17
Eddison, Robert, 23
Edwards, Hilton, 23
Edwards, Thomas R., 14
Eldon, John Scott, Earl of, 91, 122
Eliot, T. S., 14, 17, 42, 83, 137, 141
Ellis, F. S., 10
Ellis, Steve, 17
Engell, James, 16
Enscoe, Gerald, 16, 17
Erdman, David, 10
Evans, Bertrand, 15
Everest, Kelvin, 7, 21

Ferguson, Frances, 151
Fichte, Johann Gottlieb, 30
Fischer, Michael, 13, 17
Fish, Stanley, 154
Fletcher, Bramwell, 23
Fletcher, Richard M., 15
Foakes, R. A., 16
Fogle, R. H., 17, 19
Foot, Paul, 19
Ford, Boris, 10
Ford, Newell, 5, 7
Forman, Harry Buxton, 152, 153
Fraistat, Neill, 15
Franklin, Phyllis, 49
Frazer, James George, 80
Freud, Sigmund, 70, 100, 118, 158, 160
Fricker, Sara, 69
Frost, Robert, 141
Fry, Paul, 15
Frye, Northrop, 15, 17, 43, 90, 91, 143,
    144, 145
Furst, Lillian R., 13

Gaull, Marilyn, 10
George III, 90, 120
George IV, 120
Gerard, Albert, 16
Gleckner, Robert, 17
Godwin, William, 18, 77, 127, 158
Goethe, Johann Wolfgang von, 8, 97
Goslee, Nancy Moore, 14
Gottlieb, Erika, 15

Grabo, Carl, 18, 20, 21, 93
Gray, Thomas, 103–06
Green, David Bonnell, 9
Guiton, Derek, 20

Hall, Jean, 19
Hall, Spencer, 62
Halperin, David, 161
Halsted, John B., 17
Hardy, Thomas, 43, 141
Harris, R. W., 14
Hartley, Robert A., 9
Harvey, A. D., 10, 14, 121
Hayden, John O., 10, 121
Hazlitt, William, 6, 97
Heath, William, 6
Hildebrand, William, 21
Hilles, Frederick, 17
Hillman, James, 34–35
Hitchener, Elizabeth, 94
Hoagwood, Terence, 18, 19
Hobsbawm, E. J., 14
Hodgart, Patricia, 20
Hodgson, John A., 134
Hoffman, Harold, 21
Hogg, Thomas J., 156
Hogle, Jerrold E., 19, 116
Holloway, John, 23
Holmes, Richard, 11, 22, 83, 93, 106, 157,
    158
Homans, Margaret, 157, 160
Hopkins, Gerard Manley, 43
Hughes, Daniel J., 19, 160
Hugo, Howard E., 6
Hume, David, 57, 115
Hungerford, Edward B., 161
Hunt, Leigh, 68, 92, 154–55
Hutchinson, Sarah, 96
Hutchinson, Thomas, 4, 7, 78, 153

Ingpen, Roger, 7, 8, 94, 153
Isaiah, 82

Jack, Ian, 10, 17
Jackson, James Robert de J., 10
Jaye, Michael C., 17, 22
Jeffrey, Lloyd, 20
Jesus, 79, 81, 114
Johnson, Samuel, 100
Jones, Frederick L., 8, 68, 81, 90, 94,
    129, 134, 158
Jones, Howard Mumford, 14
Jordan, Frank, 10, 143
Jordan, John E., 6

Keach, William, 12, 19, 54, 106, 151
Keats, John, 8, 10, 14, 19, 23, 34, 43, 51, 84, 87, 96–97, 100–02, 132–36, 138, 143, 158
King, Edward, 101
King-Hele, Desmond, 20, 90
Klapper, Roxana, 8
Knerr, Anthony, 8, 161
Knight, G. Wilson, 15–16, 93
Korshin, Paul, 15
Koszul, A. H., 154
Kramer, Lawrence, 16
Kristeva, Julia, 160
Kroeber, Karl, 16, 17
Kubler-Ross, Elisabeth, 100
Kumar, Shiv K., 17

Lacan, Jacques, 160
Lamb, Charles, 96
Langbaum, Robert, 130
Larrabee, Stephen, 16
Lavater, John Casper, 105
Lawrence, D. H., 141
Lawrence, James Henry, 158
Lea, Frank A., 19
Leavis, F. R., 17, 28, 83
Le Brun, Charles, 105
Lederer, Wolfgang, 159
Lefevbre, Georges, 121
Leighton, Angela, 19, 84
Lessing, Gotthold Ephraim, 98
Levinson, Marjorie, 15
Litz, A. Walton, 140
Locke, John, 29
Locock, C. D., 154
Lonsdale, Lowther earls of, 124
Lovell, Ernest J., Jr., 13

McElderry, Bruce R., Jr., 5
McGann, Jerome J., 14, 143, 152, 153
Mack, Maynard, 6
McNiece, Gerald, 19
Mahoney, John L., 6
Marks, Lawrence E., 160
Marsh, Jean, 22
Massey, Irving, 152
Massey, Marilyn Chapin, 157
Matthews, G. M., 4, 7, 80, 133
Mavrocordato, Prince, 124
Medwin, Thomas, 156
Mellor, Anne K., 143, 157, 159
Metternich, Klemens von, 123
Metzger, Lore, 15
Miller, J. Hillis, 13, 144

Milton, John, 14, 23, 34, 42, 43, 67, 70, 77, 100, 101, 102, 110, 125, 134, 135
Mingay, G. E., 121
Moore, Marianne, 140, 141
More, Thomas, 122
Moschus, 100, 101
Murphy, John, 20
Murray, E. B., 8, 152

Nelson, James, 157
Neville-Andrews, John, 22
Norfolk, Howard dukes of, 124
Notopoulos, James, 8, 18, 114
Noyes, Russell, 6
Nye, Andrea, 161

Ollier, Charles, 90, 98
O'Malley, Glenn, 20, 160, 161
Onorato, Richard J., 130
Otten, Terry, 15

Parker, Reeve, 60
Paul, 79
Peacock, Thomas Love, 5, 6, 13, 42, 81, 111–14, 115, 116, 117, 119, 122, 123, 129, 134
Peck, Walter E., 7, 8, 94, 153
Pennington, Sarah, 157
Perkins, David, 6, 15, 61, 98, 147, 149
Peterfreund, Stuart, 92
Plato, 8, 18, 94, 114
Pottle, Frederick A., 43
Powers, Sharon B., 3, 4, 7, 143, 145, 150, 153, 158
Price, Vincent, 23
Prickett, Stephen, 17
Pulos, C. E., 11, 19, 54, 57, 142, 143, 158
Punter, David, 14
Purkis, John, 22

Quayle, Anthony, 23
Quennell, Peter, 22
Quigly, Isabel, 4

Raben, Joseph, 80, 155
Raine, Kathleen, 16
Rajan, Balachandra, 15
Rajan, Tilottama, 13, 143
Rameses II, 65
Redpath, Theodore, 10
Reed, Arden, 13, 17

Reiman, Donald H., 3, 4, 7, 8, 10, 12, 16, 17, 19, 20, 21, 93, 107, 121, 124, 142, 143, 145, 150, 152, 153, 154, 158
Reni, Guido, 22
Richardson, Ralph, 23
Ridenour, George, 21
Rieger, James, 18
Roach, John, 14, 121
Robinson, Charles E., 20
Rodway, Allan, 14, 15
Rogers, Neville, 4, 7, 18, 153, 154
Rosenbaum, Jean Watson, 93
Rossetti, William Michael, 153
Rousseau, Jean-Jacques, 18, 97, 107, 141
Rubin, David, 93
Russell, Ken, 23

Sacks, Peter, 15, 102
St. Clair, William, 124
Sales, Roger, 14, 15
Salvensen, Christopher, 23
Schapiro, Barbara, 16, 41, 157
Schneidau, Herbert, 118
Schulze, Earl J., 19
Scrivener, Michael Henry, 19, 91
Shakespeare, William, 14, 28, 144
Shawcross, John, 5
Shealy, Ann, 21
Shelley, Clara, 68
Shelley, Harriet, 157
Shelley, Mary, 3, 5, 7, 68, 76–78, 154, 155, 156, 157, 159
Sidmouth, Henry Addington, 91
Sidney, Philip, 101
Silverman, Edwin, 21
Silverman, Kaja, 160
Simpson, David, 13
Singer, Irving, 16
Smith, Eric, 15
Speaight, Robert, 23
Spender, Stephen, 4
Spenser, Edmund, 94, 100, 101, 104, 137
Sperry, Stuart, 20
Stendhal, 96, 97, 98, 99
Stern, Daniel N., 160, 161
Stevens, Wallace, 63, 137, 140–41
Stillinger, Jack, 6
Swift, Jonathan, 122

Tetreault, Ronald, 20
Theocritus, 100
Thompson, E. P., 13, 121
Thompson, F. M. L., 121

Thorpe, Clarence D., 17
Thorslev, Peter, Jr., 16
Tokoo, Tatsuo, 152, 154
Trevelyan, G. M., 14
Trilling, Lionel, 6
Turner, Joseph Mallord William, 16, 22
Twitchell, James, 15, 16

Veeder, William, 93
Vergil, 42, 100, 107, 139
Viviani, Teresa (Emilia), 94, 98, 99
Volney, Constantin-François Chasseboeuf, 122

Waldoff, Leon, 130
Walling, William, 16, 17
Walsh, William, 23
Warren, Michael J., 156
Wasserman, Earl, 11, 19, 21, 30, 38, 41, 54, 102, 109, 142, 143, 144, 146, 147, 149, 151
Watson, J. R., 10, 17
Weaver, Bennett, 17, 21
Webb, Timothy, 4, 8, 12, 20, 133, 155
Welburn, Andrew, 18
Werkmeister, Lucy, 157
West, Benjamin, 91
Weston, Jessie L., 80
White, Newman Ivey, 10, 11, 22, 36, 121, 157
White, R. J., 14
Whitman, Robert F., 86
Wilkie, Brian, 15
William IV, 120
Williams, Helen Maria, 144
Williams, Jane, 103, 106
Williams, Raymond, 13
Wilson, Edwin Graves, 9
Wilson, Milton, 18
Wimsatt, W. K., Jr., 38, 147
Wittreich, Joseph, Jr., 14
Wollstonecraft, Mary, 97, 144, 145, 157, 158
Woodberry, George Edward, 5, 152
Woodings, R. B., 21
Woodman, Ross, 18, 159, 161
Woodring, Carl, 6, 14, 123
Woof, Robert, 22
Wordsworth, Dorothy, 96
Wordsworth, Jonathan, 22
Wordsworth, Mary, 96
Wordsworth, William, 5, 14, 20, 36, 41, 44, 50, 51, 54, 56, 58, 64, 69, 72, 73,

76, 77, 87, 96, 111, 112, 113, 123, 124,
127–31, 132, 143, 152, 157
Worlock, Frederick, 23
Wright, John, 19

Yeats, W. B., 14, 18, 20, 43, 137–40
Young, Art, 19

Zillman, Lawrence J., 7, 153